best practices
in action

PUBLICATIONS

best practices in action

Guidelines for Implementing First-Class
Business Incubation Programs

REVISED 2ND EDITION

BY Corinne Colbert, Dinah Adkins,
Chuck Wolfe & Karl LaPan

MCNAUGHTON & GUNN | SALINE, MICHIGAN

NBIA gratefully acknowledges these sponsors
who helped underwrite production of this book:

**Other Books Published by the
National Business Incubation Association**

This work has been made possible in part by support from Claggett Wolfe Associates and Maryland TEDCO.

Published by
McNaughton & Gunn
960 Woodland Drive
Saline, MI 48176

telephone: 734.429.8757
www.bookprinters.com

ISBN-01: 978-1-887183-69-7

Design by: Ullman Design
www.ullmandesign.com

PUBLICATIONS

CONTENTS

foreword

Publication of this new, completely revised and expanded *Best Practices in Action: Guidelines for Implementing First-Class Business Incubation Programs* follows some nine years after the original. Thus, the near decade of progress in the industry should be readily evident here. Despite the fine models and examples presented in the earlier edition, this new volume has been enriched by the vastly increased sophistication of business incubation as it is practiced today in the United States and elsewhere.

Since the nascent years of the 1980s, our understanding of how to serve entrepreneurial firms, commercialize technologies, create wealth, and promote entrepreneurship in our communities has increased exponentially. Therefore, we are pleased to present on these pages many activities, policies, techniques, and other examples of best practices—recognizing that there are few practices that will fit our needs in every situation or that do not require adaptation.

In some settings, even use of the term "best practice" is controversial, due to concern that it seeks to prescribe universal solutions. Given that the practice of incubation in China, France, the United States, and other nations varies based on individual cultures, resources, and needs, we are not so foolish as to suggest such iron rules.

And though we still take very seriously the principles and practices approved by NBIA's board of directors in 1996, we know they must inevitably evolve.

But we believe that the managers of the programs presented here have striven for excellence. They have aspired to be more than "good enough." Far from being prescriptive, the examples here show the creative abundance that has emerged from programs devoted, quite simply, to serving entrepreneurs in the "highest and best" manner possible.

It is our hope that—inspired by this volume—readers will incubate hundreds of new ideas and propel their programs into a future that is exemplary of its own time.

I am grateful to have participated in this exciting industry for twenty-eight years and have lost not an iota of excitement in anticipating your future successes.

Dinah Adkins
NBIA PRESIDENT EMERITA

Acknowledgments

This book is the result of nearly three years of work by a core group of NBIA staff and NBIA members who collaborated at every stage, from planning through editing. It has been a long, sometimes painful process, but the result is worth it. Deepest thanks go to:

- Meredith Erlewine, NBIA's longtime director of publications, who gathered a stellar panel of incubator managers and consultants to thoroughly revise and update an NBIA Publications classic. Meredith left NBIA in the spring of 2008, but her dogged pursuit of quality continues to inspire her former colleagues.

- Dinah Adkins, NBIA's president emerita, whose unparalleled knowledge of the industry and its practitioners was key to identifying the practices and programs to highlight. Dinah also returned to her roots as a reporter to investigate and write about many of the specific practices that follow.

- Chuck Wolfe, of Claggett Wolfe Associates, and Karl LaPan, president and CEO of the Northeast Indiana Innovation Center, not only served on the book's steering committee but also traveled around the United States and beyond to check out best practice programs and write about them. Special thanks go to the Foellinger Foundation, which funded LaPan's travels.

- David Terry, executive director of the West Texas A&M University Enterprise Network, provided not only his insights but also his Texas twang and sense of humor to long steering committee conference calls.

- Jasper Welch, director of the San Juan College Enterprise Center, and Joel Wiggins, president and CEO of the Enterprise Center of Johnson County, read early drafts of the chapters and provided both their points of view and a number of examples from their excellent programs.

- Linda Knopp, NBIA's director of news and information, lent her careful editorial eye at a critical stage, improving the tone and depth of the book. No writer could ask for a better editor or colleague.

- Mary Ann Gulino, NBIA bookstore manager, whose ability to sort, organize, and analyze data was a godsend for tracking all the examples.

- Tracy Kitts, NBIA's vice president and COO, whose persistent queries about the book's progress may have been annoying at times but always kept the project at the top of my mind even when other work crowded forward.

- Rick Huard, late of the Ohio University Press, whose sharp copyediting and proofreading whipped the final manuscript into shape (and prevented many a typo).

- Tina Ullman and Alix Northrup of Ullman Design, who patiently endured multiple rounds of changes and still made a gorgeous book.

Thanks also go to David Monkman, NBIA's new president and CEO, who came along as the BPIA whirlwind was reaching its climax and remained unfazed. I look forward to producing more books under David's tenure.

The book revision would not have been possible without support from two old friends. The Maryland Technology Development Corporation, which underwrote the original BPIA, again offered its financial support for the book's production. Likewise, Chuck Wolfe—a coauthor of the original edition—provided funding as well as his time and talent. NBIA is deeply grateful to both of these longtime supporters for their continued generosity and faith.

Finally, thanks go to the dozens of NBIA members who submitted proposals for inclusion in the book; who agreed to repeated rounds of interviews; and who answered my calls for help on the NBIA Member Listserv. Once again, you have proven that the incubation industry is not only innovative but also unfailingly generous with its time and ideas. I am constantly amazed and inspired by the work you do; I wish I could tell each of your stories! But that is another book.

Corinne Colbert

DIRECTOR OF PUBLISHING, NBIA
JANUARY 2010

introduction

Any discussion of business quality will include the term "best practice." But what, exactly, does that phrase mean in business incubation? Isn't it just a meaningless bit of jargon?

NBIA's Board of Directors—all working incubator managers and developers—don't think so. In 1996, the Board adopted NBIA's Principles and Best Practices of Successful Business Incubation, which lays out the standards by which all incubation programs should operate. It isn't a long list—just two principles and ten practices—but it remains a blueprint for incubation effectiveness and sustainability.

Simply put, best practices are the standard by which the industry measures itself. Adhering to these standards helps ensure that a business incubator truly is an incubator and not just another landlord.

Best practices also are a yardstick for stakeholders. Increasingly, those who provide funding for new or existing incubation programs want proof that their investments are yielding returns. Some of that performance can be measured quantitatively in numbers of clients served or jobs created or in dollars invested or tax revenues generated. But incubation programs also are being measured qualitatively: stakeholders want to know if the programs they support are viable. They want to see models of best practices.

That quest led to the original edition of *Best Practices in Action*. In 2000, the Maryland Technology Development Corporation (TEDCO) turned to NBIA for help in measuring the practices of the incubation programs it funded. With funding from Maryland TEDCO, NBIA researched and produced *Best Practices in Action: Guidelines for Implementing First-Class Business Incubation Programs*, the industry's first-ever guide to industry best practices. Published in 2001, the book became one of NBIA's all-time best sellers.

But what was groundbreaking in 2000 was antiquated by 2006. The incubation industry constantly evolves to meet the needs of new entrepreneurs, new markets, and new innovations. The industry also continues to grow, increasing the number of programs and, in turn, the number of ways to do the business of incubation. So in 2007, NBIA again assembled a team of incubation professionals to consider the state of best practices in the twenty-first century. We invited our members to tell us about their practices so we could share the best of them with their peers. You hold the result of that nearly three-year effort in your hands.

Like the original, this edition is organized into chapters that explore a related set of best practices, illustrated with examples of how those practices are implemented at incubation programs around the world. It also features a number of case studies that highlight incubators that are masters of multiple practices.

We hope that you will find inspiration in these pages. And if you are an exemplar of best practices, please let us know (news@nbia.org). The programs featured in this book are by no means the only ones that make "best practices" the way they do business and not merely a catchphrase. We're always on the lookout for terrific programs and services that are putting best practices into action. Maybe yours is one of them.

Principles and Best Practices of
Successful Business Incubation

Two principles characterize effective business incubation:

- The incubator aspires to have a positive impact on its community's economic health by maximizing the success of emerging companies.
- The incubator itself is a dynamic model of a sustainable, efficient business operation.

Model business incubation programs are distinguished by a commitment to incorporate industry best practices. Management and boards of incubators should strive to:

- Commit to the two core principles of business incubation
- Obtain consensus on a mission that defines the incubator's role in the community and develop a strategic plan containing quantifiable objectives to achieve the program mission
- Structure for financial sustainability by developing and implementing a realistic business plan
- Recruit and appropriately compensate management capable of achieving the mission of the incubator and having the ability to help companies grow
- Build an effective board of directors committed to the incubator's mission and to maximizing management's role in developing successful companies

- Develop an incubator facility, resources, methods, and tools that contribute to the effective delivery of business assistance to client firms and that address the developmental needs of each company
- Seek to integrate the incubator program and activities into the fabric of the community and its broader economic development goals and strategies
- Develop stakeholder support, including a resource network, that helps the incubation program's client companies and supports the incubator's mission and operations
- Develop stakeholder support, including a resource network, that helps the incubation program's client companies and supports the incubator's mission and operations
- Maintain a management information system and collect statistics and other information necessary for ongoing program evaluation, thus improving a program's effectiveness and allowing it to evolve with the needs of the clients

Developed by NBIA, with credit to M. Rice and J. Matthews, *Growing New Ventures, Creating New Jobs: Principles and Practices of Successful Business Incubation* (Westport, Conn.: Quorum Books, 1995).

governance

Many of NBIA's Best Practices of Successful Business Incubation pertain to governance, and for good reason. Without a clear mission, an ambitious—yet achievable—strategic plan, an engaged board of directors, and a committed and loyal base of stakeholders, your incubation program cannot be effective. Laying a firm foundation for how your incubation program operates is vital to the program's long-term viability and success.

Management and boards of incubators should strive to

- Obtain consensus on a mission that defines the incubator's role in the community and develop a strategic plan containing quantifiable objectives to achieve the program mission

- Build an effective board of directors committed to the incubator's mission and to maximizing management's role in developing successful companies

- Develop stakeholder support, including a resource network that helps the incubation program's client companies and supports the incubator's mission and operations

- Seek to integrate the incubator program and activities into the fabric of the community and its broader economic development goals and strategies

■■ mission

Central to any incubation program is its mission, which tells everyone why it exists and guides the program's activities and development. Developed as part of the feasibility study or business plan process, a mission statement serves as a point of reference for creating and achieving goals and staying on task.

A mission statement should describe an organization's fundamental purpose clearly and succinctly. Imprecise language and wordiness can lead to unclear goals, conflicting expectations, and, ultimately, a mission that's impossible to achieve. When crafting or revising a mission statement, be sure to avoid generalities and trim the statement down to essential information.

Questions to consider include:

- What is the ultimate value the incubator brings to its clients and supporters?

- What is distinctive about the incubator? What differentiates it from other business development programs or services?

- Do you serve all types of companies, or are you focused on a specific industry sector?

- What are your goals? For example, do you want to foster entrepreneurship in your community regardless of company size? Or do you want to stimulate economic expansion by building high-growth businesses?

A mission statement ought to reflect these specific purposes. Because a mission statement guides an incubator's activities, it should be in written form and easily accessible to staff and board members. This makes it easier to keep the incubator's mission at the center of discussions about new goals, programs, or services and to confirm that these goals, programs, or services are compatible with the program's stated purpose. Conflicts with the mission could indicate the need to rethink the new idea or to revise the mission statement. Ideally a mission statement is a stable document that can stand the test of time, but significant changes in the business environment might necessitate revisions.

If every member of an incubator's board or staff has a different idea of what the program's mission is, the incubator will never be able to satisfy everyone, and the force of the program will be wasted in nonproductive endeavors. A confusing mission statement will interfere with a coherent marketing message, limiting your ability to attract quality clients. An overly broad mission can lead to a haphazard lineup of services, strangling your effectiveness and confusing clients.

The discussions that lead to the creation of the mission statement provide important opportunities to consider and discard ideas and come to a consensus on the core purpose of the program. That's why it's important to involve board members, major stakeholders, and key staff members in the writing or revision process. A mission statement that inspires commitment from these key players helps everyone focus on and work toward the same purpose, thus promoting the success and longevity of an incubation program.

Mission statements also provide a basis for identifying key criteria that will be used to judge whether the program is, in fact, achieving what it sets out to do. The impact data the incubator management collects should be directly related to the program's mission (see chapter 5, "Program Evaluation"). Again, this means securing consensus and support from stakeholders and sponsors on the mission statement—and how the mission is being achieved.

Equally important is to review your mission statement periodically—perhaps when you revise your three- or five-year strategic plan—to see if any refinements or enhancements need to be made based on how the organization or the community in which it operates has evolved since the program's inception. For example, perhaps your community has achieved its goals for creating a critical mass of software companies and now needs to focus on developing another sector. Perhaps your mixed-use incubator serves a far higher percentage of technology companies than it did originally, or it may find itself with more manufacturing space than it can lease out.

Mission Statement

- Focuses incubator management and governing board on what the program wants to achieve
- Clearly defines the incubator's value proposition to potential clients
- Reflects consensus among all stakeholders on the program's purpose
- Provides a basis for criteria that can be used in judging the incubator's performance

BEST PRACTICES IN ACTION

A Vision/Mission Statement
West Texas A&M University Enterprise Network, Amarillo, TX
David Terry, executive director
www.IncubationWorks.com

David Terry, executive director of the West Texas A&M University Enterprise Network in Amarillo, Texas, knows the value of a mission statement. The incubator's own mission statement is multileveled, including sections articulating its "mission," its "vision," and its "core values."

Terry explains that these represent different levels of specificity.

The incubator's mission statement, for example—"To grow and diversify the economic base of Amarillo and selected regional communities by utilizing the tools of business incubation, entrepreneurial development, and entrepreneurial education"—is pretty specific.

"It really tells you why you exist, what it is that you are trying to accomplish, and gives you a sense of purpose for coming to work every day," Terry says.

The vision statement, on the other hand, is "the overarching statement of what we want to accomplish—it's something bigger," he says. Terry compares the vision statement's level of broadness to Bill Gates's dream of "putting a computer on every desk."

WTAMU's vision statement defines the goal—"to create a network of business incubators"—and focuses on the types of values those incubators will provide, such as allowing entrepreneurs to reduce risks and lower capital and operating costs.

The combined mission/vision/values statement gives WTAMU a real touchstone that it can use to assess its own performance, and it provides quite practical guidance at times.

For example, Terry recalls, in a review of programs offered by the incubator, his team realized that one was "really geared toward helping inventors primarily." Nothing wrong with that—except that it didn't do the specific things the mission statement says the incubator should be doing.

"It was a great thing, but it really was not geared toward entrepreneurial development or education or incubation," Terry notes. "So we killed that program."

Of course, a mission statement can't be too highly detailed—it needs to be concise, after all. Though the statement talks about "diversifying" the economies of a defined geographic region (encompassing twenty-six counties in the Texas and Oklahoma panhandles), Terry points out, "it really does not talk about the kinds of companies" that the incubator should foster in order to do that.

That word "diversifying" does offer concrete guidance, however, and a way to measure the incubator's success.

"I think you could look at our mission statement and ask, 'Are we really diversifying economies?'" Terry says. He notes that the inclusion of this factor in the mission statement reflected "a real need of communities in the Texas panhandle," long dominated by ranching and oil. Business leaders in the area communities made it clear, Terry says, that "if we're not increasing the diversity of their economies, they had no need of our services."

WTAMU's mixed-use lineup of client companies clearly reflects this aspect of its mission. They include a tech company that produces advanced absorbents and filtration systems; a graphic design firm; a basketball training business; a utility construction company specializing in power lines and substations; an alfalfa grower; and a soap manufacturer.

Ultimately, Terry stresses, mission statements are working tools, which are crucial to keeping an incubator on track.

"You've just got to have them to align your focus," he says.

Tying the Mission to Community Needs
USC Columbia Technology Incubator, Columbia, SC
Joel Stevenson, executive director
http://incubator.research.sc.edu

Joel Stevenson, executive director of the University of South Carolina Columbia Technology Incubator, doesn't hesitate when he's asked to describe the exact focus of his incubator's mission statement.

"It's about jobs," Stevenson declares.

More specifically, it's about creating highly skilled jobs in technology-oriented companies—employing the talents of the students and faculty of the University of South Carolina, Midlands Technical College, Benedict College, Allen University, or Columbia College—and keeping those jobs in Columbia, South Carolina, and the surrounding region.

If a potential client doesn't have a clear plan to do those things, Stevenson says, "we're not going to help you. I don't care if you've got the cure for cancer, and are going to make a gazillion dollars."

The tight focus of the incubator's mission—"to increase the vitality of the regional economy by recruiting and nurturing start-up companies that advance technological development, employ highly skilled workers, and contribute to the economic development of the area"—is no accident.

Stevenson recalls that Michael Reischman, former associate dean for research and economic development at USC's College of Engineering and Computing, watched as the city of Charleston's $3.5 million incubator ran out of money, in part from lack of stakeholder support. "He said, 'We are not going to make the same mistake. We're going to start talking to the community right from the get-go,'" Stevenson says.

Reischman wanted to make sure that a new incubator gave the area business community—including potential donors—what it really wanted from such a program. For a year between 1997 and 1998, Reischman painstakingly gathered input from academics and business leaders around the region about what an incubator could and should be doing for the area. "He put boots on the ground and interviewed people at Georgia Tech, Texas, Arkansas, and Louisiana incubators," Stevenson says. "He went door-to-door."

The result was an incubator mission firmly rooted in the area's economic needs. "If the community didn't want it, then the university didn't want it," Stevenson says. The incubator's mission statement, accordingly, is "as direct and concise a mission statement as I have seen," according to Stevenson.

In return, the incubator receives solid stakeholder support. It leases a 43,000-square-foot building from the city of Columbia for only a $1 a year, on a five-year lease with a two-year renewal option. It also receives administrative support from the university. The remaining $450,000 in operating funds comes entirely from local supporters. Client rent covers expenses such as janitorial, maintenance, water/sewer, phone, trash pickup, and Internet hookup.

Stevenson isn't worried that the city will be raising his nominal rent amount any time soon, given what he sees as the clear benefits the incubator brings to the area.

"The Columbia City Council has told me, as long as we're helping to create jobs, we'll be here," he says.

Honing the Mission Statement
Rutgers Food Innovation Center, Bridgeton, NJ
Lou Cooperhouse, director
www.foodinnovation.rutgers.edu

The Rutgers Food Innovation Center is in many ways a unique incubator program. And according to Director Lou Cooperhouse, its mission statement was crafted to precisely reflect that uniqueness.

When he and his staff first wrote the statement, Cooperhouse says, "We spent a considerable amount of time in meetings, working and massaging every word." (When they got it right, it was adopted by their board as is.)

The mission: "To stimulate and support sustainable economic growth and prosperity to the food and agricultural industries in the mid-Atlantic region by providing businesses with innovative research, customized practical solutions, resources for business incubation, and a trusted source for information and guidance."

No exotic terms here—but Cooperhouse can justify the statement phrase by phrase.

Take "stimulate" and "support." Because the incubator serves both start-ups and established businesses, it needs to signal that it will both stimulate new firms and provide ongoing assistance for established ones to keep them successful— "that we won't go away."

"Sustainable" means the incubator pushes companies to think beyond a single product or line of products to maintain their success; instead, they have to think about related products, branding, marketing, differentiating, say, their line of sauces from all the others out there. "The great idea is not just an idea, but a series of ideas," Cooperhouse stresses.

The "mid-Atlantic region" part was a revision of the original statement, which said "New Jersey." The change was made to emphasize that while Rutgers is a New Jersey university, its incubator won't limit its sights to Garden State companies but will reach outside the state or even the country to work with companies that create jobs.

The commitment to "innovative research, customized practical solutions, resources for business incubation, and a trusted source for information and guidance" is also tightly honed to reflect the uniqueness of the incubator.

It uses a "hotel model" where clients don't have to lease space, but can come in and pay for services or facility use by the day. This "highly service-centric" approach has meant that with a budget of about $1.2 million, ten full-time employees, and six consultants, the incubator has been able to help some 1,200 clients since its founding in 2001.

With the resources of Rutgers, the incubator can provide highly specific solutions to the wide range of specialized problems that arise in developing new food products. One client might need a method to increase a product's shelf life, while another might need help with precise temperature control during preparation.

By "trusted source," the incubator signals its ability to advise its clients—who work in a highly regulated industry and for whom food safety is a constant challenge—and act as a liaison with state regulators to help companies achieve compliance. Clients can be confident that the incubator won't run to the authorities if a company seeks help, but will work with the firm and the state to get violations fixed.

The statement, according to Cooperhouse, has provided staff with specific guidance to stay on mission while allowing flexibility.

"We do get asked to do things on a regular basis that might be seen as 'mission creep,' as they say," he admits. The statement helps clarify which projects don't fit, and which can be tweaked to make them fit.

When a $200,000 U.S. Department of Agriculture grant became available to create a co-op development program, for example, Cooperhouse had to worry that the project fell outside the mission. "The reality is, co-ops can be food-based, or can be non-food-based," he notes. In that case, the incubator managed to make the project fit by overlapping its food mission with its work with other types of co-ops—by, for example, using a library co-op as a resource to provide entrepreneurs with information about the food industry.

Strategic Plan

- Delineates goals and objectives necessary for the incubator to achieve its mission

- Assigns responsibilities and time frames for tasks and strategies

- Includes quantifiable ways to measure achievements

- Keeps the incubator focused on its mission and objectives to achieve the mission

- Documents progress and success of the incubator and focuses board discussions on macro issues affecting the success of the incubator

■■ strategic plan

Fulfilling a mission requires strategic planning: mapping out where the incubator is headed in the next year or more and how it's going to get there. A strategic plan provides a clear picture of quantifiable goals, objectives, and tasks within a given time frame and keeps an incubator focused on its fundamental purpose. (This is separate from a business plan; for information on business plans, see chapter 3, "Finances.")

An incubator's staff members, often in conjunction with its board of directors, are usually responsible for developing a new strategic plan on a regular basis—at least every three years, but no less than every five years. You should review the strategic plan at least annually to ensure that it still makes sense given any significant changes in the environment or in clients' or stakeholders' needs.

BEST PRACTICES IN ACTION

Strategic Plan on a Page
Northeast Indiana Innovation Center, Fort Wayne, IN
Karl LaPan, president and CEO
www.niic.net

Something about the standard strategic planning retreat always bothered Karl LaPan. "My feeling was strategic planning should be about advancing rather than retreating," says LaPan, president and CEO of the Northeast Indiana Innovation Center.

His issue was more than semantic, however. The whole idea of a strategic plan was troublesome. "For most boards, strategic planning is kind of perfunctory," LaPan says. "You wind up with a seventy-two-page strategic plan that nobody's going to read but me."

LaPan wanted a way to get the depth of a strategic planning process, but without the doorstop that often results. He wanted to engage his board without overwhelming them. He wanted to tie strategic goals to the incubator's mission and to a handful of measurable results.

He wanted a strategic plan on a page. Not finding anything in standard business literature, he created one himself.

LaPan's Strategic Plan on a Page (SOAP) workbook walks users through a process to think through strategic goals as they relate to mission and to focus on the most important measurable outcomes. Then all the most important information is gathered on a single legal-sized sheet of paper.

The single-page approach has been especially helpful in keeping his stakeholders informed about NIIC's progress. "Most of these people don't understand the nuances of incubation, and they don't want to," he says. "They don't spend enough time in the organization to get into the nitty-gritty." SOAP highlights the three most important goals for the year; at each board meeting, LaPan reports on how the staff is progressing toward achieving each goal. "It gives them a really clear look at the organization," he says. "Here are the most important things they should be asking us about every time they see us."

The plan also has been popular with funders, LaPan says. "I met with a foundation before the [2009] holidays, and they said they had never seen anything like this from a nonprofit," he says. "It was a differentiator for us."

LaPan also ties staff performance to the plan. "In our goals for each year, every person's key measurable goals are connected to one of the five key goals of the organization," he says. "It's great for building ownership, accountability, and for simplifying thinking."

That's important, he says, because it is so easy for busy incubator managers and staff to focus so much on their daily to-do lists that they forget to consider the big picture. "We have to work on ourselves as agents of change and connect our to-do list to results," he says. "If all we do is come in and do all the tasks of the day, we never have time to do that strategic thinking."

And that's what LaPan was after: a process that would allow him to think big. "Most of us put together strategic plans that are incremental—'we're going to do 3 percent more than last year,'" he says. "SOAP encourages me to think in a dynamic way that says, 'What if?'"

"Today we have a ten-person staff and and six major focus areas, so we feel the need to plan and focus and discuss the allocation of resources."

– Charles D'Agostino, executive director, Louisiana Business & Technology Center

The result is that single page, which LaPan laminates and keeps on his desk. "Every morning I think, 'What are the three to five things I can do today to advance us toward our objectives?'" he says. "SOAP is a living, dynamic, iterative document that helps me do that."

Strategic Planning Retreat
Louisiana Business & Technology Center, Baton Rouge, LA
Charles D'Agostino, executive director
www.bus.lsu.edu/lbtc

The Louisiana Business & Technology Center is much more than a business incubation program. It also operates the Louisiana State University Small Business Development Center; facilitates work of the Louisiana Technology Transfer Office, which includes liaisons with NASA research centers and running the state's SBIR program; manages an Incubator on Wheels rural outreach project; administers the Business Disaster Counseling Center's hurricane recovery operations; and coordinates Access LSU, a community outreach program.

"In our early years, with a smaller staff and fewer programs to manage, we did not need as much [strategic] planning," says Executive Director Charles D'Agostino. "Today we have a ten-person staff and six major focus areas, so we feel the need to plan and focus and discuss the allocation of resources."

That process starts in an annual half-day, all-staff retreat to brainstorm and discuss the focus of each project, review funding sources, and assess all the services offered. From that meeting, D'Agostino prepares a report for his advisory board to gain their input, either at a regular board meeting or a specially scheduled session, depending on the meeting agenda. D'Agostino uses the board's feedback to develop action items for each unit and each staff member.

The planning process has paid dividends beyond keeping everyone on track, D'Agostino says. "It's very beneficial for the staff to see the big picture and how their unit is an integral part of LBTC, but not more important than the others," he says. In addition, "the board appears to like being involved more than merely listening to reports at their meetings," he says.

Boards of Directors

■■ board of directors

Strong leadership and support from the board of directors is essential to an incubation program's success. The board provides strategic direction and leadership, and it supports the incubator director's performance. Board members should be selected for their commitment to the organization's mission and expertise—such as specific skills or connections—that support the program's growth and success. Board members whose sole motivation is personal benefit or who have a personal agenda can be devastating to incubator effectiveness.

The vast majority of North American business incubation programs are nonprofit entities (94 percent in NBIA's *2006 State of the Business Incubation Industry* report), so this discussion will reflect the roles and responsibilities of a board for nonprofit incubators. All the responsibilities of a nonprofit board have a single underlying objective: ensuring that the incubator attains its mission. Typical responsibilities include:

- Hiring and evaluating the incubator director/CEO
- Assisting with developing and updating the incubator's strategic plan
- Serving as the liaison with government representatives and other stakeholders
- Marketing the incubator to potential stakeholders and client companies
- Supporting the incubator director in establishing and managing the professional services network, mentor network, and investor network
- Supporting the operation of the incubator and monitoring incubator budgets
- Supporting fundraising activities
- Supporting the development of successful client businesses
- Ensuring regular evaluation of incubator outcomes that align with the program's mission

By attending to these responsibilities, the board can ensure that the director stays focused on his or her responsibilities to the incubator and its clients.

The size and composition of the board should reflect the incubator's needs at its current stage of development. At first, the board should comprise the smallest number of members necessary to carry out its duties in terms of strategic direction and support to the director. Additional members should be added to meet the incubator's needs over time. However, incubator management must weigh the costs of each additional member (such as staff time to communicate and coordinate with them) against the benefits the individual brings to the board. A large board brings the maximum number of resources to the incubator; a small board has greater flexibility and is more economical.

The board of a successful incubator will include a mix of individuals with different characteristics, skills, geographic representation, gender, and so on. This group might include:

- Community leaders or champions who have a clear vision of the incubator's mission and the ability to motivate and sustain the board's commitment to that mission
- Professionals with connections to investors, professional service providers, and the larger business community
- Business operations and real estate professionals who can help the director with facility operations and management issues
- Professional business service providers and mentors who can advise clients and facilitate their use of resources
- Venture capitalists, angel investors, and bankers who understand new venture equity and debt financing
- Entrepreneurs who have developed successful ventures and who can ensure that the incubator's services are responsive to its clients' needs
- Technologists who can assist the director in evaluating the technical components of potential clients
- Incubator graduates who bring firsthand knowledge of the program's operations and value proposition

In addition to supervisory and advisory roles, nonprofit governing boards in the United States have fiduciary duties toward the organizations they govern. Fiduciary duties are both legal and financial:

Entrusted with guarding the organization's assets and reputation, board members must make prudent decisions that are in the best interest of the organization, without subjecting it to unnecessary risk…. A board member's oversight role entails setting and maintaining high standards of financial accountability; establishing and adhering to guidelines for ethical and legal behavior; and operating in a transparent manner so that … stakeholders understand how and why critical decisions were made. [Board Source, *The Nonprofit Board Answer Book*. San Francisco: Jossey-Bass, 2007.]

Good governance also requires that the board approve policies related to the election and rotation of new board members, avoidance of conflict of interest, requirements for regular attendance, and assessments of the board itself. The board should consider whether it is optimally organized to conduct business on behalf of the incubator, whether it reflects the current needs of the program, and whether it has taken care to ensure the succession of incubator management. Incubator management can work with the board chairman or executive committee to ensure that the board is educated about its responsibilities and receives training in good governance.

BEST PRACTICES IN ACTION

Working With a Large Board
Innovation Depot, Birmingham, AL
Susan Matlock, president and CEO
www.innovationdepot.net

The Innovation Depot has a large board of directors (thirty members in 2009), representing a broad cross section of its stakeholders, including financial supporters, the University of Alabama at Birmingham, the investment community, the city of Birmingham, and utilities and private corporations (which comprise two-thirds of the board). Board members include CEOs and senior-level vice presidents. The board has been structured strategically to include prominent individuals from both the public and private sectors with a primary focus on increasing value to clients and the incubator (i.e., sustaining its role in the broader economy and validating stakeholder investments).

Key benefits from having such a large (and skillful) board are:

- Keeping stakeholders, including financial supporters of the Innovation Depot, engaged on a regular basis so that they take ownership of the program and share in its success and challenges. For example, Innovation Depot President and CEO Susan Matlock relied heavily on her board members to help raise $11 million of the $18 million needed to renovate a 140,000-square-foot Sears store (empty for twenty years) that is now the home of the incubator.

- Providing direct access to resources beyond the walls of the Innovation Depot. Incubator board members serve on the boards of other organizations, including TechBirmingham and the Birmingham Venture Club,

which has assisted in integrating the Innovation Depot into the technology fabric of the region.

- Engaging board members with client businesses to increase their involvement and understanding of the program and to provide clients with valuable insights (mentoring), connections (via each board member's contacts), and access to capital (including pre-VC introduction evaluation and coaching).

The Innovation Depot developed after the Entrepreneurial Center (an incubator managed by Matlock that originated in 1987) took over management of UAB's Office for the Advancement of Developing Industries in 2001. The two programs merged in one location in 2007; previously, the incubators had been separated by more than ten miles.

Matlock's efforts to build a large, powerful, and sophisticated board for the new incubator were facilitated by the very positive recognition the Entrepreneurial Center and OADI had gained over the years, both as national models (they won many NBIA awards) and in Birmingham. It also was made possible because Matlock, a seasoned executive with wide community recognition, had the executive skills necessary to work with a large board made up of individuals who themselves were community and business leaders. (For more on Matlock and her staff, see chapter 2, "Staffing.")

The Innovation Depot Board of Directors has direct interactions with incubator clients. Regular networking receptions are held at the incubator, at which client companies interact and build relationships with board members. Additionally, individual board members have invested in many of the companies in the program, and they have helped make introductions to strategic business partners and new customers. Board members also serve on many client company advisory committees.

Board Retreat
William M. Factory Small Business Incubator, Tacoma, WA
Tim Strege, executive director
www.williamfactory.com

The William M. Factory Small Business Incubator, a specialty construction trades and applied technology incubator, is governed by a board of nine members that meets monthly. Members are high-powered, and currently include Rev. Arthur Banks, pastor and chairman of the Eastside Baptist Church and commissioner of the Tacoma Housing Authority; Wendell Brown, president of Centro Latino and a former county council member; Kathy Kingman, an engineer with the Washington State Department of Transportation; Susan Moblo, a commercial banker who was among the first female West Point graduates; and five others, including an attorney, two accountants, a corporate executive, and a former city manager. Together they bring passion and resources to the business incubation program.

Beginning in January 2004, though, the board decided its monthly meetings with staff reports didn't give members enough time to consider broader issues. The board agreed to

"The results of the board retreats provide direction for the program and staff."

– Tim Strege, executive director, William M. Factory Small Business Incubator

begin an annual retreat to get a better picture of the mission and activities of the incubation program and permit members to engage in a free flow of discussion. The retreat takes about two-thirds of a day, beginning at breakfast and incorporating a working lunch and after-lunch activities. While the retreat was originally facilitated by a professional, the board decided after several years that they should facilitate it themselves. Accordingly, the board chairman informally presides over retreat discussions, engaging and soliciting input from board directors. Incubator staff observe and provide background information and comments as requested.

The results of board retreats provide direction for the program and the staff. For example, incubator Executive Director Tim Strege explains that "one of the first discussions occurred as the incubator was opening its new building in 2003. The board wanted to decide whether [it] should pursue a second building and build a greater entrepreneurial campus." During their retreat discussions board members "quickly came to a consensus that they wanted to go beyond one building." As a result, the incubation program opened a second, connected structure in late 2009 that will permit it to grow to sixty client firms, thus doubling its impact on its eastside Tacoma neighborhood.

At another monthly meeting, the board began to discuss involving the incubator in a community energy efficiency project in which its client companies could play an active role. "They decided this was a much bigger topic and set it aside to discuss at their retreat," says Strege. "They recognized there was an opportunity to more explicitly relate what the incubator does within the building with community objectives outside the building." In 2007 the retreat focused on regional economic priorities and how emerging clusters fit within the incubator's role, mission, and objectives. This resulted in greater alignment with Puget Sound regional initiatives and helped the incubator identify potential clusters of firms for its emerging campus. Building upon the incubator's original foundation of specialty construction trades, new facilities and services will assist in the start-up and growth of firms related to information technologies, transportation logistics, and green energy/clean technologies.

Before each retreat, Strege works with the board chairman to develop an agenda and provides a written briefing to members so the event is pure business. Retreats are held off-site, and board members must turn off their cell phones. Both bed-and-breakfast and hotel sites have been utilized.

According to Strege, benefits have included:

- Creating a motivated, engaged board that is better informed and more cohesive in its understanding of the role the incubator plays, even though they may not be in total agreement on every issue. "By being engaged, board members buy into the concepts of what the incubator is doing and become drivers of the initiatives they have chosen to pursue," he says.

- Setting the stage for the rest of the year and then providing a backdrop for reviewing the accomplishments of the previous year.

- Ensuring the board becomes more excited about what the incubator is accomplishing. The process is "incremental and has resulted in their continually setting the bar higher for the future."

- Challenging management on their financials and operating plan and ensuring that management is focused on "smart staffing" and sustainability.

Thus, a common retreat discussion centers on the relatively tight-fisted financial practices of the executive director and the extent to which additional operating resources will be needed to accomplish ever-expanding incubator objectives. According to Strege, the board has impressed incubator staff with the need to move from a "small staffing" to a "smart staffing" model in which staff are augmented with contract personnel, collaborative agreements with outside entities, carefully selected and recruited professional volunteer mentors, and incremental paid staff. Says Strege: "While financial and personnel issues are frequent topics of monthly board meetings, the retreat discusses these topics on a macro and strategic level: What amount of incubator dollar and staff resources should be utilized to achieve heightened expectations of the incubator?"

- Contribute to the long-term sustainability and effective management of the incubator
- Relieve the incubator manager of some duties to ensure the program focuses on client services
- Provide depth and advisory capacity to incubator management and client companies
- Provide a sounding board for incubator management and can support management's decisions

■■ advisory boards

Advisory boards offer advice and counsel but do not have the same legal fiduciary duties as governing boards. Such boards can be helpful in some settings, such as incubators that operate under a host such as a university, college, or economic development organization that governs the program. Advisory board members could include incubator stakeholders, entrepreneurs, financiers, and other members of the business community, and they may provide advice to the program and to its clients.

Since the governing board of the incubator's host or sponsor (e.g., university board of trustees or economic development agency board) may have responsibilities of which the incubator is only a small subset, a dedicated advisory board can focus specifically on the incubator and its clients' needs. Advisory boards can fulfill many of the tasks and responsibilities described for governing boards above, although they would not hire the incubator CEO or have legal duties to guard the financial strength of the organization. Nonetheless, a strong advisory board can provide significant value to a business incubation program. For example, a strong advisory board can give added weight to decisions regarding incubator operations and services by serving as a sounding board and by providing objective advice from a group with a wide array of experiences and expertise.

BEST PRACTICES IN ACTION

LBTC Advisory Board
Louisiana Business & Technology Center, Baton Rouge, LA
Charles D'Agostino, executive director
www.bus.lsu.edu/lbtc

Like many university-based business incubators, the Louisiana Business & Technology Center does not have a governing board. LBTC is a division of the university, which has its own board of supervisors that holds governance and fiduciary responsibilities for the entire university. However, LBTC Executive Director Charles D'Agostino has developed an advisory board that proves such a group can be a powerful resource.

LBTC's advisory board includes the university vice chancellors for research/economic development and finance; five deans (business, engineering, basic sciences, agriculture, and veterinary medicine); the secretary of the Louisiana Department of Economic Development; the president of the Baton Rouge chamber of commerce; three bankers, including two CEOs; and a CPA, a patent attorney, and several business owners. This advisory board of eighteen powerful people can run interference for the incubator and its clients, and it advises the incubator manager on strategic issues.

Once a year the incubator holds a morning retreat (time is limited due to members' busy schedules). "We throw out our issues and the board helps us shape our strategic plan," D'Agostino says. "The board is also available one-on-one, either on the phone or I can go to their offices."

D'Agostino's board protects incubator funding and ensures that "I get instantaneous response," he says. "Literally, there isn't a door that I can't get open for the incubator or my clients." For example, D'Agostino notes that when his program gave up space to an LSU unit following Hurricane Gustav, board members who weren't affiliated with the university spoke to the chancellor about increasing incubator funding to offset losses in rental income and encouraging the speedy relocation of the unit. The top officer of the Louisiana Department of Economic Development also has protected state contributions to LBTC's NASA contracts.

"Having the mix of the academic and business representatives gives me the best of both worlds," he explains. It also improves town/gown relations as the academic deans are kept in touch with community doings and vice versa.

The board also assists clients. At each meeting, held every other month, one or two client companies give ten-minute presentations; the board responds with suggestions, comments, and possible connections. "This is extremely valuable to the clients who normally would not have access to such individuals on a one-on-one basis. In addition, the board often follows up or connects a client with potential suppliers, customers, investors, lenders, and other resources," D'Agostino says. LBTC maintains a listserv though which incubator clients also can request assistance. The requests are screened by incubator staff, who forward them to the advisory board if merited.

Stakeholders

- Foster program success
- Provide ongoing support to the incubation program
- Raise the incubator's visibility in the community
- Require strong, clear communication about expectations

Though the advisory board started with just twelve members, D'Agostino expanded it whenever he identified a potential strong contributor. However, some positions (the LSU deans and chancellors, and the state official) hold ex officio positions, meaning that whenever a new individual comes into the job they become automatic board members. "We got a new dean about a year ago, and I sent him a message, 'You're on my board whether you like it or not,'" D'Agostino explains.

The advisory board doesn't have formal term limits, but D'Agostino will have a private conversation with members who aren't contributing and ensure a smooth transition to a suitable replacement.

BEST PRACTICES IN ACTION

Incubator Advisory Board
TowsonGlobal-International Incubator, Towson, MD
Clay E. Hickson, director
www.towsonglobal.com

As an incubator in Phase I of its own development, TowsonGlobal–International Incubator founded in 2007, relies on a seventeen-member advisory board to assist with a variety of strategic issues, including incubation program marketing, strategic alliances, and fundraising as well as client company assistance.

With seven clients in 5,100 square feet, the incubator is a division of Towson University, which serves 22,000 students in the Baltimore suburbs. Towson is the second-largest university in the Maryland system, has the state's largest business college, and has computer science, electronic media and film, and other departments that have contributed to creation of robust clusters of businesses, such as those based on video gaming and simulations, says incubator Director Clay E. Hickson.

The incubator also serves as a landing pad for nondomestic firms, and it works with companies that have or intend to have international markets and alliances. In support of its international focus, TowsonGlobal board members include representatives of the Maryland Port Administration and the Maryland/Israel Development Center; the managing director for the International Trade and Development division of the Maryland Department of Economic Development; the vice president for worldwide marketing in microbiology systems for BD Diagnostics; the Towson vice president in charge of the Division of Economic and Community Outreach; a

director of supply chain management for Northrop Grumman; and the vice president of finance for Black & Decker. Advisory board Chairman Fred Lissauer is vice president for global export business development for McCormick & Company. In addition, Hickson has a long history of international business experience and speaks fluent Mandarin Chinese. He has been president and is chairman emeritus of the Maryland-China Business Council.

Formed after the incubator opened its doors, the advisory board started with twelve members and expanded to seventeen; it meets quarterly. In addition to members noted above with international expertise, the board includes representatives of venture capital firms and the state's Technology Development Corp. (TEDCO), as well as a banker, an expert in human resources, an attorney, and a CPA.

Committees focus on incubator marketing, fundraising, and client mentoring. Members also serve on review committees of three or four that vet potential incubator companies. The board's resource team on fundraising has been identifying potential corporate sponsorships and grants for future incubator expansions (to 25,000 square feet in Phase II and to 35,000 square feet in Phase III). Board Chairman Lissauer has met with representatives of the U.S. Economic Development Administration in hopes of gaining expansion funding.

The advisory board also helps incubator management look at the big picture, such as a recent examination of the program's distinguishing characteristics that began with the discussion, "Why TownsonGlobal?"

"We looked at other regional incubation programs and created a grid for use in better understanding how we could market ourselves as a mixed-use incubator with close university ties and solid global programming initiatives," Hickson says. As a result, the incubator revised its brochure, Web site, and other marketing materials. It now places greater emphasis on its distinguishing factors in discussions with prospects, and the board has helped TowsonGlobal make contacts with many smaller accounting and law firms that contribute to incubator deal flow.

In addition to focusing on issues of strategic importance to the incubator, the advisory board provides services to clients, speaks at brown bag luncheons, and participates in the incubator's annual Globalization Forum.

Board members also provide clients—which represent industries including solar energy, business intelligence gathering, furniture imports, food contaminant testing, and study-abroad counseling—with access to their own contacts. For example, the advisory board representative of the Maryland/Israel Development Council helped TG client Transcending Cosmetics make Israeli contacts. The videogame simulations firm Exis has developed simulations for defense contractors; the advisory board's Northrop Grumman representative has provided mentoring and guidance in making contacts, managing relationships, and negotiations. As a result, Exis has landed some Northrop Grumman contracts.

■■ stakeholders

Over the years, business incubation professionals and scholars have defined stakeholders both narrowly and broadly. Some use the term to refer simply to financial sponsors, while others use the term to describe everyone in a community or region who stands to benefit from an incubation program.

NBIA considers a stakeholder to be anyone who is not on the incubator staff and has a vested interest in the success of an incubation program. This broad definition might include donors, sponsors, service providers, board members, entrepreneurs, community leaders, economic development organizations, academic and research institutions, and even community residents who would benefit from a strengthened economy.

Stakeholders can foster an incubator's success by marketing the program, encouraging promising entrepreneurs to apply for admission, and providing client firms with resources and expertise.

Although many of an incubator's fundamental and enduring stakeholder relationships are formed during its development stage, more relationships will arise as the incubator begins and maintains operations. Regardless of the origin and length of the tie, stakeholder relationships require careful nurturing. Incubation professionals must work diligently to ensure their programs are relevant and visible in their communities or face possible loss of funding or commitment from its original stakeholders.

A healthy relationship between stakeholders and the incubator manager depends on each having appropriate expectations of the time, energy, and other resources invested in the relationship. The time an incubator manager spends maintaining stakeholder relationships should be on par with the expected benefits. A good way to handle the stakeholder-vs.-client dilemma is to deputize your board members to work with stakeholders. Even better: make sure your board includes representatives of various stakeholder groups.

It's imperative that the incubator professional calibrate stakeholder expectations of what the incubator can accomplish in a given time frame. Educating stakeholders about the business incubation process and setting realistic goals from the outset are two good strategies for managing expectations. As an incubator professional once said, "If our results were quick, we would be called a microwave and not an incubator." It's better to meet or surpass realistic projections than to make fantastic promises you can't keep and risk losing stakeholder support.

Taking time to manage relationships with stakeholders and acknowledge the service and support they provide is important to the incubator as well as its client companies. Without the support of stakeholders, the incubator's value to clients diminishes considerably.

WORKING WITH POLITICIANS

Enlisting political support for a business incubation program is vital—but tricky. While senators, representatives, and other politicians should be invited to the incubator and kept informed about its successes and needs, getting them involved in operations or otherwise entwining your future with theirs may be unwise.

"If the incubator becomes too closely allied with an individual mayor, for example, there is always the possibility that the new mayor won't support it," says NBIA President Emerita Dinah Adkins. "I have seen programs close down because of this problem."

Having a politician or political appointee on your board should be considered carefully. In some cases you may want to ensure that the board seat is an ex officio seat, meaning that the next incumbent of that position will take over the board position, Adkins says. "There is also a chance they won't show up and will contribute in name only. To avoid such a situation, the board should also have rules regarding regular attendance and participation by board members."

Politics and business incubation do sometimes mix, however. The Northeast Indiana Innovation Center in Fort Wayne, for example, receives financial support from both the city of Fort Wayne and from Allen County, so it has four political representatives on its board: two from the city (one appointed by the mayor and another by the city council) and two appointed by the county council. Despite political splits in governance—the city tends to be run by Democrats and the county by Republicans—NIIC President and CEO Karl LaPan says the arrangement has worked well. "Buy-in, attendance, and support have been good even though there is a high level of contention between the city and county," he says.

He attributes that goodwill to the involvement of both the city and the county in the incubator's development, as well as to his own dedication to accountability. "They appreciate that we're making a difference that is tangible and measurable," LaPan says of his political stakeholders. "It gives them comfort in knowing that the dollars they invest in us are achieving what they intended." (For more on LaPan's accountability efforts, see this chapter's section on strategic planning.)

Because the representatives are appointed by the current administration, the appointees must resign if the political regime changes. Because LaPan stays in constant communication with the mayor's office and with the county commission, he leverages those relationships to make sure he has input on their appointments. "I spend a lot of time working with politicians at all levels so that we're a part of that process, instead of having it mandated to us."

BEST PRACTICES IN ACTION

Effective Stakeholder Relationship Management
Louisiana Business & Technology Center, Baton Rouge, LA
Charles D'Agostino, executive director
www.bus.lsu.edu/lbtc

Established in 1988 as a joint venture between Louisiana State University, the Baton Rouge Area Chamber of Commerce, and the Louisiana Public Facilities Authority, the Louisiana Business & Technology Center is owned and operated by LSU as a component of the E. J. Ourso College of Business. It also has a number of contracts with city, state, and federal agencies to provide business counseling and other economic development services.

LBTC historically has leveraged its stakeholder relationships to define a broad mission beyond business incubation and job creation. Working with its stakeholders, LBTC has established itself as an economic development engine for the area and, more broadly, the entire state of Louisiana. For example, LBTC operates Small Business Development Centers, is the liaison for SBIR grants from the state's NASA labs, and offers entrepreneurship outreach in rural and disaster areas.

"We expanded services and mission to take advantage of market conditions and funding opportunities," D'Agostino says.

Keeping all those government stakeholders happy is simple, D'Agostino says: "Give the stakeholders what they want." He believes incubator management should determine what motivates stakeholders and what they want out of the incubator and their association with it. "In the case of LBTC, we have two separate sets of stakeholders [clients and supporters], who to a great extent want the same thing: to be associated with a quality program that accomplishes the economic development goals set out by the board," he says.

The quality program part is not a problem: LBTC was NBIA's 2005 Randall M. Whaley Incubator of the Year, was a finalist for NBIA's 2007 Incubator Innovation Award, and won the Incubator Innovation Award in 2009. Its recognition is external as well: LBTC staff and programs have won awards from the Association of University Research Parks, the Federal Laboratory Consortium, the Louisiana Department of Economic Development, the Southern Growth Policies Board, the U.S. Economic Development Administration, and the U.S. Small Business Administration.

To spread the word about the incubator's accomplishments—and provide tangible proof of such to stakeholders—D'Agostino maintains an active publicity effort, sending press releases on incubator activities or clients nearly every day. (He drafts the releases or has an intern do it; LSU's public relations department polishes and sends them.) Once a week, D'Agostino collects press clippings and any other information on LBTC to send to stakeholders.

The incubator also publishes an annual report with data on patent activities, job creation, payroll/tax base, capital formation, and revenue of all client companies in the aggregate for both the current year and historically.

"Stakeholders fund and support winners," D'Agostino says. "Clients and affiliates seek help from winners. Publicity implies that entrepreneurs need to seek out LBTC to maximize their success, and the numbers reported in the press and elsewhere tell funding groups to get behind a winner."

Stakeholder Surveys
San Juan College Enterprise Center, Farmington, NM
Jasper Welch, director
www.sanjuancollege.edu/gcb

For the first six years of his incubator's existence, Jasper Welch—director of the San Juan College Enterprise Center in Farmington, New Mexico—gathered feedback on his program and services with short questionnaires and informal discussions. By 2006, however, he was ready for a more formal approach.

"We felt we had enough history that we could ask our customers how we were doing," he says.

For $2,000, Welch hired a professional market researcher to interview fourteen stakeholders such as local bankers, politicians, college officials, and the directors of local Small Business Development Centers. In personal interviews lasting thirty to seventy minutes, the researcher asked just eight questions about the stakeholders' perceptions of the incubator; their willingness to refer clients to the incubator; what is and is not working in the program; the program's value to the stakeholder's organization; and whether their organization could support the incubator financially.

The results were both gratifying and eye-opening. Stakeholders held the incubator and its umbrella organization, the Quality Center for Business, in high regard. The problem, they said, was that the incubator did not promote itself as thoroughly as it could and that Welch was stretched too thin.

As a result of that study, Welch implemented a regular review of the incubator's marketing plan, which is updated every two years. He also stepped up publicity efforts in the regional business journal. In terms of staffing, the survey helped him make the case to his board to beef up his personnel; he now has a half-time coordinator and a half-time secretary, a one-third increase in staffing.

"The stakeholder interview process was very helpful in moving our program forward," Welch says.

Integration into Broader Economic Development Goals
University of Central Florida Business Incubation Program
Orlando, FL
Tom O'Neal, director
www.incubator.ucf.edu

Tom O'Neal would appear to have enough on his plate: as director of the University of Central Florida Business Incubation Program, he oversees operation of seven facilities with eighty clients (more facilities were scheduled to open in 2010). However, he makes the time to be involved in myriad community activities to ensure that UCF remains a player in regional economic development.

O'Neal is a council member of the Florida High Tech Corridor Council (FHTCC), which includes three universities, more than twenty local and regional economic development organizations, and fourteen community colleges serving a twenty-three-county region.

One benefit of his involvement is that FHTCC now views incubation as an important component of its agenda to grow, attract, and retain high-tech industry in the region. "There are very few high-wage, high-value projects that will not involve UCF," says Ray Gilley, president and CEO of the Metro Orlando Economic Development Commission.

UCF clients have benefited, too: several have used the FHTCC's industry matching grants program to secure SBIR or other funding in partnership with the university. In 2005, the grant program provided more that $2.3 million to match more than $4.9 million from industry to conduct leading-edge research.

O'Neal's other commitments include serving on the mayor's task force for high-tech economic development and being a board member of the Disney Entrepreneur Center, Bio Florida, the StarTech Incubator in Largo, and other economic development organizations. These partnerships and associations between UCF and the leadership of the greater community provide the strong linkages and integration necessary to create the innovation ecosystem that will sustain a strong local economy.

Don't just take O'Neal's word for it, though.

"UCF is central Florida's premier partner for increasing the region's capacity and capability for invention, innovation, and entrepreneurship," says Orange County Mayor Richard Crotty. "This is our springboard for staying competitive."

Integration into Broader Economic Development Goals
Northeast Indiana Innovation Center, Fort Wayne, IN
Karl LaPan, president and CEO
www.niic.net

As a result of a strategic mandate to serve a thirteen-county region in Indiana, the Northeast Indiana Innovation Center has partnered with myriad local community entities—such as economic development agencies and private businesses—that possess local knowledge and resources since 2004. The local entity benefits from regular access to NIIC's entire portfolio of resources and programs and from cobranding and reciprocal privileges with NIIC's programs and services.

NIIC raised $200,000 for its community outreach initiative from the U.S. Department of Agriculture's Rural Development Action grant, as well as ongoing funds from participating counties and communities.

These partnerships have led to collaborative (and successful) federal, state, and foundation grant proposals; paid research projects and feasibility studies for county initiatives (outside of Allen County, where NIIC is based); and the development of entrepreneurial resource capabilities and centers in the more rural counties. These initiatives are facilitating the development and growth of new business enterprises employing knowledge workers and highly skilled individuals. This "hub-and-spoke" model has several advantages:

- Reduced redundancies, eliminating duplication of services and delivering the services more cost-effectively
- Greater depth and sophistication of services available to regional entrepreneurs
- A coordinated and geographically distributed one-stop shop for the entrepreneur to access consistent, high-quality services

Through this initiative, the Innovation Center has established a regional node called Venture Works in collaboration with the Huntington University Enterprise Resource Center and the Huntington United Economic Development Corporation. This program serves Huntington County and the surrounding counties and has provided entrepreneurial training to high school students, run business idea/concept competitions, and offered direct entrepreneurial coaching services as well as some preincubation and incubation services.

In Wells County, the Innovation Center is partnering on the potential feasibility and launch of a specialty foods incubator/test kitchen. NIIC has conducted the stakeholder interviews and the feasibility assessment and has developed the business plan.

In Adams County, the Innovation Center is working with the Adams County Economic Development Corporation to identify the components of a success/engagement center that will provide, among other things, retraining services, entrepreneurial coaching, and comprehensive business support and development assistance services.

In South Whitley, Indiana, the Innovation Center partnered with a local engineering firm to develop a business model and case for support for economic revitalization of the downtown area, which included an assessment of entrepreneurial needs for a more vibrant downtown.

Integration into Broader Economic Development Goals
William M. Factory Small Business Incubator, Tacoma, WA
Tim Strege, executive director
www.williamfactory.com

The William M. Factory Small Business Incubator, in operation since 1986 in Tacoma's poorest East Side neighborhood, has been highly successful working with 80 percent minority disadvantaged businesses. Yet the incubator doesn't advertise itself as an incubator for minorities and women. Instead, it focuses on a mission to revitalize its eastside neighborhood, bringing jobs and wealth to that community and contributing to the overall economic health of Tacoma.

The incubator has helped its clients become involved in many projects in Tacoma and on the East Side, building its reputation throughout the city and bringing clients recognition for their efforts to rehabilitate Tacoma's old industrial area. As a result, Executive Director Tim Strege says the incubator has become a "beacon of hope" in its neighborhood.

Early incubator supporters were pastors, deacons, and members of largely African American churches in East Tacoma. Initial incubator leaders also were active with neighborhood organizations that provided vocal support for the incubator and took pride in incubator accomplishments. These church and community group participants still visit the incubator frequently, attend annual incubator fundraising banquets, and regularly testify before public agencies on incubator-related issues such as small business contracting policies, commercial zoning proposals, and contracts between the incubator and government entities. The White House Office of Faith-Based and Neighborhood Partnerships (previously the White House Office of Faith-Based and Community Initiatives) recognized the incubator in 2007 for its positive relations with its surrounding constituencies. All of this has increased stakeholder pride in the neighborhood, its institutions generally, and the incubator.

The incubator also maintains formal partnerships with other community-based and regional organizations that help to ensure William M. Factory clients have technology transfer, workforce training, marketing assistance, and other services at hand when needed. These include:

- African American Prosperity Partnership
- Bates Technical College
- Clover Park Technical College
- Seattle Urban League
- University of Washington School of Business
- Washington State Division of Child Support
- Washington State WorkFirst (a welfare reform program that helps residents obtain and retain jobs)
- WorkSource Pierce County (a program of the Workforce Development Council)

Additional incubator stakeholders include local government, the construction industry sector, and minority communities in Tacoma and the East Side at large.

Both the incubator's board and its management have worked to align incubator activities to community objectives. For example, a 2008 board retreat looked at regional economic priorities—green technology, information technologies, and transportation logistics—and how these emerging clusters fit within the incubator's role, mission, and objectives. The William M. Factory incubator has now expanded services to these new sectors.

In another example of the incubator's dedication to its community stakeholders, all leases include first-source hiring agreements in which clients agree to consider unemployed neighborhood residents for available job openings. These agreements create beneficial relationships between the businesses' growth and the residents' well-being. In effect, the employment clause helps incubator companies feel ownership of the East Side and encourages a desire to increase the quality of life in the neighborhood even after they graduate.

Encouragement of the incubator's efforts to expand from specialty construction trades to transportation logistics, clean technologies, green energy, and other desirable, growth-oriented economic clusters has come from members of the same religious congregations and neighborhood groups that supported the incubator in its early years.

The White House Office of Faith-Based and Neighborhood Partnerships recognized the incubator in 2007 for its positive relations with its constituencies.

staffing

Except for facilities, the single largest expense for most incubation programs is payroll—which should be no surprise. Staff are the incubator's most important asset and can make or break its success with clients and stakeholders. In addition to regular full- or part-time staff are myriad individuals who interact with clients and enhance incubator services, such as volunteers, interns, and service providers from the community. Although they are not staff per se, the quality and qualifications of these supporters are almost as vital to your program's success as those of your paid staff.

Management and boards of incubators should strive to

- Recruit and appropriately compensate management capable of achieving the mission of the incubator and having the ability to help companies grow
- Develop stakeholder support, including a resource network that helps the incubation program's client companies and supports the incubator's mission and operations

Incubator Staff

- Have company-growing skills
- Communicate effectively with sponsors and the business community
- Have financial and operational skills to ensure the incubator is sustainable

■■ qualifications

Often the first staff member hired—typically early in the incubator's development—is an executive director, manager, or CEO who hires and supervises other incubator staff and oversees the incubator's operations and finances. (In some cases, the incubator is managed by an outside firm that contracts with the incubator's board.) No matter what the title, this individual must be dynamic and have business experience in the industries the incubator will support. Other desirable characteristics include:

- Ability to effectively market the incubator to potential clients, sponsors, and stakeholders
- Ability to identify clients' needs, coach clients effectively, and facilitate their access to outside resources
- Ability to work with the board to impart the incubator's vision and mission to the general public and, through the selling of that vision, enlist support

It's unlikely that a single individual will be fully knowledgeable in all aspects of entrepreneurship. Therefore, the director must recognize his or her own weaknesses and be able to bring in outside assistance when needed and, if necessary, to enlist mentors to help build capacity. Additional staff may be hired as the incubator develops, depending on the program's budget, the level of services provided, the number of clients served, and the support provided by the board and stakeholders.

While some programs are generously staffed, many make do with just a few people. Large programs may have a director who oversees all operations; a facility manager who focuses on the building; and entrepreneur support staff who deal directly with clients. But that situation is likely the exception, not the rule: In NBIA's *2006 State of the Business Incubation Industry* report, average full-time-equivalent staff at responding North American incubation programs was 1.8—down from 2.8 in 1998.

Nearly all incubation programs have a full- or part-time administrative assistant or receptionist who handles duties such as light bookkeeping, scheduling, responding to inquiries from potential clients, and assisting existing clients with basic services and information. About two-thirds of incubation programs have a full- or part-time assistant manager or client services manager who focuses primarily on working with client companies. However, the majority of incubation programs—97 percent, according to NBIA's *2006 State of the Business Incubation Industry*—call upon outside service providers to assist clients as well.

BEST PRACTICES IN ACTION

Staff Qualifications
Innovation Depot, Birmingham, AL
Susan Matlock, president and CEO
www.innovationdepot.net

Qualified management is the key to the Innovation Depot's success. In addition to a strong board of directors (comprising thirty community leaders), President and CEO Susan Matlock possesses the interpersonal, technical, and managerial skills to bring together diverse stakeholders working together toward a common vision. Matlock's resume reads like a listing in *Who's Who in Corporate America*, showing that highly successful incubators possess leaders who could just as easily be the CEOs of major corporations. She also has hired highly qualified and effective staff. Current staff includes the president and CEO, chief financial officer, chief operating officer, director of IT services, director of facility operations, and administrative personnel.

See abbreviated resumes below:

Susan Matlock is the president and CEO of the Innovation Depot, Inc., a business incubation program that assists in the development of emerging biotechnology/life sciences, information technology, and service businesses. Matlock was named one of the "Top 25 Most Influential People in the Southeast Technology Community" by *TechJournal South* in late 2007. She was founding president of the Entrepreneurial Center and executive director of the University of Alabama at Birmingham incubator known as OADI. The Entrepreneurial Center was named a 2000 Business Incubator of the Year by Dun & Bradstreet and the National Business Incubation Association.

Powerhouse Ventures in New Zealand, is
both stategic and methodical about building
a managment team.

Matlock is a member of the board of directors of both Regions Financial Corp., a Birmingham-based bank, and of St. Vincent's Health System (where she serves as vice chairman); she also is on the board of managers of Ascension Health Ventures, a $325 million investment fund based in St. Louis. She is a past chairwoman of the board of directors of the Birmingham Venture Club, a founding member of the Alabama Information Technology Association board, and a member of the Biotechnology Association of Alabama board. She was 2004 chairwoman of TechBirmingham.

Matlock is a member of the board of directors of the United Way of Central Alabama and serves on the advisory board of the UAB School of Business. She also served as the chairwoman of the board of directors of the National Business Incubation Association from 1994 to 1995 and was an NBIA board member for six years. In 2004, Matlock was named by Ernst & Young and the Ewing Marion Kauffman Foundation as one of the three finalists for the national Supporter of Entrepreneurship Award.

In 1992 and 1993, NBIA and Coopers & Lybrand recognized a graduate of the Entrepreneurial Center as an Incubator Graduate of the Year; in 2002 NBIA recognized an OADI tenant as a Tenant of the Year; and in 2004 and 2005 OADI graduates were named Graduate of the Year (the award was then sponsored by Turnstone, a division of Steelcase). Matlock was founding chairwoman of the Alabama Business Incubation Network and has been recognized by the Birmingham Area Chamber of Commerce as Small Business Advocate of the Year and by the U.S. Small Business Administration as the Financial Services Advocate of the Year for the State of Alabama.

She has a master's degree in public administration from the University of Alabama at Birmingham and has taught the entrepreneurial course offered to students seeking a master's degree in public and private management at Birmingham-Southern College. She completed an executive in residence

program at Harvard Business School and is a member of the Kiwanis Club of Birmingham and a graduate of Leadership Birmingham and Leadership Alabama.

Matlock is a contributing author to two books on business incubation and has spoken on the topic at many conferences on six continents.

Devon Laney is the chief operating officer of the Innovation Depot. Prior to joining the incubator, as an analyst with Accenture LLP in Atlanta, Laney worked on a broad range of marketing, IT, and strategic organizational projects with various Fortune 500 companies. Previously, he worked on the development, redesign, and launch of Energen Corporation's intranet, and he also served as the entertainment editor for nationally distributed *Family Issues* magazine during its first eighteen months of publication.

In the Birmingham community, Laney serves as vice president on the board of the Birmingham Venture Club, where he is also chair of the Marketing Committee. He is the youngest member ever to serve on this board. Additionally, Laney serves on the board of Operation New Birmingham's Magic City Art Connection, the Alys Stephens Center Young Patrons board, and the UAB Comprehensive Cancer Center's Young Supporters board. He is a member of the inaugural class of Leadership UAB and is also a member of the Biotechnology Association of Alabama, TechBirmingham, and the Young Leaders Society of the United Way of Central Alabama. He also was selected as one of the *Birmingham Business Journal*'s "Top 40 under 40" in 2009 and is a member of the 2010 class of Leadership Birmingham.

Laney has a master's degree in business administration and a bachelor's degree in international business, both from the University of Alabama. He also has completed studies at the International Business School in Gröningen, the Netherlands.

Gerry O'Toole joined the Innovation Depot (then the Entrepreneurial Center) in March 1994 as the director of administration and finance. He was named vice president/

CFO in June 2000. O'Toole was an integral part of the team when the Entrepreneurial Center was named a 2000 Incubator of the Year by the National Business Incubation Association and Dun & Bradstreet.

O'Toole oversees operations of tenant facilities and has overall responsibility for internal operations, as well as all financial forecasting and reporting for the organization. He also runs and maintains a small accounts receivable/working capital lending program for the clients of the Innovation Depot.

O'Toole has a strong background in finance and technical skills and earned a bachelor of science degree in mathematics from Duquesne University in Pittsburgh, Pennsylvania.

He is a current member of the Birmingham Venture Club, the Alabama Information Technology Association, the Biotechnology Association of Alabama, and the National Business Incubation Association, and he represents the Innovation Depot in the Woman's Business Ownership Council.

Entrepreneurial Personality Tests

Powerhouse Ventures, Christchurch, New Zealand
Stephen Hampson, CEO
www.cii.co.nz

Powerhouse Ventures in Christchurch, New Zealand, is both strategic and methodical about building a management team that is able to help its thirty clients (eighteen in-house) grow profitable companies.

Powerhouse clients focus on language learning software, water purification, electronic payroll, 3-D computer animation software, and data security hardware. When hiring management staff for its three incubation programs, Powerhouse looks for individuals with entrepreneurial skills, technical background, and prior management experience with start-ups. Currently Powerhouse employs fourteen people, nine of which are management team members.

Since early 2006, the incubator has been using a commercially available entrepreneurial personality test to determine job candidates' entrepreneurial traits. Powerhouse staff learned about entrepreneurial personality testing after working with a client company whose expertise was in the field of recruitment screening tools. That client's product wasn't suited to Powerhouse's entrepreneurial requirements, so Powerhouse sought out another commercially available product through an expert in entrepreneurialism.

There are multiple products available, according to Stephen Hampson, Powerhouse CEO. Powerhouse uses two testing options, ranging in price from NZ$50 per test for a basic report to NZ$480 for more extensive reports.

One of the tests assigns a primary and a secondary color to each candidate on the basis of entrepreneurial traits. In brief, Powerhouse seeks red (highly entrepreneurial), blue (analytic), and yellow (people-oriented) individuals.

Additionally, Powerhouse seeks individuals with a strong technical background and whose industry sector strengths complement those of other staff members.

As of this writing, Powerhouse's team included management staff with the following credentials:

- A managing partner with a strong track record of working with technology start-ups, helping create a number of successful companies. He has substantial hands-on experience leading companies in Europe and New Zealand. His experience with New Zealand start-ups spans eight years and more than thirty ventures.

- A partner who led a technical management team through the evaluation stages of a business proposal to develop proprietary technology and to source and commercialise third-party intellectual property. That technology has since been used successfully in the airline passenger management sector.

- A manager who was a founding employee of a Christchurch-based corporate spin-out. The company generated world-leading technology in the field of biodegradable expanded foams. The technology was sold to a European firm.
- A technology entrepreneur who founded her own software start-up in 2000. The company developed generic configuration management software for mobile telecommunications network operators.
- A general manager who, as head of a corporate technology spin-out, successfully negotiated a license for the technology to that industry's premier company, based in Italy.
- A manager whose experience includes managing the branch of a nuclear contracting firm and leading a team developing advanced combustion systems.

Additionally, the incubator has found entrepreneurial assessment software to be useful in working with clients. It helps incubator staff find out what areas a particular entrepreneur is weak in and helps guide the staff's interaction with the entrepreneur. Incubator staff also have helped clients use the test as part of their own recruitment processes.

Aligning Staff Evaluation with Operating Goals
Northeast Indiana Innovation Center, Fort Wayne, IN
Karl LaPan, president and CEO
www.niic.net

Every year, the Northeast Indiana Innovation Center establishes five major operating goals that are consistent with the incubator's strategic plan (see chapter 1, "Governance," for more on NIIC's strategic planning process).

Each of NIIC's twelve staff members must establish measurable, achievable personal goals that are aligned with the plan. Throughout the year, they must demonstrate and track their personal progress toward their goals. (For more on how NIIC uses innovative technology for performance evaluation, see chapter 7, "Leveraging Innovation.")

"We want to get people focused on their activities and have a direct line of sight between those activities and the results the organization is trying to achieve," says Karl LaPan, NIIC's president and CEO.

Because the self-evaluation process is continuous, LaPan and his managers can see how well staff are progressing toward their goals. Those who are struggling can get help—"Maybe we need to provide more coaching," LaPan says.

There is a tangible reward involved: NIIC offers profit sharing in good years. When the program does well, employees can get up to 3 percent of their salary added to their 401(k).

Compensation

- Attracts and retains high-quality management and staff
- Reflects the program's commitment to providing the best management possible
- Contributes to program outcomes and other success measures, including incubator sustainability

■ ■ compensation

Finding and hiring good staff is only one part of the equation. Appropriately compensating those staff members is just as important. Incubator boards—driven by a nonprofit, public-sector mentality—often are tempted to skimp on salaries. This is a mistake. Attracting and retaining the type of talent needed to sustain a successful incubator requires competitive compensation and benefits packages.

NBIA research has shown a correlation between outcomes—such as incubator sustainability, job creation, and graduation rates—and adherence to best practices such as appropriately compensating incubation program management and staff. While it is impossible to provide causative links between staff compensation and incubation program performance, there can be little doubt that paying low wages limits a program's ability to hire talent that has the skills and expertise needed to grow companies—or the incubator itself. Incubator sponsors that hire a program "concierge" rather than a qualified professional will forgo the positive impacts successful programs can generate and may doom a project to failure. For example, a poorly paid and ineffective manager could fail to develop or maintain a financially sustainable program or provide appropriate services to emerging companies.

Median salaries for full-time incubator executives in all sectors reached $79,325 by 2009—more than double the median in 1990. Still, that figure is significantly lower than salaries for similar positions in private firms. Although some individuals will be attracted by the pure benefits of working with early-stage ventures, contributing to the community, or the recognition and prestige attached to the incubator, many talented people will eventually be drawn away by more lucrative offers.

Salary levels within the incubation industry vary by incubator type. In NBIA's 2009 compensation survey, full-time executives of technology incubators averaged $92,151 per year, while full-time biotechnology incubator managers earned an average of $131,800. In contrast, full-time leaders of mixed-use programs reported an average salary of $76,500. Geography plays a role, too: Managers of urban incubators reported average salaries of $88,217, while their rural counterparts were paid an average of $82,119.

In addition to salary, incubator staff compensation often includes vacation, paid holidays, and health insurance. Some incubation programs also make contributions to a retirement account for their managers. In 2009, about one-third of U.S. incubation programs offered bonuses to executives; in most cases, these bonuses were linked to incubator performance and financial sustainability measures.

- Relieve the incubator manager of some duties so that he or she may better focus on growing companies
- Bring special expertise to serve the needs of client companies

■■ volunteers and interns

In addition to paid staff, many incubation programs rely on volunteers from the community, industry, colleges, and other resources. Volunteers may serve as receptionists, tour guides, office assistants, facility managers, or business experts. Matching these resources with the needs of each client is a complex process and should be carefully coordinated to ensure value to both parties. To keep staff focused on client services, you might delegate volunteer training to a board member or a senior, experienced volunteer.

Many incubation programs benefit from the services of interns from nearby colleges and universities. Interns' roles can range from administrative and clerical duties to client counseling, depending on the talent pool available.

BEST PRACTICES IN ACTION

Utilizing University Interns
Louisiana Business & Technology Center, Baton Rouge, LA
Charles D'Agostino, executive director
www.bus.lsu.edu/lbtc

The E. J. Ourso College of Business at Louisiana State University offers its students immersive experiences in education. A prime outlet for those efforts is the Louisiana Business & Technology Center, the university's business incubation program. "Real-world application of classroom theory is invaluable as a learning experience," says LBTC Executive Director Charles D'Agostino.

LBTC pairs clients with MBA students who apply their knowledge and know-how to help the firms develop business, marketing, and financial plans as well as provide other research services. The students are matched with companies based in part on their expertise and backgrounds; for example, several MBAs with undergraduate degrees in engineering have worked with LBTC's engineering technology and manufacturing clients.

The college of business offers ten positions as paid graduate assistantships, a competitive process that yields the best students, D'Agostino says. "They send us resumes to review and we interview and select the GAs. Because of the reputation for stimulating work and greater starting salaries after two years with LBTC, we generally get the cream of the crop."

LBTC also works with other university departments. Through a partnership with the LSU School of Art, for example, LBTC pairs clients with senior graphic design students who devise logos, Web sites, and other graphic identity standards for them. In 2009, three of four clients implemented the entire graphic identity the students devised for them; the fourth did a partial implementation. Interns from other departments work on information systems and marketing projects. Although they are not paid, they receive course credit for their work.

Small Business Clinic
Springfield Business Incubator, Springfield, MA
Deborah King, former executive director
www.stcc.edu/sbi

Clients of the Springfield Business Incubator in Springfield, Massachusetts, have access to an enviable perk: free legal and business assistance worth thousands of dollars.

The Small Business Clinic is operated by the Law and Business Center for Advancing Entrepreneurship, a joint program of the Western New England College schools of law and business. The center rents space in the incubator building and staffs it with law students operating under a supervising professor's license, as well as MBA candidates.

The program was the brainchild of Eric Gouvin, a professor at the law school who wanted to give his students practical experience in business law. In the early 2000s, he approached Deborah King, who was then the executive director at the incubator, a program of Springfield Technical Community College. King immediately recognized the opportunity.

"These entrepreneurs are basic start-ups—they don't know how to hire employees or put employee documents and policies in place," she says. And having dedicated legal expertise at her disposal was hugely attractive. "The law is always a work in progress, and it's not my job to keep track of it," King says. "You have to have resources in place to do that."

At first, teams of WNEC law students worked with clients of STCC's student incubator. That was so successful that the students' services were offered to all SBI clients and then to the community at large. The students draw up employee contracts, perform intellectual property research, and provide other legal services.

"Some of these are critical legal issues that an entrepreneur might tend to put off because cash flow is tight," King says.

Over time, Gouvin and King found that legal issues crossed over into business issues. So Gouvin pulled in MBA students from the WNEC School of Business to provide that expertise. That led to the development of the Law and Business Center, which now has a dedicated faculty member and $1.6 million in funding from the college and other stakeholders.

WNEC's commitment to the project—especially Gouvin's drive—was vital, King says. "To get it set up, it was key to have someone who really believed in it and wanted it to work," she says. "The person at the law school is the key piece."

Of course, King played a role, too, in providing a pipeline of viable clients. "The worst thing that can happen, from their point of view, is to have students who are engaged and have a bad experience because they have bad clients," she says. Bodies in chairs weren't enough; the clients had to present an opportunity for quality legal work.

That has never been a problem, King says. "Entrepreneurs can get themselves so screwed up doing the wrong things, when it's not so hard to get set up right," she says.

An Internship Partnership
The Boston University Business Incubation Program
Boston, MA
Clifford Robinson, former director
www.bu.edu/otd/about/incubation

Boston University's president, Robert Brown, came to the university in 2005, at about the time Clifford Robinson took over the BU Business Incubation Program. Brown wanted three things. While the incubator had previously been exclusive to the BU Photonics Center, he wanted it to be a resource for the entire university and to incubate companies that were representative of BU strengths across all disciplines. Second, he wanted to change the program from an equity-based to a fee-for-service business model. And third, he wanted to include students so they could gain educational experience from working with the incubator companies.

Robinson worked closely with Jonathan Rosen, director of the Institute of Technology Entrepreneurship and Commercialization that Brown created within the Graduate School of Management, to make the third mandate a reality. For example, Rosen and Robinson built a program in which ITEC students were assigned projects to work on with incubator clients. The CEOs and founders helped define the project and work with faculty to develop it so that the project was of legitimate educational value and provided real value to the company.

ITEC students came from myriad backgrounds, and not all were business majors. Many were from the sciences, engineering, or medical departments; some were law students, while others came from liberal arts colleges. Through the internship program, all got a real-world look at entrepreneurship. "Working day-to-day in a start-up company is an excellent way for a student to determine whether or not they have what it takes to be an entrepreneur," says Robinson, who led the incubator until his retirement in September 2009. "Many interns described it as a 'life-changing experience.'"

"It was a win-win-win for everyone," says Robinson. "The company gained a student to work on a project at no cost, the students received educational value and course credit, and the university itself used the company as a living case study and provided its students with on-campus experiential learning in a way that other universities could not."

To ensure the continuous involvement of students, Robinson created a policy requiring all companies in the incubator to agree to accept students as part of their license agreement with the university. By working with the university's Office of General Counsel to draft appropriate language, Robinson was able to implement this policy without its being onerous or burdensome for client companies. It worked well. In almost all cases, companies agreed they had benefited from the students' work.

However, not all students were working with companies as part of an educational program. Sometimes a company would simply need work to be done and would hire and pay a student who was not receiving course credit to work as an intern for a semester, summer, or sometimes a year or more. From 2006 to 2009, more than eighty students worked as interns with twenty companies, funded by close to $100 million. Ten students found full-time employment with incubator companies after graduation.

- Expands the range of technical and professional expertise available to incubator clients

- Provides credibility to the incubation program by showing strength in the range of value provided to clients

- Allows the incubator to expand its reach into industry clusters that may be beyond the expertise of staff (e.g., clean tech, biotech)

- Helps incubator staff focus on coaching and facilitation rather than technical assistance

- Promotes the incubator's purpose and mission in the broader community by serving as an effective outreach mechanism and referral vehicle

- Increases the number of stakeholders interested in supporting the incubator

■■ service provider network

The service provider network, or professional services network, is a collection of experts from the region who provide services to incubator clients but are not paid staff of the incubator. These experts typically include:

- Senior-level accountants
- Attorneys
- Marketing specialists
- Venture capitalists
- Academic researchers/professors
- Experienced entrepreneurs
- Technology specialists
- Human resource professionals
- Insurance professionals
- Drug approval process experts (for life science incubators)

In addition, you may know of other people in your community with expertise and a willingness to support client businesses. Because these individuals are not typically available to or affordable to early-stage ventures, their cooperation with your program offers great value to your clients—and they are a great marketing tool for your incubation program.

The types of providers you line up will depend in part on who your clients are. For example, artists and designers will need to be versed in the legal aspects of trademark and copyright laws, while those who are commercializing new technologies will have additional needs involving patent law. Food businesses and biotechnology enterprises, on the other hand, will need guidance through industry-specific government approval processes.

Expertise is not enough, however; neither are low- or no-cost services. The service provider must supply a clear benefit to your clients and have a sincere interest in giving back to the community, without expecting a guarantee of future work from either the clients or the incubator. The incubation program must clearly articulate and reinforce this point so there is no misunderstanding.

That is not to say that the service provider should get nothing. You may arrange for the expert to provide a certain number of hours per month to your program for free, with a reduced rate for services over that limit. Such an arrangement prevents clients from taking advantage of the provider and reinforces the value of the provider's time and expertise. And, of course, you should recognize the provider's affiliation with your program on your Web site and in marketing materials.

Finding the right experts may take time and may require you to reach outside your local community. The process will become easier as your program establishes itself as a valuable source of support for successful ventures.

There are a number of ways to find top-notch professionals for your network. One is to get out into the community (which you should be doing anyway) and meet people. Another is to ask people you trust to recommend candidates. Your clients and board members, chambers of commerce, bar associations, university business departments, and successful businesses are all good places to look, too.

Before inviting a professional to join your network, take time to get to know him or her. You may want to institute a formal screening process with an interview and reference check. In other cases, a simple face-to-face meeting may provide all the assurance you need that your choice is the right one. Give new service providers a trial project to make sure the fit is good and to work out any kinks in the relationship.

Professionals may choose to work with your clients for a variety of reasons:

- To obtain new, potentially appealing customers as businesses graduate from the incubator and pay market rates for professional services
- To find prospective partners and strategic alliance opportunities among other providers or to maintain industry awareness
- To identify investment opportunities
- To enhance their public relations profile
- To give something back to the community

Regardless of their reasons, you must regularly acknowledge their contributions and manage your relationships with them well—because without them, your program's value to new ventures diminishes significantly.

BEST PRACTICES IN ACTION

Service Provider Network in Lieu of Staff
Mi Kitchen Es Su Kitchen, New York, NY
Kathrine Gregory, director
www.mikitchenessukitchen.com

Kathrine Gregory, the founder and director of Mi Kitchen Es Su Kitchen, a food incubator in New York City, views herself more as a coordinator than as anything else. Her program has no dedicated facility, and she is its only staff member.

"I'm the intermediary, the go-to person," she says. "I'm fine with that."

Gregory leases space in commercial kitchens around New York for her clients to use, so she has few facility management tasks. And she relies on outside service providers for the business support services that are the hallmark of an incubation program.

"I find that entrepreneurs don't want anything until they're ready for it, and usually they're ready for it when they're in a crisis," Gregory says. "At that point, I have to be prepared to either answer their questions directly or give them the name of somebody who's very reputable."

For general business assistance, she refers clients to the local Small Business Development Center. With them, she runs a twice-yearly, ten-week seminar on starting a food business. Anyone who has perfect attendance gets a certificate to use one of Gregory's kitchen facilities for one shift at no charge.

For more specific needs, she calls upon a "consortium of consultants" that she personally has vetted. "You go out into the industry and find people who are willing, really knowledgeable, and have the right mindset," Gregory says.

Providers who pass that test sign an agreement to work with clients Gregory sends to them. The first five hours are given at a reduced rate; after that, the provider and the client can decide on an agreeable rate. Gregory gets no piece of the action, preferring not to appear biased in favor of a provider who is giving her money. "I decided to be Caesar's wife, above reproach," she says.

In return, the providers get a pipeline of customers. Even those who stop after the first five hours may become regular customers later on. "I have three insurance brokers I recommend all the time," Gregory says. "They have all the legal learning I require, and they know my standards. I must have given them $40,000 to $50,000 in business, each."

To address the very specific needs of food entrepreneurs, Gregory works with providers that have that expertise. For example, she will arrange for a company that does product packaging to offer a two-hour seminar on packaging at its showroom. Clients can bring their products to test different packages, guided by the provider's staff. "These are people who do food packaging, so they know all the rules and regulations," Gregory says. Her clients get good advice, and the provider gets to showcase its wares and abilities to potential customers.

> "I find that entrepreneurs don't want anything until they're ready for it, and usually they're ready for it when they're in a crisis."
>
> – Kathrine Gregory, director, Mi Kitchen Es Su Kitchen

Detailed Client Needs Matching

Ben Franklin TechVentures, Bethlehem, PA
Wayne Barz, manager of entrepreneurial services
www.bftechventures.org

The Ben Franklin Business Incubator in Bethlehem, Pennsylvania, has always drawn on a broad network of service providers. But in 2002, the incubator—now Ben Franklin TechVentures—decided it needed to do more than pass along phone numbers.

The incubator dedicated three staff members to what it christened the Solutions Network, giving them a mission: recruit the best service providers possible, match clients with the appropriate provider, make sure the relationship gets off to a good start, and monitor the interaction.

If someone from BFTV hears about or meets someone who might be a good addition to the network, a Solutions Network staffer schedules a meeting. If the potential provider has expertise that BFTV clients might need, that individual is added to the network. Each Solutions Network staff member has a particular focus area; for example, one team member concentrates primarily on establishing relationships with venture capital firms, angel investors and networks, and federal funding programs such as SBIR grants.

"We're lucky to be located where we have a pretty sizable pool of resources to draw on," says Wayne Barz, manager of entrepreneurial services for Ben Franklin Technology Partners of Northeastern Pennsylvania, which operates the incubator. As a result, team members meet with new potential providers almost weekly.

That also means BFTV has a large roster of service providers—certainly more than can fit in a Rolodex. And the incubator wanted to keep detailed records of each provider's background and areas of expertise, the clients each had worked with, and the outcomes of those interactions. So the incubator expanded its custom client database to include a module for service providers.

"I can look up Company X in that database and look at all the stuff we've done with them, the clients we introduced them to, and the outcomes," Barz says.

The database is key to the Solutions Network's primary function, which is to match clients with exactly the right resource. Using the database, BFTV can sort through all the providers in a given field—say, those with experience as chief financial officers—and find the ones that have experience in the client's industry niche or that have worked well with similar clients in the past.

"We send those resumes to the company and let them decide whom to meet with," Barz says. "It's very targeted to the company's area of interest."

But that's not the end of it. BFTV facilitates that initial meeting to make sure the fit is good. "A lot of it is the chemistry between the company and that person," Barz says. It also gives BFTV a firsthand look at a service provider's interaction with clients. That way, Barz says, "you know when you have a service provider who isn't getting the job done."

Building a Network through Professional Associations

La Cocina Business Incubator, San Francisco, CA
Caleb Zigas, program coordinator
www.lacocinasf.org

San Francisco's Mission District is an ethnically diverse and economically vulnerable neighborhood that thrives in part because of the many small, informal businesses that serve the community. As is the case in many cities, food lies at the heart of this community, and you don't have to look far to find hidden entrepreneurs in the kitchens of many homes.

La Cocina—which means "the kitchen" in Spanish—was founded to serve as a platform for low-income entrepreneurs launching, formalizing, or expanding their food businesses in the Mission District. The program provides affordable commercial kitchen space and industry-specific technical assistance to low-income entrepreneurs in order to bring their businesses quickly to a point of self-sufficiency.

The incubator's staff of five focus on technical issues related to food processing. For general business assistance services, La Cocina leverages a network of local organizations and industry specialists to support the day-to-day interaction provided by its staff. Among those who provide general business assistance services to La Cocina clients are the Renaissance Entrepreneurship Center, a San Francisco incubator for low- to moderate-income entrepreneurs, and the Women's Initiative for Self-Employment, which also offers entrepreneur training and education to high-potential, lower-income women.

In addition, La Cocina used its connections in the community to recruit high-quality partners in the food industry, including Mattson—the largest independent developer of new products for the food and beverage industry—and Bon Appétit Management Company, an on-site restaurant company that provides café and catering services to corporations, colleges and universities, and specialty venues with over four hundred locations in twenty-eight states. Mattson offers nutrition testing and education and training to La Cocina clients, while Bon Appétit provides advisory services and industry connections.

Human Resources Services Program
Purdue Technology Center, West Lafayette, IN
Tim Peoples, director
www.purdueresearchpark.org

Human resources is one of the most important functions in a start-up company but is among the least appreciated and understood by early-stage companies. Purdue Technology Center in West Lafayette, Indiana, takes a unique approach to helping its clients recruit, manage, and organize employment practices. Launched in 2005, Human Resources Services assists start-up companies with the professional insights and HR staffing that clients so desperately need but can't afford.

The program began when the staff of the Purdue Research Foundation—which operates the Purdue Research Park, where the incubator is located—realized that technology park companies could better utilize and leverage its core competence in HR. The program provides selected services to park residents and incubator clients upon request and as needed by the on-site incubator professional management team. (The client's HR needs often are identified during regularly scheduled business coaching sessions.) Initially, the program offered only basic services, such as performance coaching and employment law–related questions. As more clients opted in to the program, additional services such as recruitment and job posting were provided in response to client demands.

The scope of HR Services includes recruiting; background checks; health and retirement benefits; training and professional development; employee relations issues (hiring and firing); and preparation of handbooks, policies, and other employment practices. This comprehensive portfolio of services is provided at no cost to companies located within Purdue Research Park (except for any out-of-pocket expenses, which are passed on to the client). For example, advertising positions, conducting background checks, and interviewing prospective employees incur additional costs.

In addition, the HR team hosts a monthly roundtable for all park companies, with pizza and a discussion on a topic of concern in human resources, organizational development, or legal issues. The HR team markets these events by offering a high-quality experience—good food (not your typical box lunch), good and relevant content, and frequent follow-ups to bolster attendance. Originally, it was expected that a nominal fee would be charged for these events, but to increase participation, PTC clients can attend at no cost. Guests can attend one roundtable event at no cost before having to become a client.

PTC Director Tim Peoples advises adding a small markup—5 percent to 10 percent—on any out-of-pocket expenses to help cover program overhead. He also is considering tiered HR services, with a basic package with an established number of engagements in each area per quarter or per year, and charging by the service for any needs above the basic level. For example, the program might assist in writing a certain number of job descriptions or screening a defined number of job resumes and charge a per-use fee for additional writing or screenings.

The HR Services program also is a sales tool for the Purdue Technology Center. It is prominently identified in the brochure marketing the incubator's services, and its operation is a key element of new client orientation.

The human resources team hosts a monthly roundtable for all companies, with pizza and a discussion on a topic of concern in human resources, organizational development, or legal issues.

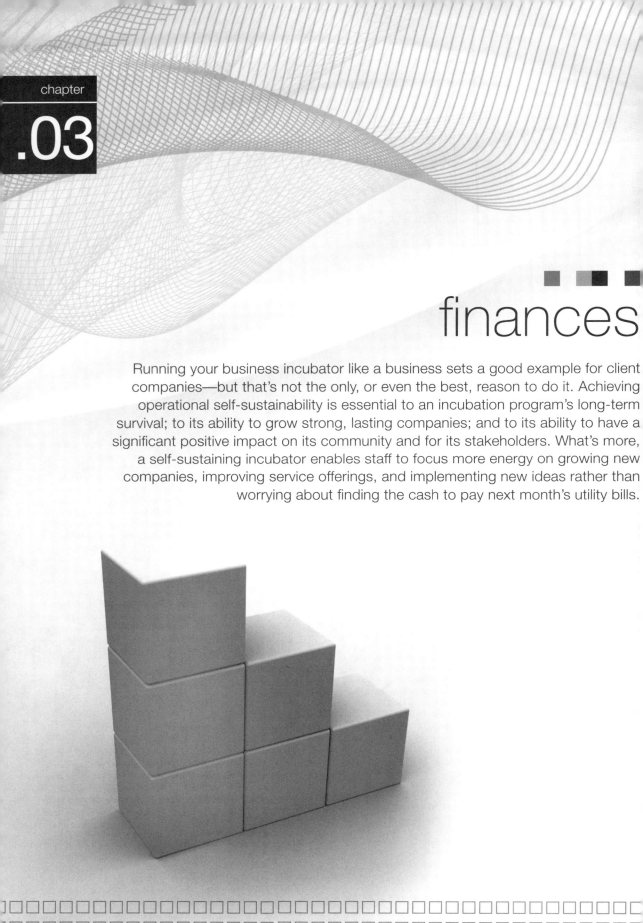

finances

Running your business incubator like a business sets a good example for client companies—but that's not the only, or even the best, reason to do it. Achieving operational self-sustainability is essential to an incubation program's long-term survival; to its ability to grow strong, lasting companies; and to its ability to have a significant positive impact on its community and for its stakeholders. What's more, a self-sustaining incubator enables staff to focus more energy on growing new companies, improving service offerings, and implementing new ideas rather than worrying about finding the cash to pay next month's utility bills.

Principle 2

> The incubator itself is a dynamic model of a sustainable, efficient business operation.

To uphold this principle, an incubation program must establish quantifiable value to its clients and stakeholders that can be translated into revenue to sustain operations. Incubators provide value to clients and stakeholders in many forms; it is the job of incubator management to monetize this value into viable revenue streams.

One of the most obvious and significant sources of revenue is rent. According to NBIA's 2006 *State of the Business Incubation Industry* report, 59 percent of revenue of North American incubation programs comes from rents and/or client fees. With this in mind, it is important to understand the factors that can influence rental income and client fees.

Determining existing or potential demand for incubator space and services at a given price is an essential part of the process. Before the program opens, you can determine an anticipated level of demand by conducting a market feasibility study. If you are already in operation, a comprehensive market analysis may clarify your opportunities for generating revenue from rent and fees. In either case, the result should provide reasonable projections for the amount and type of space that may be rented and the rates clients may be willing to pay for it.

When establishing rental rates, it's important to remember that a best practice incubation program provides significantly more to its clients than just space. The strategy of charging below-market rates might help attract price-conscious clients in the short term, but it can backfire in the long run when rental income is insufficient to cover the costs of providing the business development services that are the true driver of your value proposition. Prospects and clients will compare apples and oranges to the detriment of the incubator because the market rents they are comparing you to don't include any services. Be sure that prospective clients understand your pricing structure and how it compares to mere real estate rental.

Some programs are moving away from a rent model by establishing prices based on the value of the services offered. In some cases, client rates are broken down into rent and services; in others, the program charges a flat service fee that encompasses both space and services. Such an approach establishes the incubator as a program designed to build and grow businesses—not a real estate operation with benefits.

In setting prices for space and services, consider these questions:

- What value am I providing to current and potential clients?

- What value am I providing to current and potential stakeholders?

- What is the market price for each of the services I provide my clients, and what price is my target clientele willing to pay for them?

Management and boards of incubators should strive to

> - Structure for financial sustainability by developing and implementing a realistic business plan

- Can I establish sufficient value for my current and potential stakeholders and supporters to secure and sustain their financial support?

- Can I sell services independently or bundle them in more attractive packages to stimulate demand, improve the perceived value to the client, and generate more revenue?

- How can I position these items in the marketplace relative to the actual or perceived competition?

On the other side of financial sustainability are the costs associated with providing the value needed to attain the program's mission and goals. When considering operating costs, it is important to determine:

- The optimum level of services needed to satisfy clients' and stakeholders' perceptions of value.

- Opportunities to reduce the cost of administration or service delivery by leveraging other organizations, other programs, and other individuals.

- Ways to minimize fixed costs and maximize variable costs to lower the program's break-even point.

- The incubator's ability to provide sufficient value with the funds available. For example, if a key sponsor or subsidy falls through, the incubator might be forced to raise rates and thereby risk losing clients. This is another reason to position your incubation program as a supportive environment in which to grow a successful business rather than a space offering cheap rent.

In addition to client rents and fees, an incubator's sources of revenue might include support from sponsors (e.g., private industry, government, colleges and universities), contracts to provide services outside the incubator, and revenue from equity or royalty agreements with client companies. (Caution: Incubators should not build their operating budgets around long-term payments that might be achieved partially through equity agreements. These payments will likely be highly volatile and unpredictable.)

While it would be ideal to reach a point where the program no longer needs outside support for operating expenses (e.g., real estate and capital expenditures, administrative costs, staff salaries), many programs will require operational support in the long term. This can cause political problems for your incubator if you have not positioned it as a program that grows companies rather than a rental space. That allows you to make the case that the incubator is a vital economic development program that creates jobs, increases tax revenues, and strengthens the overall economy. If you have taken steps to demonstrate your program's value and impact, you should be able to maintain long-term stakeholder and political support.

Business Plan

- Helps the incubator run like a business
- Models good practices for clients
- Helps incubator management measure progress toward goals
- Encourages short- and long-term planning for sustainability and effectiveness
- Allows the incubator to share its strategies, goals, and results with its donors, prospects, clients, and community stakeholders

■■ business plan

Incubator management must develop and implement a realistic business plan to deliver value so the program can generate the revenues needed to support operations. A reliable business model provides the operating framework in which to implement the program's value proposition, monitor financial performance through a consistent budgeting process, and apply sound accounting practices. The business plan, combined with continual monitoring, also provides the tools required to make operating adjustments when necessary. Senior staff should review the incubator's business plan annually, making sure that its goals have been attained, that financial projections reflect viable future revenue streams, and that operating expenses fall in line with the realities of the incubator's daily operations.

Many incubators model best practices by developing business plans similar to those they may require of their clients. Developing a business plan helps the incubator run like a business and ensures a thorough annual review of the program's operations and financial matters. A business plan also includes marketing and public relations plans and describes core programs. It is important to tie these sections together to ensure that the incubator's value to its clients and stakeholders is clearly understood, both in terms of what is to be achieved (goals) and how the incubator will achieve them (tasks).

While not all sections of a business plan need to be updated annually, reviewing the plan and updating financial pro formas and other sections can help the CEO manage the incubator responsibly and promote regular consideration of program organization, client services, and other factors.

Incubator business plans vary in content and format—depending on the project focus and who prepares the document—but most contain some common elements. For example, most business plans begin with an executive summary describing the origins, purpose, and general background of the incubator project. The executive summary reviews the work already accomplished on the project and lays out what is planned for the program in the future.

The opening section of the business plan also should include your incubator's mission, because the business plan must show how the incubator will meet that mission.

The following is a sample outline of an incubator business plan, as found in *Developing a Business Incubation Program: Insights and Advice for Communities* (Athens, Ohio: NBIA Publications, 2006):

Executive Summary

- Mission and Objectives
- Client Focus
- Organizational Structure
- Legal Structure
- Board Composition
- Services and Programs
  - Services for incubator clients
  - Programs for entrepreneurial assistance
  - Business assistance providers
- Marketing, Public Relations, and Client Recruitment
  - Marketing and public relations plan
  - Client recruitment strategy
- Client Application, Selection, and Graduation Process
  - Application guidelines
  - Selection and screening process
  - Sample application
  - Graduation policy
- Staffing Plan
  - Staffing structure and job descriptions
  - Staff selection and training plan
- Facility
  - Description of incubator facility
  - Technical requirements
- Budgets
  - Operating pro formas for at least three years

BEST PRACTICES IN ACTION

A Strategic Business Plan
Innovacorp, Halifax, Nova Scotia, Canada
Dan MacDonald, former president and CEO
www.innovacorp.ca

Business planning at Innovacorp starts in December of every year—almost four months before the beginning of the new fiscal year in April. And it always starts the same way: with a couple of very long meetings.

At those meetings, Innovacorp managers undertake an honest and thorough assessment of the organization's strengths, weaknesses, opportunities, and threats (SWOT). "It's a long, ugly list," says Dan MacDonald, Innovacorp's president and CEO until early 2010.

That's not because Innovacorp has so many problems, but because of MacDonald's dedication to the process. "I make sure everybody understands what the S, W, O, and T mean, then we go around the room person by person until we've exhausted the topic," he says. "It's fascinating to watch people listen to each other. It gives everybody an opportunity to speak in turn, one at a time, so no one person can use up all the oxygen in the room."

The resulting list is circulated among the management team, and each member ranks items in each category as number 1, 2, or 3. A consensus usually emerges fairly quickly, and that's what MacDonald is after. "We want to pick the items that people violently believe are important," he says.

That narrower list is shared with the board for their input. "The board isn't involved in wordsmithing, but they are involved directionally," he says. By involving the board at a fairly early stage, MacDonald ensures that everyone is on the same page about the organization's future.

Staff are involved as well, but not at the most basic stages. "As we craft the SWOT, managers are encouraged to go back to their teams and ask what they think," MacDonald says. "It wouldn't make sense to have thirty-five people locked away [in meetings], but we have to make sure they're aware of where we're going."

As consensus on the SWOT emerges, so does a plan to capitalize on strengths and opportunities and to mitigate weaknesses and threats. "It starts to jump off the page," MacDonald says.

The plan also is tied to the organization's long-range strategic plan. "The organization has to have a North Star: where are we trying to go?" he says. "You have to challenge that direction through the business planning process."

For example, in 2007, Innovacorp set a strategic goal of adding clean technology companies to its portfolio. That year's business plan included a goal to explore the clean tech sector. The following year, new goals were added—"We know what clean tech is, now we need to do this and this," MacDonald says. "We just get closer and closer to that North Star."

Other initiatives born of the business planning process include the I-3 Technology Start-Up Competition, which was a response to a weakness identified in the SWOT exercise. "We have a provincial [mission], but we could not hold our heads high and say we were active outside Halifax," MacDonald says. "The challenge for us was, how do we handle that? We can't put people out in every hamlet." Instead, Innovacorp started a provincewide business plan competition in 2008 to identify potential clients outside the capital city. (For more on I-3, see chapter 6, "Client Entrance and Exit.")

The final plan is submitted to the board for approval, then sent on to the provincial government, which funds the incubation program. In all, managers put in about a week and a half over a three-month period, MacDonald says; he and the communications and financial managers spend about three weeks over the same period. "Once you get into a rhythm, it's the time you'd expect to put into a business plan," he says.

Planning for Sustainability
William M. Factory Small Business Incubator, Tacoma, WA
Tim Strege, executive director
www.williamfactory.com

The William M. Factory Small Business Incubator of Tacoma, Washington, prepares a five-year financial plan, which is approved by its board of directors. Updated annually, the financial plan includes a summary of actual expenses for two to three years and projections for five years. In addition, the incubator has a narrative business plan that is updated as needed, generally every two years. Updates include information on how the incubator has tracked earlier plans as well as projected future activities. The plan uses short paragraphs, numbering, and bullets that ensure key information is easy to find.

The plan includes:

- Executive summary
- Background (including the incubator mission and history)
- Description of the nonprofit organization (its legal entity and important dates)
- Current status and prospects of the industry
- Products and services (including daily on-site support services)
- Features that may give it advantages over competition
- Market research and evaluation
- Customers
- Market size and trends
- Competition
- Estimated market share and sales
- Marketing the incubator
- Space in the new facility
- Design and development plans
- Construction and operations plans
- Management team
- New facility construction schedule and financing
- Critical risks and assumptions (related to financing the new facility and assumptions about clients' ability to pay)
- First-source hiring agreements
- Community benefits (both specific and general)
- Financial plan and projections

- Ensures operating expenses are covered by predictable, reliable sources of funding
- Ensures multiple sources of funding and requires that subsidies do not represent the sole or even a majority of income sources
- Is based on detailed, disciplined projections and planning, as well as careful tracking of cash flow

The incubator's mission is

> to nurture carefully selected, smaller local entrepreneurs through their formative years by providing advisory, professional, and technical assistance and affordable office space and services. Recruiting and assisting those businesses with high potential for growth equates to increasing job opportunities for lower-income and unemployed Tacoma/Pierce County residents. This sets the stage for future growth, job generation, creation of an expanded tax base, and revitalization of the Eastside Tacoma community.

The incubator has been in operation since 1986, so the business plan is clearly not that of a start-up operation. While it describes projected activities of the incubation program, including construction of a new Phase II facility (which began accepting clients in late 2009) and the new, expanded services it will offer, the plan demonstrates the incubator's excellent achievements thus far. In doing so, it assures readers of the incubator's history of sound management, thus giving confidence in its projections.

Basic services are clearly described in a way that reveals how the incubator staff understand the incubator's service offerings and how these have been able both to attract clients paying above-market rents and to ensure the success of its clients and graduates. New service offerings indicate how the incubator will use innovative technology to assist client growth.

In addition to basic services, the incubator offers twice-monthly meetings with large contractors that are looking for subcontractors, and it advocates with both government and the contracting industry about the qualifications of its clients and legal issues related to minority contracting.

The five-year approach to its financial projections allows the incubator "to prepare for future expenses such as personnel benefits, increased telecom costs, and building maintenance and serves as a basis for increasing lease rates, which are currently raised by $1 per square foot per year," says Strege. "This approach also enables the incubator to calculate—as part of our building expansion plan—which costs can be held to smaller incremental amounts versus which costs will increase proportionately to size" as the incubator expands.

(For more on how the incubator has achieved financial sustainability and how careful investments have helped it manage expenses, see the following section on sustainability.)

■■ sustainability

NBIA defines financial self-sustainability as an incubator's ability to cover expenses with predictable, reliable sources of funding. A self-sustainable incubator generates income that contributes to its operational budget; does not depend on a single source of external support; and makes sure that outside funding is either reliable or replaceable. Some incubation programs take the concept a step further and make it a goal to cover all expenses from their own operations (known as "financial self-sufficiency").

The first step toward financial self-sustainability is securing multiple sources of funding. Some incubation experts recommend having six to ten revenue streams, which might include:

- Rents and service fees
- Income from contracts
- Cash operating subsidies
- Revenues from selling conference room or shared services or sponsorships
- Investment income

While subsidies—significant infusions of cash from a single source unrelated to performance of a specific incubator initiative—are fine, they are typically short-lived because they are not based on a perceived return for the investment. This source of revenue can be helpful during the start-up phases of the program when it is establishing its value, but should not be relied upon as an ongoing source of revenue. If it is the sole or even the majority source of an incubator's revenue, the program has greatly reduced its opportunities for long-term survival. Most incubators will require some amount of subsidy for a period of time—and perhaps for a long period of time—because they are not able to support themselves with fees collected from rent and services alone. A developing or newly opened incubator may rely on such significant subsidies for a time (say, its first four to seven years), but for long-term stability it must move to other sources of revenue or minimize subsidies so they are like the icing on the cake: a bonus to enhance the program's core value with new or desirable (but not necessary) services. According to NBIA's

A subsidy is not tied to performance is more like a gift, and thus its continuation relies on the granting agency's goodwill.

State of the Business Incubation industry surveys, subsidy as a portion of overall revenues has decreased from 57 percent in 1989 to 15 percent in 2006. In the 2006 survey, 32 percent of North American incubators reported receiving no subsidy at all; only 23 percent said they would have to discontinue operations if their current subsidy disappeared.

Caution: Incubators should be careful about providing sponsors or funders a definitive date when they will not require investment. The important thing is to track earned income as a percentage of total revenue and other statistics to show the incubator's progress toward financial self-sustainability rather than committing to a certain date for achieving it.

A subsidy that is not tied to performance is more like a gift, and thus its continuation relies on the granting agency's goodwill. A performance-based arrangement, such as compensation for business services provided under contract, is a more stable form of revenue. Similarly, long-term or permanent free use of a building that is appropriate in terms of size, cost to maintain, location, and other factors can help an incubator get off the ground with no debt load, a key to eventual self-sustainability. (This plan can go awry, however, so have a backup plan just in case.) This does not mean you should accept the donation of just any building; programs that are founded primarily on the availability of a free facility are unlikely to succeed in the long run. It is preferable to achieve free space by obtaining grants from government and industry to cover the cost of construction or renovations. (For a thorough discussion of the pros and cons of "free" buildings and the relationship between facility size and financial sustainability, see *Developing a Business Incubation Program*, Athens, Ohio: NBIA Publications, 2006.)

Incubation programs that operate as a program of a larger organization (for example, a university or county economic development organization), in particular, sometimes receive cash or in-kind subsidies for expenses, including personnel, rent, or building maintenance. These subsidies allow the programs to operate with much less overhead but can be dangerous when political winds change because they could be terminated at any time for political or other reasons. More than one university has seen a successful incubation program go down the tubes because a new president chooses to make sweeping changes in university priorities.

One way to avoid such problems is to establish an arm's-length relationship between the incubator and its larger sponsor. Although institutional ties can remain close, an incubator might operate under the umbrella of a university foundation or technology park as opposed to being an actual program of the larger institution. Large institutions such as universities, some economic development organizations, and local governments usually have missions that are much bigger than business incubation. For example, the university may see its role primarily in education and research, and a city government will likely prioritize justice, water treatment, and public safety more highly than entrepreneur support. Having the incubator report to a smaller government-funded economic development initiative or a university research foundation or research park—an organization aligned more closely to the same interests as the incubation program—may ensure greater sustainability for the program. Likewise, some incubator sponsors have "spun out" the incubators they created to stand on their own feet, with their own nonprofit status and an independent board of directors for which the incubator itself is its first concern. This strategy could ensure the longevity of a business incubation program during management transitions in the parent institution.

Factors in the size and duration of subsidies include:

- Facility size
- Ratio of leasable to nonleasable space
- Debt load
- Program age (because it takes time to lease up a building)
- Program type (kitchen and biotech incubators, for example, must make significant investments in expensive infrastructure and equipment)
- Amount of space designated as common areas
- Differential between incubator rental rates and correlating costs to the incubator operating costs
- Occupancy levels

Many cash flow problems can be avoided with detailed, disciplined, clear-eyed projections and planning both for the short term and for the long term. This means doing a line-item annual budget, broken down month by month and based on previous fiscal years, with flags on anything that may need adjustment.

Cash flow analysis requires tracking annual and monthly inflows and outflows of cash, as well as a clear idea about what constitutes a truly reliable source of income. Once an incubator has a line-item monthly budget in place, it must manage cash flow judiciously so that its day-to-day operations reflect its projections. To achieve this, managers should load their actual inflows and outflows into their accounting program regularly (week by week, if not day by day) to determine how closely their financial situation conforms to what the budget calls for.

BEST PRACTICES IN ACTION

Co-location With Compatible Programs
Business Incubator Center, Grand Junction, CO
Christina Reddin, executive director
www.gjincubator.org

Founded in 1987, the Business Incubator Center is a four-legged stool of entrepreneur support and development. This model not only provides a continuum of service to BIC clients but also earns revenue for the center.

The center is housed in a 60,000-square-foot multiuse facility that dates to the 1940s, when it was used by the U.S. Department of Energy. Now owned by a nonprofit formed by the city of Grand Junction and Mesa County, the site has considerable development challenges and therefore is leased to the center for $1 per year. The incubator in turn rents space to clients, thus generating earned income. Additional BIC revenue sources include fees for business development services and Internet access.

In addition to the incubator itself, the center operates—under the same roof—the regional Small Business Development Center. "It's a way to get a lot of counseling hours for your clients without having to hire staff," says BIC Executive Director Christina Reddin. Reddin and her two staff members are also SBDC counselors, working with the SBDC director and a half-time assistant. The SBDC is funded by the U.S. Small Business Administration, plus a small fee charged to workshop participants.

Also under the BIC umbrella is the Business Loan Fund, which manages a $4.5 million portfolio of debt capital provided to incubator clients as well as the local business community. BIC administers the fund, earning income in fees and interest (both that paid by clients and what accrues on available funds). The earned income pays the salary of the one and a half full-time-equivalent employees who are responsible for it. Any profit the loan fund earns is plowed back into the incubator program.

As BIC executive director, Reddin sits in on loan fund meetings. "I don't have a vote [on investments], but it gives me all the knowledge and experience I need with the loan fund," she says.

The fourth leg of the stool is the Mesa County chapter of the Colorado Enterprise Zone, which the center administers for the state. The state Enterprise Zone program offers tax credits and other incentives for economic development in distressed areas. "The state was looking for somebody in western Colorado to administer the local program, so we applied to do it," Reddin says. The center receives the administrative fees paid by businesses that participate in the EZ program.

Having all four programs in one organization achieves significant economies of scale, Reddin says, noting that even in the boom-and-bust economy of western Colorado, the center remains 75 percent self-financed.

Leveraging Existing Facilities
Mi Kitchen Es Su Kitchen, New York, NY
Kathrine Gregory, director
www.mikitchenessukitchen.com

Kathrine Gregory runs a successful kitchen incubator program—with no kitchen of her own. Instead, she arranges to use commercial kitchen facilities around New York City when they otherwise would be empty.

One of the four kitchens her clients use was originally built for a job training program that ran from 1 p.m. to 6 p.m., four days a week. "Here is this 5,000-square-foot facility with all this top-notch equipment, and it's only being used not even one-third of the time," Gregory says. Now her clients use the kitchen at night and on weekends.

Another of her kitchens is in a church. "They had a walk-in fridge and a walk-in freezer, both empty," Gregory says. "And three reach-in refrigerators with only staff lunches." The kitchen was used rarely: during the week to make meals for the homeless, on Sundays for coffee with the pastor, and occasionally rented to caterers on the weekend.

The key to this approach, she says, is knowledge of her clientele. Most of them have regular day jobs and are just beginning to build a food business. The only time they have available is nights or weekends—when many commercial kitchens are empty. Even if they had the time during the week, Gregory adds, "most don't have the money or sales revenue to afford [kitchen] space Monday through Friday."

The same model could apply to any highly specialized industry, Gregory says. "I know [clothing] designers who have a job someplace else and sew at night in their apartments," she says. An incubator could arrange to rent out a space with sewing machines at, say, a vocational school after hours.

"The object is not to keep people [in a building]," Gregory says. "The object is to allow them to grow at their own rate going forward."

Long-Term Financial Planning

William M. Factory Small Business Incubator, Tacoma, WA
Tim Strege, executive director
www.williamfactory.com

The William M. Factory Small Business Incubator prepares a five-year financial plan that is approved by its board of directors. Incubator Executive Director Tim Strege says the program's business model includes operating frugally, keeping core expenses low, investing in activities (e.g., warranties and high-quality building elements) that will lead to future savings, and earning a net income at the end of every fiscal year.

While the incubator's thirty current clients gross more than $30 million per year combined, the incubator's annual operating budget was $535,000 (including depreciation and mortgage loan interest) prior to the addition in late 2009 of a second (Phase II) building that will more than double capacity to sixty resident clients and raise total operating expenses to $750,000.

Incubator finances are managed so that 10 percent net income is earned after all annual operating expenses, mortgage loan interest, and depreciation expenses, Strege says. "Because depreciation is a 'paper expense'— depreciation is calculated as a component of the incubator's financial position, but these funds remain available for other uses—this approach provides both an operating cash flow reserve and funds that can be used for capital expansion, equipment purchases, and other incubator investments or for early mortgage payoff."

The incubator benchmarks key indicators with other model incubation programs; financial indicators include gross revenues, expenses, net assets, year-end cash, and accounts payable.

Financial projections are straightforward, using either historical averages of past revenues, expenses, and net income or two to three years of actual past fiscal year data. The incubator conserves cash by eliminating costs that are not reimbursable (e.g., false alarm fees, tax penalties, interest expenses, entertainment).

The William M. Factory Small Business Incubator raises funds through an annual banquet ($10,000) and through contracts with the county to maintain a "contract center" ($25,000) and with the regional transit authority to reach out to small disadvantaged firms ($5,000). Software manufacturers have also donated site licenses to the incubator.

Rents cover all soft services (including company advising, minor copying, and utilities, but not telecommunications), and rates are higher than those at nearby commercial structures. However, tenants of those buildings don't get on-site ready access to the technical and business assistance services provided by the William M. Factory incubator.

Strege says the strict financial controls and long-term picture the incubator maintains through its five-year budgeting process help the program make "better decisions." For example, the incubator gave notice to its largest tenant to vacate its premises following repeated violations of a smoking ban. While the loss of that tenant meant the incubator would relinquish $2,000 a month in rental income, Strege said his board was unconcerned by the financial considerations. The incubator soon found two new clients to take the previous client's space, as well, so in fact no vacancy occurred.

For the fiscal year ending June 30, 2009, the incubator raised $3.3 million in equity contributions for its Phase II. The reserve fund currently stands at $150,000. After depreciation expenses, year-end net income was $50,000. Strege termed this net revenue "encouraging," since recession-related cutbacks resulted in both Pierce County and the Port of Tacoma failing to renew substantial contracts during the fiscal year.

In addition to keeping close watch over revenues and expenses by comparing budgeted and actual revenues each month, analyzing cash flow, and gradually increasing rents, the incubator designed its new Phase II space to achieve economies of scale and other savings. William Factory opened 20,000 square feet of Phase I new space in late 2003. The Phase II space (2009) is connected to the existing incubator building, and it utilizes the 2003 Phase I area lobby. The incubator also had to build only one new restroom on the fourth floor of the new space, since available restrooms on the second and third floors of the Phase I facility can accommodate the interconnected buildings.

While the incubator charges a base price of $27 per square foot per year for Phase 1 offices, Phase II offices are base-priced at $30 per square foot per year. At full occupancy, Phase II will generate annual rental income of $300,000, while incurring less than $150,000 in additional operating and staff costs. Combined, the Phase I and Phase II buildings will be sufficient for the incubator to cover operating expenses, depreciation, and mortgage expenses while meeting its positive net income goal.

Financial stability has been achieved by investing in high-quality infrastructure and paying for lengthy warranties and modular, easily upgradable equipment. "While each of these actions costs money up front, they saved funds over time," says Strege, who notes that client revenues from telecommunications now provide net cash flow for the incubator.

Specifically, new infrastructure investments are expected to reduce operating costs by:

- Incorporating an Internet-controlled room-by-room HVAC system
- Obtaining lifetime warranties for Hewlett Packard chassis switches with modular components for ease of additions and upgrades in the incubator's IT hardware systems
- Including on-site warranty coverage for Cisco Voice-Over-Internet-Protocol (VOIP) devices
- Purchasing telecommunications instruments with built-in Web and video conferencing solutions with upgradable cameras.
- Installing expanded video monitoring
- Specifying minimum six-year lighting fixtures, a ten-year roof, and a five-year warranty on elevators
- Including scenic but low-maintenance landscaping
- Merging the voice and data network to expand workstation capacities and combine two networks into one

The incubator's annual building expenses, including property insurance, utilities, and maintenance (excluding property taxes) amount to about $1.50 per square foot per year—half the average for commercial office buildings, according to Strege.

William M. Factory incubator management also addresses sustainability issues by focusing on a "smart staffing" model using contract personnel, collaborative agreements with outside entities, carefully selected and recruited professional volunteer mentors, and incremental paid staff. Smart staffing and other financial sustainability issues are frequently topics of annual board retreats in which the board discusses on a macro and strategic level what amount of incubator dollars and staff resources should be utilized to achieve heightened expectations of the incubator.

Multiple Revenue Streams
Louisiana Business & Technology Center, Baton Rouge, LA
Charles D'Agostino, executive director
www.bus.lsu.edu/lbtc

A fundamental concern of most incubation programs is how long will it take for the incubator to become self-sustainable. Early on, stakeholders from government to foundations to economic development organizations want to know what the path to sustainability will look like.

The Louisiana Business & Technology Center has not required an operating subsidy for the last eighteen of its twenty-two years—even though it continues to increase services to clients both within and outside the incubator. Executive Director Charles D'Agostino credits that accomplishment to a sound model for sustainability.

"One of our key objectives is that in order to provide services and make value-added contributions to client companies, the LBTC must be on stable financial footing," D'Agostino says. "LBTC management and staff must focus their time and attention on assisting clients, not raising funding to keep the doors open."

The incubator's financial model rests on strong relationships with stakeholders, both at its host institution, Louisiana State University, and within the business community. Building on those relationships, D'Agostino has negotiated agreements and contracts that support his program and increase its ability to serve clients statewide.

Under LBTC's arrangement with LSU, the incubator does not pay for its space, utilities, maintenance, or janitorial services; it is treated as any other academic department. At the same time, the agreement allows D'Agostino to keep income from rents and services under his control—not the university's—to cover salaries and other management expenses of the incubator.

Perhaps the most important aspect of his financial model, though, is the sheer number of outside contracts D'Agostino has set up with various agencies and organizations to do specific tasks with specific deliverables that enhance LBTC client and outreach services. The contracts—which account for more than 85 percent of the incubator's revenues—include an overhead fee to help offset the university's costs of operating the incubator. And they not only give LBTC income but also consolidate its position as the state's premier supplier of small business services.

PROGRAM	SOURCE	TOTAL ANNUAL REVENUE
Provide entrepreneurial services and counseling to incubator clients and outreach clients	Louisiana Economic Development Department	$300,000 (includes funding for SBIR/STTR program)
Operate a Small Business Development Center	U.S. Small Business Administration	$200,000
Stimulate university technology commercialization in Louisiana	Louisiana Board of Regents	$25,000
Promote the SBIR program in Louisiana and help entrepreneurs and small business owners compete for and win SBIR/STTR grants	NASA and Louisiana Economic Development	$65,000 (NASA)
Conduct economic development projects in Baton Rouge	Baton Rouge Chamber of Commerce	
Provide MBA graduate students to assist Louisiana entrepreneurs	Louisiana Public Facilities Authority	$50,000
Mobile classroom and rural entrepreneurship program	U.S. Department of Agriculture, Louisiana Municipal Association, Louisiana Public Facilities Authority, Louisiana Workforce Commission, et al.	$147,000 (USDA), $25,000 (LMA), $25,000 (LPFA), $20,000 (LWC)
Operate Disaster Business Counseling Center	U.S. Department of Housing & Urban Development, U.S. Small Business Administration, Community Development Block Grants	$200,000

NBIA defines financial self-sustainability as an incubator's ability to cover expenses with predictable, reliable sources of funding.

facilities management

Nearly all business incubation programs are based in a facility, although many offer affiliate programs (sometimes called "virtual incubation"; see the section on affiliate programs in chapter 8, "Client Services") that provide services to off-site clients.

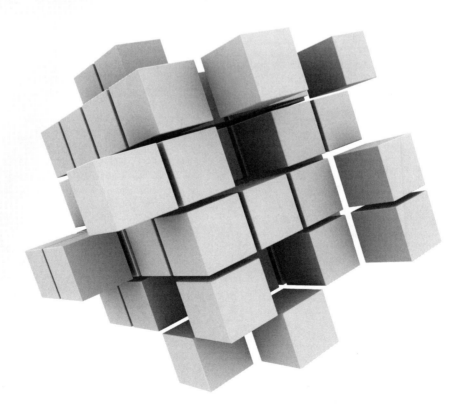

Management and boards of incubators should strive to

- Develop an incubator facility, resources, methods, and tools that contribute to the effective delivery of business assistance to client firms and that address the developmental needs of each company

While it is important not to equate an incubator with a building—an incubator is a program, not a place—the fact remains that clients and stakeholders can obtain tangible and intangible value from the facility in several ways:

- **Image.** An attractive facility with a receptionist and conference rooms makes an impressive statement to potential customers and investors, one that cannot typically be obtained when working out of the home, garage, or low-cost office space. Remember, your facility's lobby and reception area form the front door to the corporate headquarters of your clients. The hive of entrepreneurial activity in the facility helps drive support to the program.

- **Identity.** A facility provides a physical identity to the incubator that programs and services alone cannot. A facility is something that can be seen and touched, providing program stakeholders with a tangible focal point for the programmatic and operational entrepreneurial support activities that occur within its walls.

- **Operational efficiency.** A turn-key operating platform (e.g., space with furniture, telecommunications infrastructure, and support equipment) allows the client to get up and running immediately, pay more attention to the firm's core business, and spend less time dealing with operational issues. It also reduces client wind-down costs if the venture has to be closed.

- **Access to specialized assets and equipment.** Incubators that work with a particular industry can offer clients the use of equipment, design software, and other industry-specific assets they otherwise would have to pay for up front or do without, which in turn could jeopardize their time to market and chances for success. For example, an arts incubator might include a kiln for ceramics artists; a kitchen incubator might provide shared prep space and industrial cooking appliances and freezers; and a manufacturing facility might offer compressed air and machining equipment. Biotech facilities are probably among the most elaborate, offering gases, air filtration, laboratory benches, fume hoods, and access to shared high-priced equipment such as centrifuges.

- **Responsiveness.** Having a place to come to every day is a boon to the client and to the incubator manager. Clients that reside in an incubator facility have nearly immediate access to your services without waiting to schedule an appointment. And your daily contact with your clients allows you to observe situations that may need to be addressed before the client is aware of the need for help. Either situation benefits the client by mobilizing resources and support in a real-time environment.

- **Peer support.** Over time, a well-run, facility-based incubator can develop a sense of community in which clients become an integral part of the program's value proposition. The sharing of technical information, business knowledge, and business-building successes and challenges lend credence to the guidance your staff and service network provides. The intellectual and emotional support of such interaction is hard to quantify, but it can have a profound impact on sustaining your clients' entrepreneurial drive. Successful programs have environments in which clients share resources, business and marketing strategies, technologies, contacts, employees, and equipment. In some cases, client interactions have led to cooperative bidding on projects that otherwise might have been too large for either client to handle on its own.

For more information on facility features and program value, see *Developing a Business Incubation Program: Insights and Advice for Communities* (Athens, Ohio: NBIA Publications, 2006), and *Bricks and Mortar: Renovating or Building a Business Incubation Facility* (Athens, Ohio: NBIA Publications, 2000).

Although your incubator is not purely a real estate operation, its success will be influenced by a number of factors common to any real estate project:

- **Location.** You'll want your incubator facility to be in a location that's attractive to your target market or industry. For example, a technology incubator located in a distressed industrial area can impede client recruitment and service provider involvement. Other location factors include parking, security, and proximity to resources such as restaurants, copy centers, professional services, and key assets (e.g., a university or college campus or a research park).

- **Access.** If the facility is physically hard to reach, clients won't find it—and neither will their customers. And if clients will be shipping goods from the incubator, the road infrastructure must be sufficient to handle the vehicle sizes and weights, and the loading area must have a turning radius sufficient for trucks to get in and out. The dock and staging areas must be large enough to ensure use by more than one client at a time.

- **Layout.** The facility must offer space that is worth the rental fees you will charge (either in the form of rent or as a variable-priced services package that includes space), and there must be enough space (excluding common areas) to optimize rent revenues. The interior also will affect future growth. You may need to add telephone or Internet lines, tear down or put up walls to accommodate a greater number of clients, or increase electrical capacity. Flexibility should be a primary consideration, along with privacy, noise reduction, and air circulation.

- **Common areas.** An incubator should have common areas providing amenities for smooth business operations:
    - Reception area
    - Kitchenette with refrigerator, microwave, coffeemaker, and vending machines
    - Business center with high-speed copier and production area
    - Conference room (which can double as a training room)
    - Meeting and presentation rooms

- **Storage.** Many incubators overlook the need to provide storage space for clients and the incubator itself. Since most clients will maximize use of their primary space, centralized, secure, and appropriately sized storage areas can be very valuable. This added value can also translate into additional revenue.

- **Communications.** Businesses of all types now demand high-speed Internet access—at minimum, a T-1 connection. In many rural areas, a solid broadband offering can be the determining factor that makes a potential client choose the incubator over a home or a low-cost space down the street. Incubators whose clients require more bandwidth (e.g., media development and media hosting companies) might need bundled T-1 lines (commonly referred to as T-2, T-3, etc.; for more on communications, see "Wired—or Not—for Business" later in this chapter).

- **Security.** An incubator should offer a facility in a location where clients and visitors feel secure at all times of the day, evening, and on weekends. In addition, the facility should allow secured access twenty-four hours a day, seven days a week. The security system should be flexible, to permit the addition and deletion of users as clients enter and graduate from the program. As security needs increase (or depend on your target market, such as homeland security), new security technologies such as biometrics may need to be considered.

- **Utilities.** Heating, venting, and air conditioning should be zoned and controlled for flexibility in the use of space, both during and after normal work hours (e.g., evening and weekends). It may be appropriate to have individual work areas, light manufacturing, and laboratory units with their own air handling systems that meet air quality standards for the intended use of the space and control of airborne contamination. Incubators with special applications such as data centers, food processing, and life sciences should consider redundant power sources, such as a back-up generator, to ensure continuous electricity in case of a power outage.

Sufficient electrical power should be provided, including three-phase power for light manufacturing operations.

Electrical power in offices should be designed to handle increased loads, since clients will typically squeeze in more people and equipment per square foot than a conventional commercial office setting. In addition, power should be distributed in zones so that space can be reconfigured as required. Light manufacturing and laboratory spaces should be individually metered; some incubators even charge the cost of distributing power within these spaces back to the client, especially in sectors such as manufacturing that have significant power requirements.

Light manufacturing and laboratory space should have—at minimum—water and sewer stubbed out to each unit. Centralized compressed air, increased electrical power, and material handling support also may be good selling points. If your clients will generate hazardous waste, consider how those materials will be handled and be sure to incorporate waste containment systems, including floor drains, into the facility design.

- **Parking.** Incubators generally have high demands for parking because of the typical client's desire to house as many individuals per square foot as possible and its need to host visits of numerous outside visitors and customers. Four to five parking spaces per 1,000 square feet of rentable space are recommended for office space and three to four spaces per 1,000 square feet for light manufacturing. In some urban settings, parking is at a premium, and incubators have had to consider using commercial parking lots and garages with negotiated fees, client parking subsidies, and parking validation for visitors. This is not always the case when clients and visitors expect parking expenses as a normal cost of doing business. But the added cost of parking can affect an incubator's ability to attract clients and the service providers to support them.

- **Special features.** Special features that might be suitable for an incubator facility are listed below:
    - Access points and corridors of sufficient size for moving equipment and materials in and out of labs, as clients or their equipment needs change
    - Secured interior or yard space with rack space for raw materials and finished product storage
    - Corridor widths suitable for forklifts
    - Areas for use of common, incubator-owned equipment
    - Inside and outside recreation areas
    - Loading dock(s) and staging area(s)
    - Roll-up doors to each unit (to the exterior of the building or to a central corridor)

Special features for a biotechnology incubator might also include an animal storage and handling area, greenhouses, fume hoods, gas to each unit, hazardous materials storage and handling areas, safety washes, and a test lab with electromagnetic shielding.

While wireless local area networks (WLAN) have gained popularity and can play a role in opening up more space for client use (e.g., outside eating areas and casual meeting areas), wired networks are more reliable, especially in severe weather situations (e.g., lightning storms). Wired networks are also relatively easy to secure and are capable of much higher data transfer speeds than wireless networks. Wireless networks, on the other hand, win for flexibility—clients can access the network from more locations—and ease of installation, requiring only two or three wireless hubs or routers. Wired networks require installation of cabling (usually Cat-5 or Cat-6) throughout the building and to specific ports in each office, lab, or other areas. Additional hardware will also be needed to manage the network (based on factors such as the level of service provided and the number of users) and to avoid data conflicts that could affect network performance.

A compromise could be to enable wireless access in common areas and provide hard-wired Internet access in private office spaces.

No matter what type of Internet access the incubator provides, it must have a robust physical infrastructure—all the wiring, specialized rooms, and equipment—to support clients' communication needs while keeping building management simple. At the most basic level, in which all clients provide their own communications, managers should always have a protocol for phone company access and operations.

Additionally, nearly every incubator will benefit from dedicating a secure space or small room with its own power supply where telephone lines enter the building.

The advantages are many:

- Incubator staff have more control over contractors and service providers.

- Staff know where all the main telephone and data links are when something goes wrong.

- Staff know where all the subsidiary telephone and data links start when something goes wrong.

- The incubator can install a separate power supply for that room to keep communications going if other circuits need work or a client blows a fuse. A small uninterruptible power supply will keep all systems going through relatively short outages and emergencies.

- Nobody can pull out the plug (which happens surprisingly often).

- The room is secure.

If the incubator chooses to offer Internet access and other services, it might need equipment such as servers for file storage and data processing, and a networked printer, copier, and scanner. All the equipment and their data should be protected with an uninterruptible power supply, a data backup system, a firewall, and software to block computer viruses and spyware. Depending on the type of equipment, the incubator also may need to consider adequate cooling and fire suppression. And everything must be connected in a network and then to the outside world.

At the high end of IT services are videoconferencing, electronic file storage, rack space, servers to host client Web services, advanced security, an intranet that hosts collaboration software, facilities scheduling software, and links to entrepreneur resources. Some of these services require very specific equipment, and incubator staff must carefully analyze the market before investing in the infrastructure to offer them or partner with firms who provide and deliver these services as a reseller.

The Incubator Facility

- Enhances the image of the client's business
- Provides an environment for stimulating interaction between clients
- Allows for the timely identification of needs and mobilization of solutions
- Reduces the time and cost associated with starting up a new venture
- Creates a tangible focal point for stakeholders and sponsors

■■ designs to encourage networking

Effective incubation programs work diligently to establish a sense of community among their clients. This is achieved not only through programs and by having management that values and promotes networking but also through the physical layout of the incubator facility.

While long, sterile hallways and minimal shared areas designed to optimize the amount of rentable square feet may be beneficial from a revenue perspective, they do not support client synergy. Successful incubators balance maximum rentable area with amenities that encourage entrepreneurs to meet formally and informally. These touches include:

- Functional common spaces such as centralized kitchens, copy rooms, mailboxes, restrooms, and meeting rooms that draw clients out of their offices to core areas where others are likely to congregate.
- Small, visible, casual seating areas in hallways to encourage impromptu meetings.
- Use of glass walls in meeting rooms and glass sidelights adjacent to office doors to provide a more open environment, making it easier to identify company personnel and encourage interaction. (But be sure to include blinds or draperies that can be closed over glass walls when privacy is needed.)
- Artwork, lighting, and other design features that create an inviting environment.
- Open areas to link multifloor facilities, such as an open central staircase to connect clients between floors.
- Outside seating and eating areas with pleasant surroundings (e.g., plants/vegetation, shade structures, water features) to provide a nice location for clients to unwind in a more relaxed environment.

All of these suggestions will increase the cost of the facility but in the long run will increase the value provided to clients and the ultimate performance of the program.

BEST PRACTICES IN ACTION

Transforming an Unused Store into an Incubator
Innovation Depot, Birmingham, AL
Susan Matlock, president and CEO
www.innovationdepot.net

Taking a former Sears store that has sat empty for twenty years in a blighted neighborhood and transforming it into a centerpiece facility for technology development and entrepreneurship is no small feat. Yet the Innovation Depot, opened in March 2007, offers 140,000 square feet of award-winning space that fosters networking both within the incubator and with the larger community. Key design features of the incubator include:

- A large open atrium with an open staircase and glass-walled elevator that foster visual and physical linkages between the facility's two floors.
- A café (Culinard Café) with a gelato bar that opens into the atrium area on the inside of the building and has its own parking and outside entrance. The café provides an informal location for clients and visitors to interact and is a bridge between the larger community and the incubator. It also allows incubator staff and company executives and staff to eat without leaving the incubator's premises.
- A courtyard garden with a boule court and a rooftop deck with tables and chairs, as well as informal sitting areas on the first floor. These provide more intimate places for clients to relax or meet in informal settings.
- Shared meeting and board rooms with glass walls that may be covered with shades, if needed, for privacy.
- A funky industrial interior utilizing the Sears building's original terrazzo floors, visible beams, cables and utilities in open areas, and other design features that both emphasize the history of the building and give it a sense of modernity.
- Large window walls to the outside in public areas and skylights to open up the building. Staff offices also have glass walls, and the reception area is freestanding.
- A "Main Street" corridor that extends from the parking lot entry through the "Town Center" to offices and conference rooms. Centralized offices, training rooms, break rooms, a copy center, and the café surround the two-story, sky-lit "Town Center."

together these features create a sense of openness and accessibility and a hip and exciting environment that is sought by entrepreneurs. The building itself serves as a powerful attractant—to business founders and to community members who may be able to provide supportive resources to the incubator. Incubator clients and staff walking through the building's public spaces can readily identify each other and grab informal opportunities to chat and share contacts, expertise, and resources. And with sixty-five client firms and four hundred employees working in the incubator, there is a palpable feeling of "high energy."

The large atrium and other public areas of the building have become the "go-to" place for the Birmingham community's large events, which can be catered by Culinard Café. Innovation Depot President and CEO Susan Matlock makes the space available without charge to organizations that are important to the incubator's market. She just requires the opportunity to explain the purpose of the Innovation Depot and why these organizations should be supportive of the incubator and local entrepreneurship.

Examples of such events include Tech Mixer Unplugged, which draws six hundred community residents to the incubator for an annual awards ceremony and other activities, and a biotechnology mixer that draws up to 150 participants. The Birmingham angel investor network meets at the incubator monthly, and the University of Alabama at Birmingham holds two MBA program classes at the Innovation Depot each week. Additionally, the Birmingham Venture Club conducts a six-month-long accelerator program for twelve to fourteen winners of an entrepreneurs' competition at the Innovation Depot; for three years, half the class has comprised incubator clients.

Alabama Launchpad, a business plan competition for students at the state's universities, holds its annual event at the incubator. Awards for the competition include $100,000 for first place, $50,000 for second place, and $25,000 for third place. Innovation Depot staff serve as judges and mentors for this event, and the incubator gives the winner six months of free space.

After some Innovation Depot board meetings, receptions are held for the incubator's clients and the board of directors. A reception in late 2009 was held for the Indian ambassador, who subsequently attended a White House function.

Located in a formerly distressed neighborhood of Birmingham at 1500 First Avenue North, the Innovation Depot is just three blocks away from UAB, an internationally recognized research university and academic health center; the city's legal and financial district; and freeways. It is the anchor of the Entrepreneurial District, recognized by city council and

zoned for that purpose. It is purposefully sited in proximity to the future Railroad Reservation Park and the city's downtown housing and restaurant scene. Future construction, including the urban park and bike paths, will link the incubator even more closely with UAB.

Innovation Depot architects Williams-Blackstock Architects have won many awards for the design of the building, including the 2008 American Institute of Architects Honor Award for the state of Alabama, the 2007 Best Commercial Project in the Southeast Award, the 2008 Overall Design in Architecture Award from the National Association of Industrial and Office Properties, and the 2008 Merit Award for Renovation and Adaptive Reuse from the Birmingham chapter of the American Institute of Architects.

Designing for Networking
William M. Factory Small Business Incubator, Tacoma, WA
Tim Strege, executive director
www.williamfactory.com

Tim Strege, executive director of the William M. Factory Small Business Incubator, believes "incubators exist to provide a shared work environment for start-up and expanding small business enterprises. So the intent of the incubator design should include lots of functional joint use areas rather than maximizing private leased office space."

The incubator (including Phase I and Phase II facilities) totals 42,000 square feet, with interior parking, private leased client offices, and shared spaces including wide hallways, conference rooms (small, medium, and large), four fiber-optic telecommunications rooms, a contract center for construction plans and project management support, an accounting area, an atrium lobby, a kitchenette, and incubator staff and administration offices. The exterior includes an outdoor meeting area and two balconies with views of Commencement Bay and the Cascade Mountains.

"The concept is that while clients may lease a 250-square-foot or larger office, they have the presence of a much larger company due to all the shared spaces that they may use for customers, suppliers, and employees," says Strege.

Strege also notes that use of the shared areas promotes greater interactions among incubator clients. "These interactive informal and more formal communications provide valuable exchanges of knowledge and add value to the incubation experience," he says.

Shared space is used for, among other things, twice-monthly networking sessions in which large corporations are brought to the facility to meet client companies and discuss contracting opportunities. Currently, 1,000 square feet of space is being converted into an "executive lounge" or "country club" type of setting to further encourage small and larger group meetings that may result in business contacts for incubator firms.

While the first incubator complex (Phase I) has an atrium in the front of the building, the newer facility has an atrium in the middle—encouraging interactions among incubator resident clients. At the bottom of the atrium is the lounge and exhibit area with casual furniture for informal use. This space also serves as overflow space for an adjacent conference room with a built-in multimedia presentation system.

At the top of the new building, an outdoor terrace for networking events can handle up to eighty people, with an enclosed kitchen and bar refreshment area, advanced lighting features, partial covered skylight, and views of Commencement Bay. The construction project also included renovation and reconfiguration of existing offices to present a more upscale image, addition of a display area for company awards and recognitions, and a fourth communications room with modern technology infrastructure designed to meet the needs of clients and incubator management for the foreseeable future.

When the incubator's Phase I construction opened in 2003, Strege says he learned a valuable lesson. "Though I expected people outside of the building would have higher respect for those in the building" because of the fancy new infrastructure, "I didn't realize until months later that people inside the building ascended to meet and exceed that higher level of expectations." Strege believes these physical amenities—"which are extremely important to companies that are otherwise disadvantaged due to lack of wealth, venture capital, or bank lines of credit"—have contributed to clients growing to an average of more than $1 million in annual revenues per firm.

The incubator facility is now the most technologically sophisticated small office structure in the Puget Sound region (for more, see chapter 7, "Leveraging Innovation"). Building attributes and the incubator's technical and business services permit the William M. Factory incubator to charge above-market rates (in 2009, $27 per square foot per year in the Phase I structure and $30 per square foot per year in Phase II). Rental revenues should reach more than $400,000 when the facility is fully leased, or over 75 percent of the total $600,000 operating budget, with contract revenues bringing in other income streams.

Says Strege: "The best strategy is to design, build, and operate an incubator facility that best promotes start-up firms and earns the financial revenues necessary to support the incubation program."

■■ shared facilities and equipment

One of the benefits of a physical structure is the ability to offer access to shared equipment and services that otherwise would be unavailable or would sap a start-up's financial position.

Shared facilities can be bare-bones, such as meeting rooms, kitchens, and mail or copy centers. However, an incubator can increase its value proposition by providing unique spaces that are typically unavailable to or too costly for individual entrepreneurs. These include:

- Dry labs with workbenches, compressed air, specialized electrical service (e.g., 3-phase or 220v/110v outlets), and other services for use in product testing
- Retail storefronts or showrooms for displaying or selling client products (e.g., artwork and food products)
- Secured dry storage areas to handle manufacturing clients' parts or food production clients' ingredients
- Sensitive Compartments Information Facility (SCIF) space for clients developing products or providing services requiring a secured environment
- Radio frequency (RF) shielded labs for clients in the electronics and telecommunications clusters
- Server rooms with appropriate security, HVAC, and power backup for clients involved in Web hosting and other related industries
- Emergency wash areas and biohazard storage and handling areas
- Greenhouses for clients involved in the agricultural and biosciences clusters
- Animal handling facilities for clients involved in the biosciences clusters

In addition to shared space, some incubators provide shared equipment. Like shared facilities, shared equipment can be as simple as copiers, fax machines, postage scales and meters, and LCD projectors. However, providing more sophisticated equipment—particularly in specific industry sectors—can deliver great value to clients. Examples include:

- Kilns for ceramics artists
- Shared kitchen equipment, flash freezers, and short-run bottling and labeling lines for food production
- Oscilloscopes and other bench test equipment for clients in electronics and telecommunications manufacturing
- Rapid prototyping equipment (e.g., CNC, injection molding, laser cutter, and 3-D printer/modeler) for advanced manufacturing
- Autoclaves and specimen freezers for life science clients

However, be aware that adding these amenities can add significantly to an incubator's development and operating costs. You will need to consider how current (and future) lients perceive the value of such amenities and their willingness to pay for them, as well as your program's ability to operate and maintain them. A number of incubators have expended significant amounts of money to install features and equipment that went unused or did not generate sufficient value or revenue to be sustained over time.

Most facilities include common areas like a business center and access to meeting space. Specialized incubators also offer amenities unique to their clients' needs, such as wet labs, common equipment rooms, and fume hoods for life science companies; high-end commercial kitchen equipment or food companies; or precision and tooling labs for prototype development.

BEST PRACTICES IN ACTION

Specialized Supplies Procurement
Southwest Michigan Innovation Center, Kalamazoo, MI
Robert DeWitt, president and CEO
www.kazoosmic.com

As the home to more than a dozen life science firms, the Southwest Michigan Innovation Center understands how important it is for researchers to have the specialty items they need readily available—at a reasonable cost. To fulfill that need, SMIC developed an innovative, market-based procurement program that also includes an on-site stockroom for scientific supplies.

Since 2004, the Innovation Center has provided an on-site storeroom with a variety of research supplies to give clients a convenient, low-cost alternative to maintaining their own inventories. By reducing the amount of standard scientific supplies clients need to store, the program allows clients to fill their labs with the equipment and researchers they need to grow their firms.

Originally, the program was maintained by Sigma-Aldrich, an international life science product supplier. Under the agreement, the Innovation Center provided a secure room, a locking cabinet, utilities, and Internet access; Sigma-Aldrich handled all invoicing and provided the stock, the personnel, and the equipment: a refrigerator, a freezer, two chemical solvent cabinets, and a $60,000 vending system.

Sigma-Aldrich later turned over storeroom management to Single Source Procurement and donated the storeroom equipment to the incubator. SSP has expanded the products available (at an average of 30 percent off list price) and maintains personnel on-site every business day to answer questions and assist with special orders. The Innovation Center subsidizes SSP's operations with a $2,000 monthly stipend, allowing the supplier to maintain lower, more competitive margins.

SSP has since expanded its program to other incubator and nonincubator facilities. In addition, as part of its comprehensive procurement services, SSP has been involved in writing procurements, negotiating procurement costs, and managing shipping and receiving for its clients.

A Regional Network of Incubation Programs
Northeast Ohio Incubator Collaborative, northeastern OH
Wayne Zeman, former chairman
http://neoinc.org

Clients of five state-funded technology incubators in northeastern Ohio may reside in one incubator, but they have access to facilities and resources at the other incubators, as well.

The Northeast Ohio Incubator Collaborative, or NEOinc, has five members: the Akron Global Business Accelerator in Akron; Braintree Partners in Mansfield; the Great Lakes Incubator for Developing Enterprises in Lorain County; MAGNET in Cleveland; and the Youngstown Business Incubator in Youngstown.

"We attempt to provide a seamless entry point for entrepreneurs, as well as a seamless support network for entrepreneurs," says Wayne Zeman, who was vice president for venture development at MAGNET until 2009 and chaired NEOinc until then.

The collaborative was born in 2005, when the state of Ohio announced that it would be offering funding for regional entrepreneurial assistance and incubation programs. "Even though there was probably a glimmer in a lot of people's eyes, we finally said that in northeastern Ohio we ought to be functioning on a regional basis anyway," Zeman says.

Although the group considered formalizing its operations as a separate organization, they decided simply to work cooperatively to offer space and expertise to each other's clients. "Each of [us] knows what each other's capabilities are," Zeman says.

Any client of an NEOinc member incubator can use facilities at another member incubator at no charge. For example, if a client of the Youngstown Business Incubator has a meeting in Cleveland, that client can arrange to use a conference room at MAGNET instead of renting a hotel room.

In addition, member directors can call on each other's expertise and connections. "If I have someone who needs to be introduced to the deputy mayor of Akron, I know that Mike LeHere, from the Akron incubator, works with them all the time," Zeman says. "I can call Mike and say I need an introduction, and he can arrange that for me."

The group meets regularly, either in person or via teleconference, to discuss developments at their individual programs. They also created and run a Web site with a blog that reports on news from the incubators and entrepreneurship, highlights client success stories, and otherwise promotes the region's incubators.

"We each have our own individual identities, but we have a collective identity as well," Zeman says.

The collective identity is most apparent in NEOinc's work to measure and publicize its members' joint economic impact. The results of their impact measurement are reported widely in regional media, as well as on the NEOinc Web site.

The bottom line, Zeman says, is that there is strength in numbers—whether in serving each other's clients or in showing the effectiveness of business incubation.

"We can certainly talk about successes at each incubator," he says. "By pooling our resources, we get more attention."

■■ appropriate space for target clients

Space should be configured to maximize interaction among clients and to provide the greatest flexibility for handling emerging company needs. Primary incubator space can typically be grouped into office, light manufacturing, and laboratory space, each of which is discussed below.

Office Space

Anecdotally, NBIA has found that most incubators configure client offices as hard-wall spaces ranging from 100 square feet to 600 square feet, with locking doors between some of the spaces to allow a single user to expand easily. Caution: Although cubicle space is less costly to develop, it can be difficult to rent because of client concerns with security and protecting proprietary information such as intellectual property, business contacts, and marketing strategies. It is more frequently used for "hot-desking," when affiliate clients or those that are not yet full clients of the incubator stop by to work on a business plan or conduct other business that doesn't require secure office space. As with most aspects of an incubation program, managers must consider the demands of the market and adapt the facility accordingly.

Light Manufacturing Space

Light manufacturing space should be configured into units appropriate for the types of clients that will use the facility. Typical incubator manufacturing spaces range from 800 square feet to 2,000 square feet, with some configurations allowing for two smaller spaces to be linked by a connecting door. Each space should also include the following:

- A minimum of one small office (100 square feet to 150 square feet)
- Ceiling clearances of fourteen to twenty feet, which also allows for the installation of optional storage lofts above the office
- A roll-up door with a side door and access to a loading area (either to individual loading areas behind each space or to a centralized corridor that connects to the loading area)
- Floor load ratings to support the intended uses
- A loading dock for truck bed- or ground-level deliveries, depending on types of deliveries expected
- Location to accommodate the largest anticipated type of delivery truck with ingress and egress and an adequate turning radius

Laboratory Space

Laboratory space can be grouped into dry lab or testing and assembly space, and wet laboratory space for bioscience clients. Facility specifications for dry lab space are similar to those for light manufacturing, with the addition of criteria such as shielding for radio frequency electromagnetic radiation or Sensitive Compartmented Information Facility areas, depending on the types of clients to be served.

Wet laboratory space is more complicated and should be developed with a firm that specializes in this type of work. Some general considerations include the following:

- Laboratory space should be configured into single units of approximately 400 square feet to 600 square feet, with adjoining doors on some units to allow for expansion up to 800 square feet to 1,200 square feet.
- Typically, laboratory space has, at a minimum, a single small office adjoining the actual lab space. However, as clients grow, they often need more office space. Whether that space will be adjacent to the lab or elsewhere in the building is an important long-range design consideration. In developing a new facility, be aware not only of current industry requirements but also of potential changes. For example, some life science incubators have seen a decrease in demand for pure lab space and an increase in demand for office space as the industry has evolved.
- Be sure that doorways, corridors, and elevators are sized to accommodate equipment changes.

Client businesses may pay for improvements to meet their specific needs. If the improvement will benefit future clients, the incubator may make special arrangements with the client. In some cases, the incubator may split the cost with the client; in other cases, the client may pay for the changes, and the incubator may deduct the materials costs from the client's rent and fees. In a third scenario, the incubator may pay for the fit-up and amortize that cost by adding a fraction of it to the client's monthly rent and fees for an agreed-upon time, such as a year.

Such improvements are expensive not only to install but also to remove. Keep that in mind and consider whether the cost of such a specialized investment is in the program's long-term interests and conforms to the incubator's broader objectives and mission.

However, the incubator should avoid making any investments or admitting clients that are not compatible with the incubator's broader objectives and mission.

Emerging from the concept of hot desking (a working space shared by different users at different times), co-working is a rising trend among independent contractors and other self-employed individuals who find working from home isolating. A co-working space offers entrepreneurs and other business people a location to connect to the Internet—and to one another for camaraderie, support, and synergy.

It also is emerging as a new service offering (and revenue stream) for business incubation programs.

Some are embracing the concept wholeheartedly. For example, NextSpace, located in Santa Cruz, California, offers three types of membership based on space desired: a seat in a café ($175 per month), a library-type carrel ($325 per month), or an office, ranging from $600 to $1,600 per month depending on size and location. Regardless of membership type, all members have access to coaching, consulting, networking and educational events, and meetings with potential investors.

Other incubation programs are adopting co-working as a way to introduce their programs to potential clients. The Nussbaum Center for Entrepreneurship in Greensboro, North Carolina, turned a 550-square-foot office into a co-working space with Wi-Fi Internet access, six workstations, and two conference tables—one with four seats and another with six. Entrepreneurs can use the space for $100 per month. (For more on Nussbaum's services for off-site clients, see the affiliate section in chapter 8, "Client Services.")

Although some users are typical co-working candidates—telecommuters and sole proprietors who want to get out of the house—Nussbaum President and CEO Sam Funchess also uses the space as a sort of preincubation program. If a potential client isn't quite ready for full incubation, "We push them in that direction until they prove to us that they deserve to move in or they complete their business plan to a satisfactory level," Funchess says.

BEST PRACTICES IN ACTION

A State-of-the-Art Food Facility
Rutgers Food Innovation Center, Bridgeton, NJ
Lou Cooperhouse, director
www.foodinnovation.rutgers.edu

Although it began working with clients in 2001, the Rutgers Food Innovation Center did not have an incubation facility until late 2008, when it opened a state-of-the-art, high-tech, high-touch 23,000-square-foot food business incubator. Inspected by both the U.S. Department of Agriculture and the U.S. Food and Drug Administration, FIC is one of the largest incubators in North America dedicated to food science.

Until the facility opened, FIC staff assisted clients with business development, market research, product and process development, quality assurance, and food safety by going into the field—literally, in some cases. With the new facility, however, the program can offer more specialized and complex services, including product design, development, analysis, and commercialization. Clients also can use the facilities for ongoing manufacture of products for sale to retail and food service markets, making the center a true one-stop shop for the food industry.

The FIC facility has a wealth of features targeted specifically at food entrepreneurs, taking them through every step from product development through processing. The building is organized in zones to promote logical workflow and collaboration.

The Client Services Area has a separate product development research kitchen where clients can develop value-added products (such as cider from windfall fruit), nutraceuticals, and specialty products such as certified organic, kosher, halal, or gluten-free. The facility also lets clients evaluate the effects of additives, preservatives, pasteurization, processing methods, and preparation types (such as standard versus convection oven) on their developing products.

The client services area also features a number of specialized laboratories. Sensory evaluation booths let clients undertake scientifically controlled, unbiased taste tests. A microbiology lab is available to analyze raw materials and finished products and undertake shelf-life studies. In the analytical laboratory, clients can perform routine food chemistry testing and receive counseling on FDA, USDA, and other packaging and labeling requirements.

Use of the Client Services Area is included in the $85-per-hour business mentoring fee that FIC charges clients who are developing their food businesses.

The bulk of the facility is dedicated to the Shared-Use Processing Area, which features separate rooms and specialized equipment for a variety of procedures, including fresh-cut cold processing for raw produce; automated hot processing for everything from beverages to catered meals; and dry processing for baking, seasonings, and dried herbs and produce. Clients can use the cold assembly area to package refrigerated or frozen products.

Use of the Shared-Use Processing Area is charged by the hour on the basis of the type of equipment and services needed for production. Most clients at this stage are no longer paying the business mentoring fee and are using the facility only for production, not business development.

Once the product has been developed and analyzed, clients can use the Consumer Research and Focus Group Area to get feedback from potential customers on anything from the product's taste to its packaging and advertising. Trained moderators lead the focus groups; FIC clients can watch the proceedings from an adjacent room. Users are charged a daily fee for use of these facilities.

Making the Most of an Existing Building
Enterprise Center of Johnson County, Lenexa, KS
Joel Wiggins, CEO and president
www.ecjc.com

In 2001, the Enterprise Center of Johnson County opened in what had been a furniture store. Renovating the building into 22,000 square feet of incubation space cost between $50,000 and $75,000, paid for by a capital campaign that drew donations from community organizations, individuals, and corporations. ECJC leases the facility from a private landlord and re-leases the space to clients.

The building is an open V-shape, with the main entrance at the point of the V. "Everybody comes in and out of the same door," says Joel Wiggins, the incubator's CEO and president. "Our reception person gets to know everybody and knows when they're here."

The sides of the V form wings to either side of the main entrance. Each wing has a locked door; each office also has a locking door. As a mixed-use incubator, ECJC has no laboratory or dock space, just forty-five offices ranging in size from 126 square feet to 210 square feet. There also are four suites of 824 square feet to 2,181 square feet.

"It's executive suites on an incubator budget," Wiggins says. "It works out well for companies looking for expandable office space."

The monthly fee includes telephone answering for one line; a single Internet connection; wireless Internet; use of the conference room; and coffee and tea. Additional phone lines, Internet connections, copying, secretarial services, and outgoing faxes are charged separately.

Clients can reserve one of three conference rooms at no charge. The largest can seat thirty-five and includes a sound system and a digital ceiling-mounted projector. The other two rooms can seat seven or ten. Each room features wireless Internet access, a multimedia projector and projection screen, a laptop computer, a television and DVD/VCR unit, and a whiteboard.

The incubator's Resource Center offers computers with Microsoft Office and QuickBooks as well as broadband access to library and economic development databases; audiovisual equipment; and a library of business and entrepreneurship books and other materials.

In addition to its clients, ECJC also hosts several organizations with similar missions, such as the Kansas biotechnology and software associations and the Kansas Technology Enterprise Corporation, the state's technology-based economic development agency.

"We get a lot of visibility from meetings they hold with their boards and their constituencies," Wiggins says.

The monthly fee includes telephone answering for one line; a single Internet connection; wireless Internet; use of the conference rooms; and coffee and tea.

program evaluation

Incubation professionals approach program evaluation from a number of different perspectives. The most common one focuses on program outcomes that can be presented to the incubator's sponsors, directors, investors, and community stakeholders. A second approach, which is implicit in NBIA's Principles and Best Practices, is the evaluation of the program's adaptability and effectiveness in providing value to its clients and in meeting broader community needs.

Management and boards of incubators should strive to

- Maintain a management information system and collect statistics and other information necessary for ongoing evaluation, thus improving program effectiveness and allowing the incubator to evolve with the needs of the clients

Ultimately, the goal is to establish a mechanism for adapting and improving the incubator's offerings to better meet the purpose outlined in its mission statement, to reach the goals and objectives reflected in its strategic plan, and to demonstrate community impact.

Regardless of the approach taken or the information collected, the evaluation process should be manageable in terms of the time and resources needed to execute the data collection effort, compile and evaluate the results, and develop an action plan for improving operations. Although desired by many sponsors and investors, an overly ambitious evaluation process runs the risk of requiring a significant amount of time from the incubator's staff—time that should be more appropriately directed to assisting clients. Incubators should be deliberate, thoughtful, and methodical in what they measure and how they measure their results and community impact.

Program Evaluation

- Provides evidence of success to incubator management, stakeholders, and investors
- Allows incubator management to compare program effectiveness with other, similar incubators
- Provides evidence of incubation program and service quality
- Presents information necessary to ensure that programs provide value to clients and evolve as necessary
- Identifies areas for continuous improvement
- Serves as a sales and marketing document for client recruitment

■■ collection of statistics on program parameters

The most obvious data to collect are on economic impact. Collecting and reporting economic impact data can deliver ammunition for fundraising, help track program performance over time, and add to the credibility of the incubation industry.

These are the ten basic data points NBIA suggests that all incubation programs collect annually for all clients and graduates. Data on jobs, revenues, wages, and so on for graduate firms should be collected for at least five years after leaving the program.

01. Number of current clients

02. Total number of graduates since program inception

03. Number of graduate firms still in business or that have been merged or acquired

04. Number of people currently employed full-time (at least thirty-two hours per week) by client and graduate firms

05. Number of people currently employed part-time (less than thirty-two hours per week) by client and graduate firms

06. Current monthly salaries and wages paid by client and graduate firms

07. Gross revenues for most recent full year for client and graduate firms

08. Dollar amount of debt capital raised in most recent full year by client and graduate firms

09. Dollar amount of equity capital raised in most recent full year by client and graduate firms

10. Dollar amount of grant funds raised in most recent full year by client and graduate firms

For details on why and how to collect data, as well as help in analyzing and reporting results, see *Measuring Your Business Incubator's Economic Impact: A Toolkit* at www.nbia.org/impact.

"It reminds our clients of our commitment to excellence and encourages them to make the same commitment in their enterprises."

– Karl LaPan, president and CEO, Northeast Indiana Innovation Center

Economic impact is not the only measure of an incubation program's effectiveness; evaluating internal operations is vital as well. Questions to ask include:

- Does the program conform to its mission?
- Does the program have the right staff to meet clients' needs?
- Is the program operating within its budget?
- Does the program have the right mix of board members?
- Have staff become complacent, or do staff constantly try to improve?
- Has the program achieved its performance goals?
- Are performance goals aligned so the program can meet clients and stakeholders' expectations?
- Where is the program strong? Where is it weak?

Answering these questions may require some outside information to benchmark the program effectively. In some cases, the incubator can compare itself to the entire incubation industry; NBIA's State of the Business Incubation Industry reports give baseline data about overall industry averages for comparison. NBIA's online benchmarking tool at www.nbia.org/benchmark can show how the program's practices compare with those of others.

Other areas require information specific to a program's particular type and mission, so that apples are compared to apples. For example, a technology incubator associated with a university might collect data on the number of university technologies successfully commercialized through new company formation. But this same measure would not be relevant to a technology incubator not affiliated with a university. NBIA may have some of that information, as may other associations, such as the Association of University Technology Managers or the State Science and Technology Institute.

BEST PRACTICES IN ACTION

Meeting Industry Standards
Northeast Indiana Innovation Center, Fort Wayne, IN
Karl LaPan, president and CEO
www.niic.net

It's one thing to tell clients and stakeholders that an incubation program is committed to excellence. It's another to prove it. So when the management of the Northeast Indiana Innovation Center asked themselves what single thing would have the greatest positive impact on the quality of client services, they decided to seek ISO9001:2000 certification for the center.

An internationally recognized set of standards for quality management systems, ISO9001:2000 emphasizes process management—the optimization of tasks and activities to achieve quality. It requires involvement of all staff, from top management to front-line employees, using quantitative metrics to measure improvement and achievement.

NIIC management felt that the process of achieving certification would keep the organization focused on quality, organizational effectiveness, and excellence, while giving it independent verification of its own business practices. Potential clients and stakeholders could do business with NIIC with confidence.

The journey to certification began with a two-day introductory workshop in November 2004 for all Innovation Center staff. The registration audit itself came in two phases: a preassessment in April 2005, in which the auditor determined NIIC's level of readiness, followed by the actual registration audit in May 2005. All staff members participated in these audits, with special emphasis on how top management reviewed and applied quality system findings. The auditor cited some minor findings, which were addressed. NIIC achieved its first ISO9001:2000 certification on August 31, 2005, and was recertified in late 2008.

The ISO9001:2000 plaque is a highly visible asset for NIIC, says President and CEO Karl LaPan. "It reminds our clients of our commitment to excellence and encourages them to make the same commitment in their enterprises," he says. And to potential prospects, "ISO9001:2000 certification is a mark of distinction, overtly demonstrating that we walk the walk."

Incubator Benchmarking Survey
Southwest Michigan Innovation Center, Kalamazoo, MI
Robert DeWitt, president and CEO
www.kazoosmic.com

In 2006, the Southwest Michigan Innovation Center experienced a change in leadership. Some of the new CEO's first questions centered on identifying best practices and measuring the incubator's operating performance against that of its peers: other private, nonprofit life science incubators. The problem was that there were no data to show what equivalent, sector-focused facilities spent on depreciation, utility cost, repairs, maintenance, and administrative costs. So in November 2006, SMIC started a benchmarking survey to compare operating costs among similar incubators.

Eleven NBIA incubators were willing to participate anonymously, supplying these data points:

- 2006 operating costs (mostly budget)
- Depreciation (combined building and equipment)
- Utilities (gas, electric, and water/sewer)
- Maintenance and repairs (several subcategories requested)
- Outside services (computer, subscriptions, etc.)
- Administration and support (subcategories requested)
- Building square footage (gross area, usable lab space)
- Rental rate structure and pricing methodology
- Scope of services provided

After SMIC received the information from the benchmarked programs, incubator personnel analyzed the data, made additional requests for missing data and clarifications, summarized the data, blinded the responses, and sent the whole package back to all survey participants to receive feedback, comments, and updates.

SMIC staff entered final responses into a self-calculating worksheet. Key points from the data showed that

- SMIC's gross facility size, as well as net usable square footage, are equivalent to those of other facilities.
- Depreciation runs higher at SMIC than at other incubation programs.
- Utility costs are substantially higher at SMIC than at other incubators, possibly because there is no separate metering for individual client spaces.
- SMIC's administrative and other support expenses are significantly less than those of other incubation programs.
- SMIC's other support and services (administration) costs are significantly less than those of other incubation programs.
- Total operating costs are lower at SMIC than at other comparable facilities, for both gross and net square footage.

The results confirmed that while some SMIC expenses were in line with those at comparable facilities, there were other areas where—with some focus and scrutiny—SMIC could be more competitive and agile. For example, the incubator conducted an energy audit and redesigned its control system with after-hours set-backs and (unsuccessfully) lobbied the Michigan Utility Rate Commission for special utility rates for incubators in Smart Zones. Results also were communicated to the SMIC board with a road map to implement necessary changes.

■■ collection of statistics on clients and graduates

Perhaps the most important evaluation any business incubator can undertake is measurement of its economic impact or returns on stakeholder investment. Proof of an incubation program's effectiveness is vital to securing new and ongoing financial support from sponsors and stakeholders. Potential sponsors want to know that they're investing in a worthwhile endeavor; current sponsors want to know they're getting their money's worth. Measurement also can help gauge how well the program is meeting its mission.

When collecting statistics, you must include incubator graduates. Most stakeholders want to know not just the number of companies the program has nurtured, but also how those graduates perform in the long run. NBIA recommends that all incubation programs track their graduates for at least five years to demonstrate long-term economic impact. (To ensure that this information can be obtained from graduate companies, include it as an admission requirement, clearly outlining its purpose in the client contract, or rental or service agreement.)

Collecting, analyzing, and reporting economic impact data need not be difficult or overly time-consuming. Information on why, what, and how to collect this information is available free to all incubation programs in NBIA's *Measuring Your Business Incubator's Economic Impact: A Toolkit*, available at www.nbia.org/impact.

BEST PRACTICES IN ACTION

Collecting and Reporting Economic Impacts
William M. Factory Small Business Incubator, Tacoma, WA
Tim Strege, executive director
www.williamfactory.com

Tim Strege, executive director of the William M. Factory Small Business Incubator in Tacoma, Washington, understands the value of collecting data that illustrate how the incubator is contributing to the local and state economies. The incubator compiles information on client revenues, average wages, jobs created, earnings, taxes, purchases of supplies, and other data annually.

William M. Factory focuses on specialty construction trades, business services, and applied technology companies (e.g., ICT, RFID). Located in the low-income area of east Tacoma, the incubator has targeted businesses that provide high-quality jobs for minority and low-income people, although it includes a wide variety of client firms by race and ethnicity. (See elsewhere in this volume for further information on this

award-winning incubator's best practices.) Two incubator buildings—joined together—provide 42,000 square feet of client, administrative, and shared space.

Data compiled by the incubator for 2009 represent twenty-seven specialty construction trade companies, seven information technology companies, and one business service company that were clients of the incubator in that year. (The incubator opened a second, 20,000-square-foot facility in late 2009; at capacity, the incubator will house fifty to sixty firms.)

Strege provided the following data in his 2009 report:

$35,227,010.00	Aggregate client commercial revenues
$343.00	Full-time employment by client companies
$23.25	Average hourly wages of client employees
$16,589,697.00	Total wages paid by client companies
$9,612,113.00	Total client company supply purchases
$2,726,161.00	Total client company overhead and reinvested profits
$ 6,299,039.00	Total business taxes, comprising:

Federal employment taxes	$1,389,353
Federal business taxes	$544,355
State employment taxes	$490,360
State and local business taxes	$3,874,971

$3,259,875.00	Employee Social Security and income taxes
$9,558,914.00	Total business and employee taxes

The federal employment tax rate is the required FICA (Social Security and Medicare) 7.65 percent contribution and an estimated .85 percent of payroll based upon unemployment insurance rates of .008 to .062, with a maximum credit of 5.4 percent for state unemployment insurance taxes paid for the first $7,000 of wages paid. "This is about $400 per full-time-equivalent employee," Strege says.

The employee tax rate assumed a married person with four allowances—either dependents or other income tax deductions—and is based upon published IRS withholding tables. State and local taxes include business, occupation, and combined sales tax (collected by the state from companies and distributed on a formula basis to government entities).

All calculations are direct economic impacts," Strege emphasizes, noting that he also uses Minnesota IMPLAN (Impact Analysis for Planning) economic modeling software multipliers for Washington to calculate indirect and induced economic benefits.

The data are collected for each company on a quarterly basis and aggregated to obtain totals. The incubator sends its data to all its funding agencies that want employment, revenues, and wage income figures.

"We provide information on tax ratios to illustrate the cost-benefit ratio. For example, about $4.4 million of state and local taxes were produced by incubator client companies," Strege says. "The incubator received about $216,000 of government operating support in 2009, but generated $20 in state and local taxes to offset each $1 of operating support."

Tracking such data is important, but reporting them is even more so. When Strege presented the 2009 report to the Tacoma Community Redevelopment Authority, "Members were impressed that the incubator helps companies grow favorable wage employment," Strege says.

Strege provides a concrete example of client success: "One soon-to-be graduate company, Advanced Government Services, which specializes in traffic control at construction sites, has invested over $1 million in equipment purchases and for property acquisition and renovation of its new corporate headquarters." The woman-owned company grew from a two-person startup to forty-two employees during its time in the incubator.

Economic Impact Data Reports
University City Science Center, Philadelphia, PA
Kristin Hart, manager, incubator operations
Jeanne Mell, vice president, marketing communications
www.sciencecenter.org

The University City Science Center, an urban research park and business incubator in Philadelphia, partnered with the Economy League of Greater Philadelphia and Select Greater Philadelphia to conduct an impact report of its incubator services on the Greater Philadelphia region's economy. Established in 1963, UCSC was the first and remains the largest urban research park in the United States. The incubator currently provides mentoring and business advice and "fully-equipped laboratories and 'plug 'n play' offices for entrepreneurs."

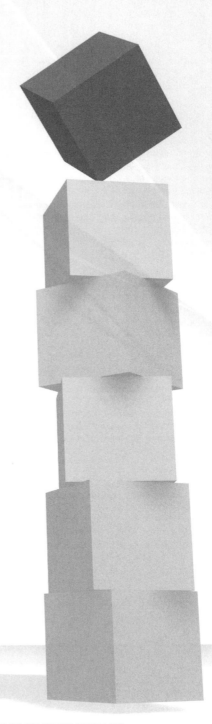

The University City Science Center—An Engine of Economic Growth for Greater Philadelphia, published in September 2009, summarizes the "impact of the Science Center's incubation services on the Greater Philadelphia region's economy by looking at the companies and organizations that received incubator services and other early-stage businesses that received a benefit by being located at the Science Center as they grew."

Findings of the Economy League report are impressive: "Of the 350-plus graduate organizations referenced in this study, the 93 that remain in the region employ 15,512 people; the Science Center's 37 current incubator residents employ another 174. These highly skilled jobs command an average wage of $89,000, contributing $22 million to the City of Philadelphia in wage taxes and $42.5 million to the Commonwealth of Pennsylvania in income taxes annually."

Average wages and indirect and induced jobs and demand created by UCSC clients and graduates were based on multipliers provided by the Minnesota IMPLAN (Impact Analysis for Planning) economic modeling software. The report also says that each UCSC-generated employee supports an additional 1.68 jobs due to such indirect benefits.

The report further notes UCSC's contribution to networks and other actors in the Philadelphia technology economy, including life sciences: "The 449 patents (72 percent in the life sciences) obtained by all Science Center–incubated and graduate organizations have strengthened connections between the region's mix of university research institutions, hospitals, and start-up organizations, reinforcing the innovation pipeline that creates new opportunities for economic growth."

In addition to the data reported above, UCSC's report also finds that the center created 15,686 direct jobs and 42,021 total jobs (the IMPLAN multiplier) and contributed to $1.669 billion in direct and $3.218 billion in total labor/wages.

To collect data, a list was developed of all organizations that received incubator services and benefited from the Science Center as they grew; the data were drawn from a variety of sources, dating to 1968. Incubator staff gathered current incubator client information.

Once the list was created, the researchers determined for each company:

- Its current address, including ZIP code
- The year it exited the Science Center, if known
- Its total employment when it exited the Science Center, if known
- The primary type of good or service it produces and its appropriate NAICS code, if known
- Organization location, employment, and current status—verified through Hoover's database or determined by direct contact

The report was distributed to Science Center stakeholders of all types, including government officials and peer organizations, such as Ben Franklin Technology Partners and BioAdvance. It is posted on UCSC's and the research organizations' Web sites. "The report was very well received and garnered positive press reports in outlets such as the *Philadelphia Inquirer*, the *Philadelphia Business Journal*, *Genome Web Daily News* and on public television station WHYY," says UCSC Vice President for Marketing Communications Jeanne Mell.

> "This extensive survey informs us of what we are doing well and what we can improve on in our services."
>
> – David McNamara, vice president, incubation, Innovacorp

■■ evaluating incubator services

An incubation professional must regularly gather feedback from clients about the perceived value they receive from the incubator and the usefulness and effectiveness of specific programs and services. Based on the feedback—and keeping the incubator's mission in mind—incubator management can eliminate or adjust ineffective services or add new programs that better reflect what clients see as most valuable.

Client surveys are a useful way to gather not only outcome data but also information on the value clients place on a particular service and their level of satisfaction with service delivery. Questions gauging client satisfaction and loyalty might cover:

- Coaching services
- Training and mentor programs
- Space and facility services, including reception services
- Networking and social events
- Efforts to assist firms in obtaining financing
- Service provider programs
- Effectiveness of service delivery

The idea is to evaluate clients' use of services and whether those services are making a difference in their businesses.

Clients will appreciate the opportunity to rate incubator programs and services as well as answer open-ended questions. They will also appreciate surveys that are easy to understand and do not take an unreasonable amount of time to complete. Consider using an online survey service that aggregates results and allows for anonymity. And be sure to include a question such as, "Would you recommend this program to a friend or colleague?" Since word-of-mouth is one of the most powerful marketing methods, it's good to know whether clients would refer others to the program.

Another effective way to gather input is to organize focus groups. Used in combination with surveys, focus groups offer additional insights and can bring out more spontaneous reactions from participants. Some managers ask graduate companies to participate in focus group sessions because graduates often have a greater appreciation for what they gained from the incubation experience. Clients may not recognize all the benefits of the incubation program until they've been out on their own for a while.

In addition to clients' perceptions, incubator managers can evaluate what stakeholders think about the program. Qualitative data help frame the program's performance, but it is important to understand how various stakeholders view this data relative to how they perceive the program. In some cases, graduating ten clients in five years may be considered stellar; in others, it may be viewed as a failure. To see how stakeholders perceive the program's progress, reach out with surveys or focus groups, just as with clients.

BEST PRACTICES IN ACTION

Client Satisfaction Survey and Gap Analysis
Innovacorp, Halifax, Nova Scotia, Canada
Dan MacDonald, former president and CEO
David McNamara, vice president, incubation
www.innovacorp.ca

Innovacorp is strongly committed to systematic and rigorous self-assessments of its performance, not only in economic impact measures and leading indicators but also in client satisfaction. In its performance measures, Innovacorp uses an objective third party to solicit client feedback on performance and value and to pinpoint specific areas that require enhancement or focus.

Since 2006, Innovacorp has contracted with an independent third party (for about C$5,000 each year) to conduct a telephone survey of clients' perceptions of Innovacorp and its services in seven areas:

01. General awareness of Innovacorp's products and services (e.g., business advice and mentoring, incubation services, shared equipment) and the degree to which clients used those products and services.

02. The specific assistance (business strategy and planning, product positioning, identification of outside resources or expertise to solve key problems) the client received and the client's level of satisfaction with the quality of those services.

03. Whether clients would recommend the organization to others in the future and the likelihood of their recommending Innovacorp to business colleagues.

04. The level of satisfaction with services and resources that clients identified as being "very important." In addition, incubation clients are asked satisfaction questions related to the cost of space and the cost of services.

05. Clients' perception of the importance of and satisfaction with Innovacorp's business advisory services (knowledge, professionalism, timeliness of service), as well as their uniqueness (depth, ties to other services, unique level of quality).

06. Whether the client has ever approached Innovacorp for investment or financing and how satisfied the client was in its contact with the Innovacorp staff; the timeliness of service; staff's understanding of the clients' business; whether Innovacorp provided quality work; and how defined the investment process was.

07. Clients' satisfaction with seminars, events, and networking opportunities provided by Innovacorp, as well as their importance to the clients.

Innovacorp measures both satisfaction with and importance of key services of the incubator. The gap analysis examines the percentage of clients who both view a service as "very important" and are less than "very satisfied" with the delivery of that service. On the basis of survey results, Innovacorp establishes operational objectives and identifies service offerings that can be enhanced to increase client satisfaction.

For example, as a result of client feedback from the survey about the quality of Innovacorp's technology infrastructure, the program invested more than C$270,000 to build a state-of-the-art, enterprise-grade integrated voice and data network and services to ensure it could deliver advanced and reliable information technology services to resident and affiliate members.

By implementing changes in response to the surveys, Innovacorp has seen steady increases in client satisfaction. In 2008–9, 96 percent of clients said they were satisfied with Innovacorp's services overall, up from 89 percent in 2005–6. Over the same period, the percentage of clients who said they would recommend Innovacorp to a colleague increased from 90 percent to 96 percent.

"We have to stay close and be relevant to our clients," says David McNamara, Innovacorp's vice president for incubation. "This extensive survey informs us of what we are doing well and what we can improve on in our services. It also tells us from year to year what our clients value most and how we are delivering on our value-added services."

Perhaps the most important evaluation any business incubator can undertake is measurement of its economic impact or returns on stakeholder investment.

chapter 06

client entrance and exit

The incubator aspires to have a positive impact on its community's
economic health by maximizing the success of emerging companies.
Having a means for selecting clients helps differentiate between business
incubation programs and other entrepreneurial support initiatives.

Management and boards of incubators should strive to

- Prioritize management time to place the greatest emphasis on client assistance, including proactive advising and guidance that results in company success and wealth creation

Client Entrance and Exit Procedures

- Promote the mission of the business incubator
- Ensure maximum return on investment on the incubator's valuable and limited resources
- Avoid a poor fit between clients and incubator capabilities
- Motivate clients and staff to measure success through achievement of agreed-upon milestones
- Make room for a continuing flow of qualified incubator clients and graduates

For example, Small Business Development Centers funded by the U.S. Small Business Administration are required by law to offer their services to anyone who asks for them, thus limiting their ability to provide concentrated, long-term support to a specific entrepreneur or business. Companies located in research parks can typically remain as long as they like if space is available and they can pay rent.

A business incubation program, in contrast, selects its clients on criteria that may include coachability, growth potential, viability, industry sector, and stage of development. And it should require companies to leave the program within a reasonable period of time, having met appropriate benchmarks and other graduation criteria. A best practice incubator goes beyond these basic measures by positioning itself to find the best clients through implementing a comprehensive application and screening process, requiring nonperforming or disruptive clients to exit the incubation program, working hard to graduate successful companies into the community, and maintaining contact with its graduates.

■■ client identification and selection

One of the first steps in identifying suitable clients is to understand the program's value proposition and how the program is positioning itself to maximize the impact of this value within its market area. Knowing exactly what the program has to offer clients is not only sound marketing but also good business. Being able to match the incubator's value proposition to client needs helps focus and channel prospects in order to select those with the most potential to succeed in the program. Incubator professionals have limited time and resources to devote to clients; they will want to choose only those companies that are truly committed to success and that are willing to accept the program's help.

At the same time, it is important to seek a diverse range of clients to increase synergy among companies and to diminish the risk of direct market competition. Even a special-focus incubator needs diversity: a roster full of cookie makers won't help a kitchen incubator achieve its mission (and is likely to lead to food fights!). A client list that includes bakers, caterers, and gourmet food producers will promote relationships between clients and strengthen the overall local economy.

An effective client identification process can not only help select optimal clients but also ensure a steady stream of new prospects to keep the incubator full as companies graduate, which contributes to financial sustainability. Of equal importance, effective identification and selection of clients will ensure a greater percentage of them graduate as successful businesses. This will allow the program to avoid a reputation as a "hospital for sick companies." Incubation professionals at best practice programs are acutely aware that their program's reputation for graduating successful companies will, in the long run, determine their ability to tap into community goodwill, access high-quality expertise, obtain additional funding, and develop helpful strategic alliances.

There are many ways to identify and reach out to potential clients. For details on market research and marketing strategies, tools, and techniques, see *A Practical Guide to Business Incubator Marketing* (Athens, Ohio: NBIA Publications, 2007).

BEST PRACTICES IN ACTION

Start-Up Competition
Innovacorp, Halifax, Nova Scotia, Canada
Dan MacDonald, president and CEO
www.innovacorp.ca

Originally established as the Nova Scotia Research Foundation in 1948, Innovacorp became a Crown corporation of the province of Nova Scotia in 1995. Innovacorp's mission is to help early-stage companies—particularly in information and communications technology, life sciences, and clean technology—commercialize their technology for export.

To help manage deal flow and prospects, Innovacorp leads a biennial provincewide contest called the I-3 Technology Start-Up Competition. The "I-3" stands for Idea/Innovation/Implementation, the early steps in the commercialization process.

"An important point of distinction is that this competition is a business competition not a business plan competition," says Dan MacDonald, Innovacorp president and CEO until early 2010. "The purpose of this competition is not to find the best or most creative writer but to find compelling Nova Scotia business opportunities that advance these companies and their ideas forward."

The purpose of the competition is "to identify and support high-potential early-stage Nova Scotia knowledge-based companies and encourage entrepreneurial activity across the province." Participants must be incorporated in Nova Scotia, primarily devoted to the knowledge sector, and have had sales for less than one year.

The competition started as a pilot for businesses in Cape Breton, Nova Scotia, in March 2006, and generated eighteen formal submissions. Management decided to run the full-scale competition every other year to allow Innovacorp a full year to work with prize winners.

For the first full-scale competition in 2008, Innovacorp segmented Nova Scotia's population of 1 million into five geographical zones and awarded prizes in each of the zones. Participants represented information and communications technology, life sciences, and advanced manufacturing businesses. Of the submissions, 52 percent served the business-to-consumer segment, and 48 percent served the business-to-business segment. A little more than half were at the idea stage; 46 percent were in prototype; and 3 percent had products in the market.

Judges include representatives of the competition's twenty-eight private-sector partners, including law, accounting, commercial, and marketing firms in each of the competition zones. Competition submissions are evaluated on business plan credibility, management experience, unique proprietary technology and/or high barrier to competitive entry, size of addressable market, and probability of obtaining a fully funded business plan. Ultimately, the winning entrants are determined by highest commercialization potential.

Winning companies in each zone receive cash and in-kind services (from private-sector partners) worth C$100,000; the second-place package is worth C$40,000. Each of the first-place zone winners is then eligible to become the overall provincial winner and vie for a C$100,000 seed equity investment from Innovacorp.

The competition not only reinforces Innovacorp's brand recognition within Nova Scotia but also yields business for the program: of 121 submissions, Innovacorp forged relationships with thirty companies it otherwise would not have known of and gained eleven new clients.

Introducing Youth to Entrepreneurship
Purdue Technology Center–West Lafayette
West Lafayette, IN
Tim Peoples, director
www.pardueresearchpark.org

In the summer of 2007, Purdue Technology Center–West Lafayette received a catalyst grant of $35,000 from the Indiana Workforce Innovations in Regional Economic Development (WIRED) program through a one-time federal grant. Purdue University opens its doors each summer to highly motivated high school juniors and seniors who have a passion for math, science, and technology (initially to those in a thirteen-county area, and subsequently to the state of Indiana as a whole).

Students from across Indiana, who have been nominated by a teacher and selected by a committee, attend an intensive, experiential, and immersive venture creation program conducted by industry leaders, PTC staff, volunteers, serial entrepreneurs, and university faculty. Wendy Kennedy, author of the popular inventor's patent book *So What, Who Cares, Why Me,* is a featured guest speaker for a day and half and provides guidance and insights on the technology commercialization process.

Students work in small teams and individually with an assigned mentor to create a new business, moving systematically from idea to proof of concept and on through business planning. The academy culminates in an elevator pitch/investor presentation day, when the students present their executive summary and compete for $500 tuition vouchers before a panel of community judges, including lawyers, bankers, venture capitalists, and economic development leaders. Winners can use their vouchers at Purdue, Indiana University–Kokomo, and the twenty-three-campus Ivy Tech Community College system.

The Purdue Research Park (which houses the incubator) provides tuition, room, board, instructional material, and program seminars and workshops for all participants. Families are responsible for transportation to and from the program, pocket money, and a $75 registration fee (although scholarships are available). Students who complete the academy and choose to enroll as undergraduates at Purdue may use the academy experience to fulfill one of the approved option course requirements for Purdue's Certificate in Entrepreneurship and Innovation Program, which is similar to a minor.

Purdue Research Park does not dedicate any full-time staff to the event, but many of the staff volunteer time outside the normal work day to deliver this program. People who are passionate about entrepreneurship and its importance to the state of Indiana serve as mentors, facilitators, and judges. However, as with any good program, there needs to be a passionate champion who drives the success, momentum, and energy of the effort.

The program has several goals, including:

- Recruiting potential students to Purdue University, especially its entrepreneurship program

- Augmenting students' understanding of technology transfer and technology-led economic development

- Sparking interest in entrepreneurship among Indiana youth

- Generating participation opportunities for community professionals

- Gaining interest and financial support from community leaders

- Promoting community awareness of the need for homegrown entrepreneurs for local economic development

Clarifying and establishing career aspirations is another dividend of the program. John Hanak, director of the statewide Purdue Technology Centers program, enrolled his son in the academy. "My son's single greatest learning was he did not feel he will [ever] be ready to be an entrepreneur, but the experience did convince him that he wanted to be a business major," Hanak says.

The academy sustains itself through cash and in-kind sponsorships from local community leaders and organizations. PTC leveraged the success of its clients and graduates and that of the research park as a whole to gain support from community and state-level service providers without jeopardizing existing partnerships and sponsorships. For example, they targeted local businesses for gifts of $500 to $1,000, so as not to cannibalize PTC's larger funders and donors. And they made the case for funding at the state level by showing the potential benefits to students' hometowns.

■■ application and screening process

Once program managers have identified potential clients and gained their attention, they must begin the process of deciding whether the prospects are a good match for the program. Most programs have a formal application that gives staff an overview of the client's business. For some programs, the application plus a face-to-face meeting yields enough information to determine whether the company would make a good incubator client. Many programs, however, have more in-depth screening processes that augment the application.

Criteria for admission to an incubation program vary, depending on the incubator's mission and its stage of development. In general, however, the application and screening process should determine whether the potential client:

- Has a viable business proposition.

- Has a management team that is willing to accept the incubator's assistance and will participate in the incubator's internal community.

- Will benefit the community's economic development in the form of job creation or create other community or sponsor benefits, depending on the program's goals. These could include providing new business opportunities for community vendors or contract agencies, commercializing technologies, increasing community competitiveness, creating wealth, diversifying local economies, or providing entrepreneurial opportunities for low-income people or other demographic groups.

- Will compete directly with an existing incubator client.

- Can pay program rents and fees while developing positive cash flow.

- Fits into the incubator's industry niche or sector focus areas.

- Has needs the incubation program can meet, whether on its own or through its network of service providers.

- Will meet the requirements of any incubator partners the company may need (e.g., a university or federal laboratory).

- Is likely to meet benchmarks for graduation.

- Will positively contribute to the culture within the incubator.

For examples of application forms and other screening materials, see *Put It in Writing: Crafting Policies, Agreements, and Contracts for Your Incubator* (Athens, Ohio: NBIA Publications, 2002).

BEST PRACTICES IN ACTION

Five-Stage Prescreening
Innovacorp, Halifax, Nova Scotia, Canada
David McNamara, vice president, incubation
www.innovacorp.ca

As a highly visible and successful technology incubation program, Innovacorp receives dozens of inquiries from prospective clients each quarter. "The relationship between Innovacorp and each client is a working partnership with the goal of achieving successful and sustained commercialization in an accelerated timeframe," says David McNamara, vice president for incubation. "We are producing clients who are exporting products and services internationally."

To ensure that it accepts clients that are the best possible strategic fit, Innovacorp starts with five specific entry criteria to vet applicants:

01. **Stage:** The start-up venture must be a Nova Scotia–based, early-stage technology company.

02. **People:** The start-up's business plan must be credible, and the team must have management experience, domain expertise, and, preferably, an entrepreneurial track record.

03. **Barrier:** There must be a competitive barrier to entry in the form of a unique and/or proprietary technology (product, system, or service), ideally with defendable intellectual property.

04. **Market:** There must be a large national or international addressable market.

05. **Fundability:** There must be a high probability or reasonable likelihood of obtaining a fully funded business plan. Consideration is given to how much money it will take to successfully go to market, to commercialize the product or service, and to achieve positive cash flow.

Prospects can review the eligibility criteria on Innovacorp's Web site or call to schedule a meeting with a senior advisor to review their business concept and its fit with Innovacorp's mission.

Innovacorp weighs those criteria against what it can offer the applicant from the program's menu of support services, including lab and office space, facilities, and services; information and communications technology infrastructure, services, and support; scientific resources; shared administrative support services; business advice and referral services; networking opportunities; and off-site affiliate client services.

On the basis of this evaluation, Innovacorp sorts applicants into one of three classifications:

Level 1. The review reveals strong prospects of commercial success. Innovacorp will engage additional resources in these high-potential start-ups to help position the company to obtain venture funding.

Level 2. The review reveals moderate prospects of commercial success. If appropriate, Innovacorp will work with the start-up to strengthen its attributes and the probability of securing venture funding.

Level 3. The review reveals weak prospects of commercial success. Innovacorp will disengage from the start-up, providing in-depth feedback detailing the rationale for doing so.

This selection process has allowed Innovacorp to have a highly robust pipeline of deal flow each quarter, including:

- Ten to twenty-five initial contacts
- Ten to fifteen detailed and critical analyses on prospects
- Two to five prospects become level 2 clients
- One to three become level 3 clients
- One to three clients graduate from level 2
- One client graduates from level 3

Drawing on Board Members as Screeners
La Cocina Business Incubator, San Francisco, CA
Caleb Zigas, program coordinator
www.lacocinasf.org

La Cocina, a kitchen incubator in San Francisco, starts its application process with a general orientation session held every three months. Each ninety minute bilingual orientation describes the incubation program, how it works, and how to apply, and it discusses the food business in general. About thirty-five participants attend a given session; of those, five or so actually apply for admission to the program.

Each applicant is expected to have a business plan in hand (or already be selling products informally in some way, such as at flea markets or street fairs) and must supply references.

Each application is reviewed by a separate three-person team from the incubator's thirty-five-member client advisory committee. Each team includes someone with financial experience, plus La Cocina staff. The advisory team looks at three key elements of the applicant's business plan: market, operations, and production. The applicant has to be able to address any issues with those areas within six months. The team also identifies any particular needs and recommends other resources to fulfill them.

The review period takes about three months. Companies identified as having weak areas are accepted into a preincubation phase, in which they work with incubator staff to fix the concerns. Once that happens, they may join the incubation program in full.

Excellence in Entrepreneurship Certificate Course
University of Central Florida Business Incubation Program
Orlando, FL
Tom O'Neal, director
www.incubator.ucf.edu

All applicants for admission to the University of Central Florida Business Incubation Program must complete an Excellence in Entrepreneurship course. Offered jointly by the incubation program and the UCF College of Business Administration since 2001, the quarterly course is taught by experienced entrepreneurs, professional service providers, and entrepreneurship faculty from the university.

Although any company can sign up for the class, it is a requirement for admission to the incubator program. About 80 percent of the students are program applicants, says Tom O'Neal, UCFBIP director.

The seven-session, four-week course helps students clarify their business concepts and walks them through the steps of planning and starting a business. The course introduces them to resources and advisors that provide invaluable support in laying the foundation for a successful company. As a result, those who complete the program are better prepared for incubation: the survival rate of incubator clients has increased from 70 percent to over 90 percent since the program began.

It's also a self-selection mechanism. The cost of $400 for the first applicant team member and $200 for each additional one weeds out entrepreneurs who aren't serious about success. Of those who do pony up and enroll, about 20 percent drop out of the course, O'Neal says, although "a large number of them do reapply later when they are in a better position to enter the program."

The course also acts as a screening tool for incubator staff. Over the four weeks of classes, the staff observe the participants to get truer insights into the entrepreneurs and their business concepts—achieving a deeper understanding than could be gained from a couple of interviews.

Upon completion of the class, those who wish to enter the incubation program submit an application. A selection committee (comprising incubator staff and others who might have input for a particular set of companies) reviews it. From there, it passes to O'Neal, who considers all the data and recommendations before making a final decision on acceptance. Only about 75 percent of those who complete the class make it into the incubator, O'Neal says.

A Comprehensive Screening Process
Meytav Incubator, Kiryat Shmona, Israel
Orit Shaked, CTO
www.meytavti.co.il

This privately owned and operated incubator, in existence since 1991, sources its deal flow from investment companies that are co-owners of Meytav, universities, hospitals, corporate spin-offs, independent entrepreneurs, and other local entities. A preinvestment "filtration system" identifies projects that:

- Represent the highest qualify of scientific research and ensure solid proof of concept, IP protection, a clear regulatory path, and commercial potential

- Are spin-offs of "existing industrial entities that are willing to assist in R&D, as well as the launching and marketing of the final product"

- Clearly identify an unfulfilled gap in the market

- Show potential to create beneficial alliances with strategic partners

- Can achieve a major milestone during their incubation period

- Are operated by experienced entrepreneurs with strong business (as well as scientific) backgrounds

Projects go through a "strict and comprehensive screening process" prior to investment. The Meytav CEO, CTO, and consultants review personal and business matters and conduct due diligence on the technology, the prospective client's "fit" with the incubator, and the project's work plan and budget. "We want somebody we can work with, who doesn't interfere all the time, who answers questions, and who, if he doesn't know something, will say so and get back to you," says Meytav CTO Orit Shaked.

The personal review of the founder or managing director and his or her team involves examining the individual's track record, ability to execute, and credibility. The business review includes examination of the possible business model and accessibility of potential partners (strategic and investment). The businesses themselves are considered for viability scientifically, technologically, commercially, and financially.

The details of the screening process—which can take up to three months—are provided on the Meytav Web site (which also has a diagram of the process):

Stage 1: Go or No-Go. The Meytav management team (CEO and CTO) and relevant consultants examine the initial proposals and decide whether to move forward.

Stage 2: Initial Meeting. The group meets with the applicant to request detailed information, and the application formally enters the screening process.

"The incubator must be selective and invest its resources in individuals who have greater chances of sucess."

– Tim Strege, executive director, Willam M. Factory Small Business Incubator

Stage 3: References and Due Diligence. Meytav management conducts an in-depth due diligence analysis of the project that includes a thorough checking of references and the track record of the proposed project team. The application also undergoes a detailed scientific and technological analysis while potential business models and strategic partners are identified.

Stage 4: Work Plan. The practical issues are now prepared as a work plan, with time frames, targets, and budgets. Upon completion of the plan, the incubator and applicant negotiate terms and conditions and prepare for official submission of the project.

Stage 5: Approvals. Once the project is approved by the CEO and CTO, it proceeds to the Meytav board of directors, which decides whether to pass it on for the approval of the Office of the Chief Scientist of the Ministry of Industry, Trade and Labor. (See chapter 9, "Case Studies," for further information about central government support for projects managed by Israel's technology incubators.) The agreements and the work plan are finalized.

The budgets for projects in Israel's regular technology incubators are expected to range from $350,000 to $600,000 and to support them for up to two years, except for biotechnology projects that are eligible for a third year in the incubator and thus may have a budget that totals $900,000 for the entire period. The funds invested by government represent up to 85 percent of the project's budget and are provided as a grant or soft loan; a 15 percent private sector investment is also required, though the project may raise supplemental funding beyond its regular budget.

The reason for the careful screening is that every process is focused on whether the potential client company is investable. The central government funding leverages private seed funding. This investment, in most cases, leads to follow-on investments by private angel, venture capital, or corporate strategic partners as the client company achieves milestones and prepares to exit from the incubator.

Since firms are supported for such a short period of time before they must be ready to raise follow-on investment and leave the incubator, incubator staff do not depend on commercializing the projects or products while clients are in the incubator. "We can't believe this could happen in two years," Shaked says.

Acceptance of companies in the incubator also is "conditional upon the recruitment of a CEO who will complement the skills" of the founding scientist or entrepreneur, Shaked says. Meytav then appoints experienced entrepreneurs, industry experts, and academics to the company's board of directors and scientific advisory board. Meytav places "paramount emphasis on the assembly of a well-balanced, professional, and experienced management team for each of the portfolio companies," Shaked says.

"The entrepreneur himself is not always the project leader or CEO," Shaked explains. "If the firm originates outside academia, the entrepreneur will be part of the staff and work in the company. If the entrepreneur is from academia, he will not join the company but will participate, perhaps as a consultant or a board member, but the CEO is really managing the company."

Meytav may assist in identifying CEOs, including serial entrepreneurs.

Screening Criteria for Special Populations
William M. Factory Small Business Incubator, Tacoma, WA
Tim Strege, executive director
www.williamfactory.com

The William M. Factory Small Business Incubator in Tacoma, Washington, serves specialty construction trades, information technology, and business services related to these sectors in a 42,000-square-foot facility on Tacoma's East Side. The incubator is located within the boundaries of the Puyallup Indian Reservation and the area first settled by American pioneers in the mid-1850s. The neighborhood is adjacent to

he Port of Tacoma, where industrial commerce historically as employed people with technical skills but only a high chool education. During the 1980s, permanent closures of nanufacturing plants in the port and nearby vicinities led to he loss of more than 10,000 jobs.

Vith some 75 percent of its companies owned by minorities, vomen, and low-income people, the incubator has a goal of reating 400-plus job opportunities with an average wage of 20 per hour and filling at least 50 percent of positions with cal disadvantaged residents by 2013.

he incubator management has recognized the dynamics f working with a population that includes minority isadvantaged businesses. "They typically bring no bank redit, no business networks, and no wealth to their ompanies," says Executive Director Tim Strege, "and ve can't take the same approach to screening clients as raditional incubators do. We can't take a hard line on their aving a fully developed business concept and sufficient unds to cover six months of rent."

trege maintains that entrepreneurship is not a common trait nd that, like many other institutions, the incubator has limited esources. "Thus the incubator must focus our resources n entrepreneurs who 'pass' at least some entrance and valuation steps prior to admission" to the program. Strege rgues with social service advocates who propose that people have a right to fail" and notes that many government-nd foundation-financed programs invest in lower-income eople, yet fail to help these people. In the end, many of hese programs themselves fail. Instead, he says the duty f the incubator is to help lower-income people save money y refraining from pursuing an unworkable business plan or oncept rather than to encourage them.

he incubator "must be selective," he says, and invest ts resources in individuals who have greater chances of uccess. To that end, he cites several "signs to look for" that epresent incubator screening criteria:

- Intent to devote oneself full-time to the entrepreneurial business. Strege will not invest in businesses that propose to be part-time.

- Payment of a $70 application fee (which weeds out "pretend" entrepreneurs).

- Evidence of premarketing activities in which entrepreneurs test their products or services on family members, friends, and others to determine pricing, customer service issues, needed add-ons, and opportunities for related products and services. (The incubator requires would-be clients to engage in these premarketing activities prior to developing a working draft of a business plan.)

- The intent to compete based on quality rather than on price in order to ensure that both customers and the company gain economic value from their transactions. "The owner must command a higher price than the cost of the product or service, enabling a profit for reinvestment into the firm," and the purchaser must obtain a "consumer surplus"—that is, a value greater than the price of the product or service. Success is more likely to occur if both sides of the table benefit, says Strege.

- Desire and willingness to use incubator services in addition to physical space. "While incubators should have desirable facilities, it's the on-site supportive technical services that are vital to a start-up's growth," says Strege. "Someone who approaches us merely to occupy an office is quickly sent to other commercial buildings. We seek entrepreneurs who don't 'know it all' and who want to use accounting, legal, engineering, project management, marketing, and other expertise available at the incubator." (The incubator charges above-market rents in order to provide these services.)

- Willingness to grow companies via revenues (bootstrapping) rather than debt or equity sales, which are usually not initially suitable to the types of clients served by the incubator. The premarketing activity the incubator requires "frequently provides the entrepreneur with a source of funds beginning day one of the business officially opening," Strege says. "These early customers are extremely important—for revenues, positive referrals, suggestions for product improvements, and requests for add-on services. Through a gradual growth of the company, the entrepreneur can manage, afford, and properly utilize company personnel and resources that enable future growth."

- Willingness to undertake short-term leases (no William M. Factory lease extends beyond the incubator's fiscal year-end of June 30). Companies are reviewed on a quarterly basis to determine whether a lease should be renewed. "We sit down with the incubator client and assess company performance and the extent to which there continues to be a 'best fit' between the company and the incubator." (The incubator asks clients to leave if they are no longer using incubator services.)

- Willingness to share company data and information on a quarterly basis and evidence that the entrepreneur and the incubator management will be able to communicate effectively face-to-face. Says Strege: "It is critical for the incubator to know of problem issues and provide immediate assistance to resolve what could be business-ending problems. That is why face-to-face communications are so important." Current resident clients are expected to be visible and keep up communications; otherwise, staff will check on them.

- Evidence that the company operates in a sector or at a stage at which the incubator can provide value. "The incubator cannot provide value to just any business," Strege says. "We build within our walls the capabilities to add value to specific commercial classifications."

The incubator has graduated more than two hundred companies, together employing over 1,200 workers. Approximately 80 percent of those firms remain in business or have successfully merged. Less than one in ten businesses accepted into the incubator washes out of the program prior to graduation. Seventy-five percent of current clients represent minority- or women-owned businesses, and one-third are African American–owned firms. A recent economic analysis of incubator clients identified thirty-three companies generating over $30 million in annual gross commercial revenues and providing over $7 million in federal, state, and local taxes.

Needs Identification

- Provides a benchmarking framework for screening new applicants, allowing staff to assess whether the ventures are ready for incubation and whether the incubation program has adequate value-added services to fill the applicants' needs
- Increases clients' perception of the incubator's value
- Differentiates the incubation program from a traditional multitenant landlord
- Clarifies actions to be taken and resources to be mobilized by clients and incubator staff during comprehensive business assistance, including coaching and facilitation activities

■■ needs identification

Clients have needs that depend on a number of factors, such as their stage of development, their founders' experience, the presence (or absence) of an advisory board, or their industry sector. Some of those needs may be urgent and require immediate attention; others may be ongoing.

Just as each client's needs are unique, so are the incubators that serve them. Incubation is not a one-size-fits-all process. Because not all clients will have the same needs, an important part of the application and screening process is determining exactly what an individual client needs and then deciding how the program can fulfill those needs.

Identifying client needs is a continuing process. When a company applies for acceptance to the program, incubator staff must clarify the prospect's needs to determine whether program services adequately fulfill those needs. The application and screening process should help with that.

Once the company has entered the incubation program, management must continue to assess its needs to make sure that the program is providing what the company requires to grow and succeed. At first, check-ins with the client's management team, whether formally or by e-mail, should occur weekly; as the team matures, the schedule probably can be cut back to monthly or even quarterly meetings. The frequency of these meetings may be spelled out in the client service agreement.

Regardless of the situation, needs identification provides the platform from which incubator staff can take action to assist their clients.

Methodology for Determining Mentoring Needs
Innovacorp, Halifax, Nova Scotia, Canada
Dan MacDonald, former president and CEO
Stephen Hartlen, vice president for mentoring
www.innovacorp.ca

Innovacorp developed a comprehensive needs identification process to assess incubator applicants; the methodology also is the architectural framework for monitoring client company growth and determining whether clients have met necessary benchmarks.

Although Innovacorp is a technology incubator focused particularly on ICT, life sciences, and clean technology, the needs identification framework could serve as a valuable model and be adapted by business incubation programs of all types, says Dan MacDonald, Innovacorp president and CEO until early 2010.

"As incubator managers we can't know everything or pretend to know everything," he says. "Our skill is in helping the entrepreneur identify challenges and then brokering the expertise needed to solve that problem."

While Innovacorp uses the methodology to help businesses prepare themselves to access seed or venture capital, the basic framework is useful in evaluating clients' relative prospects for success, given limited resources and time. In a white paper presented at the 2006 conference of the Canadian Association of Business Incubation, Innovacorp Vice President for Mentoring Stephen Hartlen noted that the method helps "increase organizational efficiency for those who assist start-up technology companies on a daily basis," pointing toward the additional assistance and mentoring that "will likely have the most positive influence and increase the likelihood of a successful outcome."

In addition to client acceptance and needs identification, Innovacorp uses the process to give all applicants useful feedback. "Too often start-ups are not given adequate constructive feedback, especially if it could be deemed negative, and they waste valuable time," Hartlen wrote. Accordingly, the incubator provides feedback to all the companies it works with, including firms that have applied for a biannual start-up competition it runs throughout Nova Scotia as a means of increasing deal flow (see section on client identification and selection earlier in this chapter for more on the competition).

Innovacorp looks for technology start-ups that have a credible business plan and a team with industry management experience, preferably an entrepreneurial track record; a competitive barrier to entry—a unique or proprietary technology (ideally defendable IP); a large and international addressable market; and a reasonable likelihood of successfully raising the funds necessary to become a self-sustaining, successful business. However, Hartlen cautions, "Rarely will a start-up be exceptionally strong in all categories; the goal should be to assess an opportunity relative to its peers."

Innovacorp classifies clients according to a matrix that positions them in one of three levels: Level 1, having many barriers to success; Level 2, with moderate chances of success; and Level 3, having the best chances for success. The classification process considers nine factors:

- **Collaborative relationship.** Will the start-up work collaboratively with the incubator, and will the incubator team be considered a valued and trusted member of the company team?

- **Barrier to entry.** Is the start-up's product or service a truly innovative approach or merely an incremental improvement? Can the barrier be increased through an enhanced IP strategy?

- **Total addressable market.** What is the TAM, based on a bottom-up analysis? Will the TAM be less than could attract venture capital (less than $25 million annually)?

Current and prospective clients often talk about their markets from the top down, "measured in hundreds of millions or even billions [of dollars] globally," MacDonald says. But while "you can buy research that says the market is $X billion, and explains how that breaks down," that information may not be helpful to a start-up. "What we say to clients is, 'Let's take your current offerings and your realistic future offerings and find out what the total addressable market is from a bottom-up perspective.' These are great conversations, and they're meant to help people break it down and vet the numbers realistically," MacDonald says.

For example, a client might contend that the total addressable market for a neutraceutical ingredient is huge: "The worldwide food market is X trillion dollars annually. We have a food additive like calcium that can be added to virtually every food and drink."

"We'd say, 'OK, that is interesting, but we must intelligently break down the market to ensure that we carefully consider the various sectors of the market that would look to use such an additive,'" explains MacDonald. "There are certain foods that normally have additives and others that do not; there are cultures that accept additives and others that do not; there are specific price-sensitive food categories that cannot afford the additive and others that can. There are beachhead markets to start in and there are other markets that are much slower to change. The magic is to help the entrepreneur understand the value of vetting the numbers—but not to do it for them."

- **Sales revenue potential.** Is it likely the firm can achieve initial sales revenue within the time frame acceptable in its industry (e.g., ICT, life sciences)?

- **Business model credibility.** How will the firm make money, and is the model familiar in the marketplace and sector or unproven? Does the company have a well-defined market, compelling business model, and value proposition?

"It's easy to get excited about the technology and all that cool stuff, but it all comes down to the business model and how are you going to make money," MacDonald says. "Are you going to align with an established business model or go after a new one?"

For example, corporations buy site licenses for information technology software, with cost based on the number of potential users. With the advent of cloud computing, however, an increasing number of vendors keep their software on a server and sell access on demand (a model known as "software as a service," or "SaaS").

"If the client says, 'Yes, we know the norms, but we're going to do it a different way,' we will make sure they know what they are doing," MacDonald says. "It's hard enough to build a start-up company and make a business successful without trying to change established buying patterns. The new way still may have merit, but the client will have to convince us and more importantly, representative customers, before we would agree."

- **Go-to-market approach.** Is this strategy well-defined and is it traditional or state-of-the-art? Is the start-up experienced in bringing products to market?

  "A client may have a great solution and a great business model, but that is not enough," MacDonald says. "How are you going to market? Are you going direct to customers, which might require building out a sales force and technical staff across North America? We need to know how the start-up company can achieve revenue and profits as quickly as possible and in what manner. If somebody says they're going horizontal and they're going to tackle every type of market at once, we raise the red flag."

- **Time to commercialize.** This varies by sector, but typically the shorter, the better compared to other opportunities.

- **Business management expertise and experience.** What is the management team's depth and breadth of experience, and is it relevant to the start-up's line of business?

- **Likelihood of securing a fully-funded business plan.** Given all the former factors, what is the likelihood that the start-up will be able to attract equity and debt funding that will enable it to get to a positive revenue position?

  A fully funded business plan may take just $500,000 for some businesses; for others, such as drug development, it can take hundreds of millions of dollars to reach phase two of federal Food and Drug Administration trials. "We try to imagine the likely magnitude of capital to take this product or opportunity to market," MacDonald says. "The investor needs to know that if they put in money at any stage, the odds are that the company will be able to achieve follow-on funding at a later stage. If it can't raise the additional money, then the investor's contribution goes down the drain."

Nobody gets an A-plus on all those characteristics," MacDonald says. For example, a client might fall at low-moderate, moderate-high, or high on the scale for the collaborative relationship factor; the go-to-market approach might be considered immature, traditional, or state-of-the-art.

According to Hartlen's methodology, the incubator would disengage from weak prospects; it would engage and begin to apply significant resources to a high-quality prospect. If the prospect is moderately favorable, the decision could be for or against. "If possible, the goal would be to strengthen the company's attributes and therefore the probability" of success, he writes. Many companies might still be important assets to the community if "they can achieve organic growth through bootstrapping," even if they would not be attractive to institutional investors, he notes. Innovacorp spends 75 percent of its effort on companies at Level 2 and Level 3.

Once this process is complete, Innovacorp tailors its support services to meet the client's needs. Assistance areas and strategies include:

01. **Strategic planning**
    - Develop value proposition and refine it
    - Obtain independent domain expert opinions

02. **Management team composition**
    - Identify management gaps
    - Assist with board composition and governance
    - Assist with human resource management

03. **Product development**
    - Assist definition of R&D plan and create milestones
    - Implement product development best practices
    - Develop patent portfolio strategy
    - Consult with industrial engineers

04. **Sales and marketing**
    - Develop marketing and communications strategies
    - Identify and facilitate targeted channels and strategic partners
    - Develop sales and distribution channel strategies
    - Acquire market intelligence and third-party analysis
    - Develop pricing strategies
    - Identify and help implement competitive positioning
    - Coach on sales pitch delivery

05. **Operations management**
    - Assist with general accounting and bookkeeping
    - Assist with facilities planning
    - Assist with advanced technology infrastructure

06. **Financial management**
    - Measure and make recommendations regarding proper capital requirements to reach the market
    - Federal Scientific Research & Experimental Development (SR&ED) claims review and filing (a Canadian R&D tax credits program that provides incentives for Canada-based research)
    - Develop financial modeling and forecasting, and financial plan
    - Position the opportunity for appropriate financing (angel, seed, venture, and private equity)
    - Facilitate and help secure cofunding commitments
    - Assist with creation of a fully funded business plan
    - Provide coaching on investment pitch delivery
    - Provide coaching on investor expectations

Innovacorp monitors client progress via an online client action plan that includes information on the company, its stage of development, financing (including cash on hand, cash reserve, and burn rate), and value proposition, as well as milestones achieved and milestones to go. An online relationship management system allows MacDonald, his staff of six full-time mentors, and investors to monitor company progress as well.

The tracking document also lists tasks, actions, categories (e.g., HR, governance, IP), priority level, resources, completion date, value of the task, criteria for success, and comments. For example, the task may be, "conduct IP portfolio review"; it may be listed as a B priority; the resource may be an external consultant; and the completion date may be December 31. The value to the business may be that the client will know if they have proprietary technology, and the criteria for success may be that the client reviews IP and recommendation.

Monitoring Client Progress

- Focuses client and incubator actions, ensuring that both the client and the incubator attain their goals

- Ensures that the client is committed to launching the venture and graduating from the incubation program

- Helps the incubation program increase its clients' success rate and solidify its position in supporting its mission and goals

- Provides data for use in documenting program performance and outcomes

■■ monitoring client progress

It can be easy to overlook a client's evolution through the various stages of venture development when one is responding to its specific daily, weekly, or monthly needs. But it is vital that incubator staff periodically take an objective look at the client's progress through the incubation program to assess its stage of development and determine how best to position the company for potential graduation—and whether it is likely to graduate. Staff can measure progress in terms of specific milestones that reflect the evolution of an emerging venture as well as the client's alignment with the incubator's mission. Examples of such milestones include completing or refining the business plan, solidifying the management team, completing proof of concept activities, successfully selling products, securing capital (e.g., grants, loans, angel investment), establishing strategic partnerships, and reaching a certain threshold number of employees or revenue level.

BEST PRACTICES IN ACTION

100-Point System
San Juan College Enterprise Center, Farmington, NM
Jasper Welch, director
www.sanjuancollege.edu/gcb

At the San Juan College Enterprise Center, Director Jasper Welch expects clients to take responsibility for their own progress and success. To encourage their active participation in his program, Welch developed a 100-point scoring system to monitor client involvement.

"While [the system] does not guarantee business success, our results have shown that companies that are more involved in these business development activities tend to have greater success during the business incubation process," Welch says.

Each client company is given an Excel spreadsheet listing forty individual activities in nine areas: financials, operations, business plan, management, civic involvement, mentoring, marketing, time management, and personal growth.

For example, clients can get points for setting up advisory boards; attending incubator functions; taking classes, including NxLevel workshops; updating business plans; and undertaking insurance and banking reviews and assessments. Some activities are available through the incubator; others are outside the incubator's purview. Each activity is assigned a maximum number of points available for completing the activity. Some are as low as five points; the highest award is fifty-five points for completion of a NxLevel workshop. The maximum total points available for all activities is 520.

Clients self-score their sheets, which are reviewed by incubator staff. Staff can change the scores if they feel the client has over- or underawarded points. At the end of the year, the three highest-scoring clients—usually with 250 to 450 points—receive awards at the annual Enterprise Center Incubation Celebration. Prizes have included paid company lunches, strategic planning retreats, and overnight hotel accommodations.

Companies that score fewer than one hundred points in the year are placed on probation. Failure to improve participation results in dismissal from the incubation program.

Self-Assessment Checklist
Oregon Technology Business Center, Beaverton, OR
Steve Morris, executive director
www.otbc.org

The Oregon Technology Business Center uses a two-page Self-Assessment Checklist to identify client needs and chart progress on actions they need to complete or should consider depending on the specifics of their business. The same checklist is completed by the client's assigned entrepreneur-in-residence. Progress and any discrepancies between the client's SAC and the EIR's version are discussed during monthly meetings between the client and Steve Morris, OTBC executive director. (For more on OTBC's EIR program, see chapter 8, "Client Services.")

Morris and longtime EIR Mark Paul, a Portland management consultant, developed the checklist. While the items on the list are pretty much "the usual suspects," Morris notes that they correlate well with the ten modules of the Ewing Marion Kauffman Foundation's FastTrac TechVenture training program that he has used since 2007.

Items on OTBC's Self-Assessment Checklist follow:

Opportunity (the customer's pain is known)

- Current/future transitions in the market clearly identified

- Unique positioning (to take advantage of the opportunity) well defined

- Specific customers (who will pay for the solution) have been identified

- Primary customer research has been performed

- Customers' needs quantified: How do you see one?

- What messages resonate with their needs?
- Market life cycle is understood
- Target customer profile is well defined/written

Market (market research and analysis have been performed)

- Market size and segments have been determined
- Specific niches well understood
- Market growth rate quantified
- How big is the market and the specific niches you will be going after?
- Distribution method known (and rationale for doing so)
- What do they buy? Why and how do they buy? (How do you know?)
- How solutions are cost-effectively sold is known
- Uniqueness, barriers to entry are well defined
- Pricing has been determined (customer/value-perspective)

Management (bankable team is on board)

- Management team filled out (CEO, CMO, CFO, CTO) and/or functions covered
- Management team bankable?
- Roles, responsibilities, and relationships defined and written
- Organization charge developed and aligned with customers/markets/solution delivery
- Board of advisors participating
- Board of directors participating
- Accountant, attorney, and banker on board
- Management team resumes written
- Testimonials obtained (where appropriate)
- Weaknesses identified and corrective action plan developed

Product(s)/Service(s) (solution is well-conceived)

- Solution to the identified customer problem is well explained
- Customers/prospects agree solution solves real "above the line" problems
- Unique selling proposition is clear (barriers to entry)
- Sustainable competitive advantage known
- Development costs/timeline well planned
- Protectable intellectual property identified, patents searched, and patent process started
- Research and development/future products clarified and described in response to market need
- Value proposition is clear and quantified

Competition (known, with weaknesses)

- Who or what else will get in the way? This should be described and organized
- Competition identified; competitive "map" presented (the map is a matrix of the competitive situation: products/services; financial benefits of the products, including cost reductions or revenue increases; management (funding, etc.)
- Competitive changes are clear, with planned mitigation
- Competing older technology explained
- Current ways of doing business (what is the financial reason to switch?)
- Other competitive challenges

Business Objectives/Strategies (well-thought-through and realistic)

- Business objectives (and timing) adequately described and organized
- Strategies to accomplish the business objectives clear and defensible
- Tactics to support strategies make sense (may be proven)

Marketing and Sales Plan (objectives/strategies developed)

- Marketing strategies and tactics to support sales objectives
- Sales strategies and tactics to support sales objectives
- Sales compensation plan in place
- Promotion efforts known to work (return on investment has been calculated)
- Sales cycle is known
- Methods to reduce sales cycle are known
- Positioning developed
- Distribution method selected and clarified (and built on reality of market)
- Pricing defined (through pricing research)
- Promotion efforts planned that align with how customers actually buy

Financial Pro Forma (relates to plan and communicates reasonable growth)

- Income statement complete
- Balance sheet complete
- Cash flow statement complete
- Assumptions identified (and reasonable)
- Past, current, future funding identified
- Cost to acquire one customer known
- Costs to replicate known
- Costs to acquire customer and replicate are tied to sales projections

Risk (identified and mitigation planned)

- Ability to continue operations; cash on hand
- What might go wrong has been identified
- Mitigating efforts planned; costs taken into account
- Sources of funds

Funding/Exit Strategy (what's in it for the investor and how they get their investment out is clear)

- Likely ways to exit are identified and are reasonable, with sufficient depth to verify
- How will investors get their money back (plus a return)?
- What equity will investors get for amount invested?
- Realistic value in today's environment?
- How to bootstrap is defined in the event of no investments
- Projected value of investment over time
- Specific information (if acquisition):
  - Potential acquirers identified
  - Why will they buy you?
  - How do you get their attention?
- Milestones staged for success?
- Current investors?

■■ systematic graduation process and requirements

A business incubation program should establish graduation policies that include specific criteria relative to its mission and its ability to provide continued value to the client. These policies should be included in all leases (or service agreements) and materials supplied to serious applicants, and management must ensure applicants understand and accept them. Further, these policies should be reiterated as frequently as necessary—at quarterly or biannual reviews, for example—to ensure clients don't forget them.

Many incubation programs set time limits on client services. According to NBIA's *2006 State of the Business Incubation Industry* report, clients spent an average of thirty-three months in incubation programs. The range, however, was one to seventy-two months, reflecting the variation in time required for different types of businesses to achieve viability. In general, life science and other firms with long research and development cycles will remain in an incubation program much longer than a light manufacturing company that can bring a product to market quickly.

While it's good to move clients out in a timely manner, time limits alone are generally not good graduation criteria. Time limits should be combined with other criteria that better reflect the company's achievement of benchmarks that will contribute to its success and long-term sustainability. And any time limit should be based on the types of companies served and the clients' stages of development and needs. Ejecting a client that is doing well simply because its time is up may not be the wisest course for that client—or for the incubator.

Examples of graduation criteria include:

- Outgrowing incubator facilities or need for a stand-alone location
- Hiring a certain number of employees
- Achieving positive cash flow
- Merging with another company
- Obtaining short- and long-term funding (either as straight capital or by issuing shares)
- Establishing an independent board of directors

"One of the most difficult concepts I have tried to convey to our clients is that just because they hire a CEO, COO, or CFO does not mean that they are giving up control of their company."

– DeAnna Adams, executive director, Mississippi e-Business Innovation Center

t the very least, a company should be required to graduate hen it has progressed beyond the incubator's capacity o provide sufficient value or the client ceases to utilize the ervices provided by the incubator.

raduates are those companies that have successfully ompleted the incubation program. But not all clients will ecome graduates. Some may stagnate, taking up staff me and resources without progress. A few may become isruptive—refusing to accept advice from staff or service roviders or even becoming hostile to other clients.

nd some will fail. For the program's own protection, it ust have policies in place that outline when a client may e required to leave without graduating. (Many incubators clude terms in their leases that require a certain level f performance or participation to remain in the facility.) emember that while receiving rent from a poorly performing ompany may help an incubator's financials, such firms are aking up space that could be used by successful companies, nd they're depressing the program's graduation rate (the ercentage of companies that successfully graduate from the cubator each year). As already noted, putting up with such rms could lead to a black eye for the incubator.

EST PRACTICES IN ACTION

raduation Requirements
lississippi e-Business Innovation Center, Jackson, MS
eAnna Adams, director
ww.innovationcenter.ms

he Mississippi e-Business Innovation Center has published its raduation requirements in a comprehensive client handbook. he policy related to client graduation notes that the MBIC rovides only temporary assistance and space to clients with he anticipation of clients graduating from the incubator within reasonable period of time, not to exceed five (5) years."

Incubator clients are required to graduate if they meet any two of the following criteria (quoted in full from the handbook):

- The MBIC has no space to accommodate further growth or expansion:

  Company occupies 15 percent or more of the MBIC rentable space

- The client has significant growth in revenues and is fiscally able to conduct business outside the incubator: Company has earned revenues in excess of expenses for the last twelve consecutive months

  Company has raised enough capital to fund its own operations outside the incubator for at least one year

- Company's lack of need for or use of shared services or management assistance:

  Company has a CEO, COO, and CFO or a consultant performing management functions

  Company has obtained its own business resources (e.g., copier, fax machine, paper shredder, binding machine, postage meter)

- The client is acquired or merges with a larger corporation

- The client makes a successful public stock offering

- The client gives appropriate notice of leaving as prescribed in the lease agreement

Director DeAnna Adams explains the third bullet point as follows: "One of the most difficult concepts I have tried to convey to our clients is that just because they hire a CEO, COO, or CFO does not mean that they are giving up control of their company. Those positions are held by 'employees' just as any other person in the organization is an employee. But once they have hired someone to fill these positions, I begin to see that they are making decisions within their organization and require less and less of our input. In other words they begin to outgrow us. And of course this is what we want them to do. We want them to grow to the point where they stand on their own feet and become strong. So I see the hiring of the CEO, etc., as a milestone of independence. Certainly if they are still struggling with issues, we would keep them in the center."

Adams also notes that the incubator is very up-front about its expectations for graduation and graduation policy. "They are aware as each client graduates and we hold our community reception for them. Also when we have our quarterly meetings with them and we analyze their businesses' progress, we bring up the goals they need to reach in order to graduate."

"Sometimes companies become very comfortable being with us, kind of like the child who never wants to leave home," she explains. "When we can point to concrete expectations that are written down in a handbook that becomes part of their lease agreement—it seems to put the emphasis back on the fact that they have three to five years to 'hit the ground running' and make this happen. Graduation looms out there and encourages them to be more proactive about their business."

Exit Policy and Graduation Criteria
Louisiana Business & Technology Center, Baton Rouge, LA
Charles D'Agostino, executive director
www.bus.lsu.edu/lbtc

A carefully thought-out document explains exit policy and graduation criteria for the Louisiana Business & Technology Center in Baton Rouge, Louisiana The document, based on incubator best practices, not only is educational but also provides a road map for exit and graduation.

The policy states:

A true business incubator is considered successful [only] if it graduates successful companies out of the incubator facility. Therefore, the incubator should begin the process of graduating the tenant on their first day in the incubator. The incubator staff and network must begin immediately in providing intensive, proactive assistance to all companies in the incubator.

Business incubators become safe and comfortable places for incubator companies, and many would never choose to vacate on their own. Others grow so fast that they run out of space quickly and must leave the incubator because of the lack of available expansion space in the facility. The business incubator must have a written exit policy to determine the graduation process. The policy, however, must be flexible.

Some companies, especially high-technology companies, may not have a product ready for the market place or any sales in their first thee years of operation. Therefore, an exit policy totally governed by time in the incubator would be an injustice to such a company. Each LBTC tenant must submit to an annual review in November and December each year to determine whether it has successfully met the milestones necessary for graduation. If not, the lease is renewed for an additional year. Companies needing FDA approvals, patent development and defense, and extensive prototype development may be allowed to stay in the incubator facility until they have established their product or process, have substantial sales, and are able to exit the incubator safely. These clients, upon graduation, are enrolled in the LBTC Affiliate Program so that the LBTC counselors can continue support services to the company.

The exit (graduation) policy should be determined by a number of criteria such as the following:

- Is the company solid enough to survive and grow on the outside?
- Has the tenant duplicated the staff, equipment, and services provided by the incubator?
- Have it outgrown its space?
- Is it financially sound and does it have the capital necessary to graduate and lease or buy a facility in the community?
- Is there available and affordable space in the community?

Or, on a negative note, companies must be asked to vacate the incubator if they:

- Do anything criminal or illegal
- Fail to pay rent and services fees (some leniency is permitted, but only after closely monitoring operation and funding options)
- Perform noxious activities that bother other tenants
- Fail to meet growth projections and refuse to adjust their business plan to meet those objectives for growth

■ policies promoting client and graduate success

would be nice if the mere fact of being an incubator client ere enough to ensure a company's success. Unfortunately, at's not the case. While the incubator's services are a rimary factor in promoting company success, expectations f them also play a significant role.

or example, the incubator may want to establish policies at encourage—or perhaps even require—clients' articipation in incubator networking and advisory services. fter all, much of an incubation program's value proposition es in the client's proximity to other entrepreneurs, access o expert guidance, and availability of experienced service roviders. Failure to take advantage of these offerings not nly wastes the client's money but also jeopardizes the ompany's long-term success.

s also important to let clients know that they are expected o share information about their company's financial situation. his may come in the form of quarterly financial statements r regular face-to-face meetings with incubator management. eeping abreast of the company's financial performance elps head off possible problems with the client's cash flow— hich affects not only the company's survival but also its bility to pay their rent and fees.

eases must establish clear policies regarding timely payment f rents and fees. Some incubators levy late fees on tardy ayments; others may waive those fees if the client gives ufficient notice of a late payment. Management may set the olicy as it sees fit to protect cash flow and ensure that a ient's temporary financial difficulty doesn't become fatal.

nally, it's a good idea to let clients know that they are xpected to share certain benchmark data on a regular asis for impact tracking. Explain to all clients—including ffiliates—that they must provide economic impact data as part of the program; reassure them that the information will e reported only in the aggregate, not individually. It may be a ood idea to share your survey instrument so that graduates an set up their own systems to track the necessary formation. Clients and graduates will be more likely to articipate in economic impact tracking if they are given lenty of advance notice and if expectations are established o front. (For more information, see *Measuring Your Business cubator's Economic Impact: A Toolkit* at www.nbia.org/ npact and chapter 5, "Program Evaluation.")

BEST PRACTICES IN ACTION

Comprehensive Policies and Procedures Handbook
Mississippi e-Business Innovation Center, Jackson, MS
DeAnna Adams, former director
www.innovationcenter.ms

DeAnna Adams, director of the Mississippi e-Business Innovation Center, gives clients a comprehensive policies and procedures handbook that covers virtually every aspect of the incubator's operations and policies. The seventy-page handbook also includes a comprehensive emergency preparedness plan. When clients need to know about almost anything that relates to rent, insurance, graduation policies, emergency egress, shared support services, space and building services, advisory services, marketing and financial assistance, or press releases and public relations, they can refer to the handbook.

In addition to the policies themselves, all applications and forms clients might need are included in the handbook.

"We looked at everything NBIA had written about best practices and took notes about what other incubators were doing, and then we customized the handbook to fit what we were trying to accomplish," says Adams, explaining the handbook's genesis.

Because the incubator staff has thought out so many issues and developed policies covering them, it has on-tap answers formulated to address many situations that could potentially cause conflict or confusion. Policies relate to the incubator's fee structure, shipping and mail services, office equipment, security, moving and delivery guidelines, maintenance requests, equipment checkout, custodial services, parking, client signage, and many other issues.

However, many incubator policies have been developed specifically to promote client (and incubator program) success. These include admissions policies and requirements related to graduation (see this chapter's section on Graduation Policies and Procedures), discontinuation of services, confidentiality in the incubator, and the advising services the incubator provides.

A few examples of such policies (excerpted in whole or in part) include:

- **Rent policy.** "Rent is due on the first (1st) of the month. In the event that the first (1st) falls on a weekend or holiday, rent will be considered due on the first (1st) working day following the weekend or holiday. Rent will be considered late on the tenth (10th) day following the due date. Late fees will apply on late rent payment. Late fees shall be calculated in accordance with your lease agreement at the rate of 4% of the current month's fees."

- **Discontinuation of services/eviction.** "Services will be discontinued upon occurrence of any of the following:
  - Client violates terms of the lease agreement or equity agreement
  - It is determined that the business model is no longer viable. Client is seeing no growth in his business
  - Client is unable to raise funds for operation or expansion
  - Client has failed to pay for invoices for services rendered
  - Client has defaulted on rental payments
  - Client has been a resident for five (5) years
  - Client's business plan exceeds the Innovation Center's capabilities"

- **Confidentiality within the incubator.** "Each client of the MBIC shall require its directors, officers, employees and agents to keep confidential any information not otherwise generally available to the public that it may receive from any other client as a result of cohabitation or collaboration on ideas while in the incubator. The receiving party shall not use or disclose or permit any use or disclosure thereof without the disclosing party's written consent. Failure to comply with this mandate may result in legal action and/or eviction from the Mississippi e-Business Innovation Center. In addition, as a matter of good business practices, clients should use a non-disclosure agreement when discussing, collaborating, or sharing information of a proprietary nature with other businesses within the MBIC."

- **Advisory, mentoring, and technical services.** "It is the responsibility of each Client to provide timely monthly reports to the director of the MBIC. A reminder that it is time for this report to be submitted is affixed to the monthly statement. This report enables the director to have up to date information regarding each client without having to require the client to make monthly appointments. In addition, the director may use this information to help determine the type of service the client may require at different points in their company growth."

- **Marketing and managerial assistance.** "Completing a market study and determining your 'target market' can be one of the most daunting yet important tasks a new client will face. The MBIC and the Small Business Development Center will conduct periodic workshops to address this much-needed topic. In addition, marketing mentors and marketing companies will be brought in to conduct basic seminars. . . . [T]he MBIC will place strong emphasis on the completion of the market study and marketing plan. In order for a client to have a clear vision of how he wants his company to grow, it is necessary to complete a business plan. . . . The SBDC and the MBIC will help the client complete and follow his business plan strategy."

- **Financial assistance.** "Upon entering the MBIC each client will be enrolled in the online Venture Capital Tools website. As soon as possible, client must complete the toolset as far as he is able. . . . Client should revisit the toolset every three months and update his profile. This profile will give him an overview of his company and pinpoint the strengths and weaknesses."

- **Press releases and public relations.** "Contacts will be established with local newspapers to highlight client company activity. Assistance may be provided for preparing press releases. You will be required to review and sign off on the information before it is sent to the area media. All press releases that refer to the MBIC must be approved in advance by the MBIC."

Clients are required to sign off on each modification to the handbook as it is updated. "We request that they reread the handbook at that time," Adams says. The handbook is also incorporated into the client lease: "It helps to be able to point to concrete expectations that are written down in a handbook which becomes part of their lease agreement," Adams explains

Transparency about Company Responsibilities
TECH Fort Worth, Fort Worth, TX
Darlene Ryan, executive director
www.TECHFortWorth.org

In earlier days, incubator managers occasionally complained about their inability to obtain financial statements, job creation data, or other reports needed to judge incubator impacts or determine whether client businesses were progressing as planned. Asking "pretty please" didn't seem to cut it.

It is much more common nowadays for incubator managers to state company requirements up front and ensure these are understood by existing and potential clients. Darlene Ryan, executive director of TECH Fort Worth, has guaranteed her bases are covered by explicitly requiring companies to participate in business incubation activities and to provide reports in the legal agreements established before firms move into the incubator.

TECH Fort Worth's acceleration services agreement clearly lays out client companies' responsibilities. Among these are (quoted directly from the agreement):

- **Employee reports.** "Company shall provide TECH Fort Worth with reasonably detailed periodic data on employees and independent contractors of Company, including the number and names of such employees and contractors, the titles and positions of such persons, and the names and positions of company's officers and directors (or equivalent positions)."

- **Periodic business milestones.** "Company shall maintain written objectives (minimum of quarterly) with respect to its growth and development, and shall provide TECH Fort Worth with copies of such written objectives. Company shall also provide to TECH Fort Worth quarterly and annual reports on Company's growth and development, in such form and including such data as may reasonably be requested by TECH Fort Worth as part of its business incubation program."

- **Regular meetings.** "Company shall hold regular meetings with TECH Fort Worth to monitor and mentor Company's growth and development. Company acknowledges that as part of the program and services provided to it by TECH Fort Worth under this Agreement, Company shall receive advice and counsel from TECH Fort Worth mentor team, including the Executive Director of TECH Fort Worth and such other person or persons as the Executive Director of TECH Fort Worth may designate. Company shall hold such meetings at least quarterly during the term of this Agreement."

- **Events, seminars, and conferences.** "Company agrees to participate and contribute to TECH Fort Worth sponsored events, seminars, and conferences. These events will be held to promote TECH Fort Worth and its program companies and to stimulate investment interest, provide networking opportunities and community industry updates, share best practices, impart knowledge, and for other purposes which enhance TECH Fort Worth's services and programs."

- **Specific responsibilities.** "Company agrees to fulfill the requirements set forth in Exhibit B, if any." Exhibit B may require no more than that the company negotiate a good-faith lease agreement with TECH Fort Worth and occupy its space within a reasonable time frame; recognize the contribution of TECH Fort Worth in all press releases and agreements, as well as allow TECH Fort Worth to arrange for press releases; and provide a link from the company Web site to www.TECHFortWorth.org.

Ryan also requires client firms to provide quarterly economic impact reports that sum up job creation, revenue, investment, and debt data:

- Number of full-time-equivalent employees during the previous quarter

- Number of FTE positions outsourced in the previous quarter to contract labor or other sources

- Gross sales for the previous quarter

- Total grant dollars received from federal or state agencies in the previous quarter

- Investment dollars received in the previous quarter

- Total amount of loans and other debt instruments received in the previous quarter

"We find that our clients willingly supply the economic impact data we need because they know up front that they will be asked for it every quarter," says Ryan. She explains, "We show only consolidated data in our reports, so clients know we are maintaining their confidentiality. They also know that, by supplying their data, they are helping us to continue to secure the funds we need to help them."

Ryan prepares a quarterly economic impact report for one of the incubator's major funders (the city of Fort Worth) and an annual report for the state comptroller. "Besides providing the metrics that these stakeholders require, the charts that we prepare provide a visible way to illustrate progress. We now have data for the past five years and are able to show that, despite the economic downturn, our clients are still growing in numbers of jobs and dollars of economic impact," she says. "As cities and states look ever closer at where their dollars go, it is important to show that we are a wise investment for them."

Critical to the success of the incubator (and its client companies) are clear descriptions of the responsibilities of both parties as set forth in interviews with potential clients, incubator policies, and lease and service agreements.

Including requirements in legal agreements and repeating information about these requirements at regular intervals, such as when leases are renewed, gives the incubation program the ammunition needed to track its own economic impacts and ensure client participation in its programs and mentoring activities. This makes it much less likely that potential clients will see the incubator simply as a purveyor of inexpensive space and helps ensure that the program can identify entrepreneurs who will be collaborative and will contribute to the environment inside the incubator.

Companies that do not comply are deemed in default of TECH Fort Worth's legal agreements. No "pretty pleases" required.

Integration into University Life
The Boston University Business Incubation Program
Boston, MA
Clifford Robinson, former director
www.bu.edu/otd/about/incubation

Robert Brown became president of Boston University in 2005, around the same time that Cliff Robinson took over the BU Incubation Program. Brown had several mandates for Robinson—including expanding the program's services beyond the university's Photonics Center. In addition to making the incubator relevant to the entire university, Robinson sought to make the university relevant to entrepreneurs.

"The first thing I did was instigate a policy that permitted incubator company employees to receive formal BU status," says Robinson, who led the incubator until his retirement in September 2009. With that status, they received university ID cards that carried the same access privileges as those accorded to faculty and staff. They also could use university amenities such as laboratories, clean rooms, the machine shop, and libraries, as well as parking, fitness, and recreation facilities.

"We wanted [company] founders and employees to be recognized as a formal, integral part of the BU community," Robinson says. "We wanted them to understand that they were important to the university and that the university valued their contributions to the entrepreneurial culture. In particular, we wanted the companies to gain value from their time while at the university and to feel that—after leaving the incubator in later years—they could look back and remember BU's contributions to their success," Robinson says. "In just the same way that our alumni are an important community for university development and fundraising, so too are our graduated entrepreneurs, many of whom will ultimately owe their financial success in part to the assistance given them in launching their businesses by BU."

The university's Human Resources Department provided BU IDs for company employees. Those employees' names then went into BU databases, and they received mailings, university news announcements, and invitations to events and functions. Some of the CEOs and founders were invited to present their companies as classroom case studies. Others joined university committees on translational research programs or became members of departments' industrial advisory boards. "All of this would make them feel part of the university and would help us keep track of company alumni after they left," Robinson explains, noting that many incubation program entrepreneurs were high-net-worth individuals and that some had outstanding business talent and could contribute to the university in meaningful ways.

At Boston University, the policies that contributed most to the success of the incubator program had less to do with the day-to-day management of the incubator operation and more to do with how the incubator was integrated into the university as a whole. Of particular importance were policies that ensured alignment with other university departments such as human resources, office of general counsel, office of research compliance, intellectual property licensing, health and safety, central services, real estate and space allocation, and alumni relations, as well as with academic colleges and departments.

"It is important to make the incubator part of the infrastructure of the university," Robinson says. "Technology commercialization has to be recognized as a core mission, alongside the existing missions of education and research. It has to begin with the university president and continue on down through the organization. Everyone must be on board."

MOVING NONPERFORMERS OUT

What if a client doesn't want to graduate? "Nudging is part and parcel of this business," says David McNamara, vice president for incubation at Innovacorp in Halifax, Nova Scotia, Canada.

And there may be instances in which an incubator manager needs to push hard. Perhaps it's the entrepreneur whose business is booming but who has grown too comfortable with the program's support system. Or it may be a firm that's not meeting its benchmarks—and just as important, not making use of incubator services. These are times that call for blunt discussions about alternatives outside the incubator. An incubator manager may have to "take them by the hand and introduce them to commercial space," McNamara explains.

Susan Matlock, president and CEO of the Innovation Depot in Birmingham, Alabama, says she once had to tell a client: "You have taken advantage of everything here and participated in the incubation process. It's time to make an alternative decision." Despite extensive coaching in areas of need, the company just didn't seem to learn or build from its experiences, Matlock says. "If we had allowed it, they would still be here in ten years."

"We wanted company founders and employees to be recognized as a formal, integral part of the Boston University community."

– Clifford Robinson, former director, Boston University Business Incubation Program

leveraging innovation

The great business fortunes of the nineteenth and early twentie
centuries were built on commodities: oil, coal, steel. But U.S. econom
growth in the twentieth century and beyond has been based o
innovation, from Ford's assembly line and Edison's light bulb to E
Gates's operating system and Steve Jobs's iPhon

Technology Commercialization

- Increases the incubator's potential client base and its impact

- Expands upon the expertise of incubator-affiliated volunteers and staff in all aspects of technology application and company development

- Increases the return on investment to the research-generating institution and binds incubation more solidly to the institution's economic development and research missions

- Increases the prestige of the incubator as an engine for developing technology infrastructure, knowledge economy sectors, and entrepreneurial economies

In fact, according to a July 2007 report by Robert J. Shapiro and Nam D. Pham, 30 percent to 40 percent of gains in U.S. productivity and growth in the twentieth century resulted from innovation. Innovation as a spur to growth and GNP (gross national product) is now spreading to a much greater degree around the globe, as is evident from the investments many nations are making in an attempt to develop the so-called knowledge economy.

We often equate "innovation" with "technology," but innovation doesn't just mean gadgets. Companies that integrate innovation into their operations gain competitive advantages such as improved productivity, reduced costs, or expanded market opportunities.

Consider eBay. The company that pioneered online auctions opened broader national and international markets for businesses of all kinds. A cottage industry of eBay specialists helps entrepreneurs set up their eBay shops and even handles fulfillment. And the need for simple, secure online payments gave a boost to PayPal (which is now a subsidiary of eBay). While technology is at the heart of eBay and PayPal, their economic impact lies not in the technology but in the way businesses use that technology to bring their goods and services to more markets with less effort and expense.

Companies can leverage innovation in a number of ways: the direct commercialization of intellectual property (the legal right to develop and sell products based on an idea); the conversion of these innovations into effective business practices; or the new business opportunities that arise from advances in innovation.

Start-up and emerging companies have a significant role in the process of bringing new innovations to market. In the twenty-five years following the passage of the Bayh-Dole Act in 1980, U.S. universities and other research institutions spun off more than 5,000 new companies. That pace doesn't seem to be slowing: Of the nearly 5,000 new intellectual property licenses granted by members of the Association of University Technology Managers in 2006, 15 percent went to start-ups.

A best practice incubation program leverages innovation by helping entrepreneurs bring intellectual property to market and integrate innovations into their businesses. Incubation professionals also can leverage innovation to improve the effectiveness of their programs.

■ ■ technology commercialization

Increasingly, those who work to bridge the gap between research and product refer to the process as "technology commercialization" rather than "technology transfer." Technology commercialization implies more substantial involvement to ensure that innovations become marketable products and services. In a 2008 paper examining the University of Utah's success in spinning out more than sixty companies in three years, researchers Norris Krueger, Brian Cummings, and Steven Nichols highlight five key elements of a successful technology commercialization effort:

- Visible, vocal leadership that establishes a clear vision and mission for technology commercialization

- Sufficient resources, deal flow, and entrepreneurial demand to support ongoing operations

- A market-oriented, entrepreneurial research culture

- A system that connects students, faculty, and researchers with entrepreneur support mechanisms

- Professionals who understand and support technology commercialization and can measure progress properly

Does that description sound familiar? It's almost a definition of a technology incubation program. Although increasing numbers of U.S. universities have offices of technology commercialization—at least five hundred, according to AUTM—many of them rely on business incubation programs to help bring innovations to the marketplace.

They focus on how the new technology might be used to change the way a particular process is currently being done.

In North America, incubators that are sponsored by or affiliated with technology generators such as universities or research laboratories can help those institutions move technology into the market by:

- **Overcoming cultural impediments to entrepreneurship.** Many universities and research institutions such as federal laboratories do not have an entrepreneurial focus. Business incubators can help bridge the gap by working with these technology generators in building forums, policies, and procedures to overcome cultural differences between the institution and its researchers and community businesses and entrepreneurs.

- **Leveraging financial incentives.** Many business incubation programs help their clients apply for Small Business Innovation Research (SBIR) and Small Business Technology Transfer (STTR) grants. These U.S. federal programs promote technology commercialization among entrepreneurial companies to achieve a better return on investment in these technologies. State and local commercialization grants can be just as effective, and other nations have developed similar mechanisms that their incubation professionals may access.

- **Promoting a seamless interface between lab and market.** Incubators operated or hosted by technology generators such as universities are best served by bringing together technology licensing and commercialization functions or otherwise facilitating technology commercialization.

- **Developing comprehensive support for commercialization.** This involves developing expertise in business incubation generally and in technology assessment, strategic partnerships, licensing, equity participation, deal making, and other components of transforming technologies into companies.

BEST PRACTICES IN ACTION

New Market Assessment
Powerhouse Ventures, Christchurch, New Zealand
Stephen Hampson, CEO
www.cii.co.nz

The Powerhouse City Incubator in Christchurch, New Zealand was established in 2001 to support technology start-ups. Its primary goal is to provide advice and access to capital to turn high-value IP into profitable, growing companies. Therefore, for the pipeline of potential clients to remain full, there must first be a pipeline of commercializable IP.

Powerhouse Ventures, the public-private organization that manages the incubator, is zealous in its quest to identify IP with commercial potential. To facilitate collaboration and to keep abreast of developing technologies, Powerhouse has incubators on the campuses of the University of Canterbury and Lincoln University in addition to the Powerhouse City Incubator. It is the responsibility of incubator staff at these offices to get to know all of the research projects under way on campus and the individuals (both faculty and students) whose expertise is behind the research.

To help the region's research institutions and universities maintain a constant flow of commercializable IP, the incubator provides opportunity assessments of new markets and new technologies. The assessments answer two important questions:

01. Who would use this technology, and for what purpose?

02. What changes must be made to this technology to take it to market?

Using a systematic approach, incubator staff communicate with industry experts, conduct focus groups, and talk to potential customers to answer those questions. They focus on how the new technology might be used to change the way a particular process is currently being done.

Powerhouse creates a customer value model by identifying

which customer segments will value a particular technology. This makes the process of innovation more predictable," says Powerhouse CEO Stephen Hampson.

The goal isn't necessarily to commercialize a technology as-is but to influence further research in hope of leading to commercialization. "We screen the opportunity and then shape it during technology incubation—on campus," Hampson says. "As the venture attracts capital, it then moves into one of our business incubators."

The research phase of new market/new technology assessment typically is conducted by graduate students with direction from incubator staff. If the research indicates that a technology has potential for commercialization, incubator staff develop a business plan. Payment for these services typically comes from universities and research institutions that contract with Powerhouse to help them identify and commercialize technologies. Individual entrepreneurs and companies also sometimes contract with Powerhouse to assess a technology or market.

Businesses that form around these technologies may or may not move into Powerhouse's incubation facilities, which have capacity to serve up to thirty-five companies. At this writing, Powerhouse was home to eighteen in-house clients, and Powerhouse staff were working with approximately fifty other potential companies—those with promise will undergo technology or market assessments, and some will ultimately form companies if there is indeed a commercialization opportunity. At any given time, between eight and twelve companies (the target is six on each of two campuses) have made it through the assessment phase and are moving through the business planning and capital raising process.

Companies formed after going through the assessment process cover a diverse range of markets, including water purification, electronic payroll, 3-D computer animation software, and data security hardware.

Here is just one example of how this service helps a company form around a developing technology.

One of Powerhouse's research lab partners had developed models of crops that can predict how plants will grow based on weather, fertilizer, and irrigation data. Some vegetable growers used it as a planning tool, but not many were interested in using software for farming. By analyzing

the needs of many potential users of the software—seed merchants, fertilizer suppliers, growers, contractors, consultants, food processors, grocery stores, and consumers—Powerhouse found that the yield prediction was of most value to the food processor.

"From this, the technology was turned into a software product for agronomists employed by big processing companies," Hampson says. "These people have the skills and motivation to use the software. They want to know how much yield they will get from different regions."

Commercialization Toolkit
Mississippi Technology Alliance, Ridgeland, MS
Randy Goldsmith, former president and CEO
www.technologyalliance.ms

Originally developed for the NASA Regional Technology Transfer Centers, the Commercialization Toolkit has since been adopted by economic development organizations, business incubators, and others around the globe. The model was developed by Randy Goldsmith, former president and CEO of the Mississippi Technology Alliance, which drives innovation and technology-based economic development for the state of Mississippi.

The model emphasizes product, process, and service innovations that are investor-focused, high-growth, intensive (innovative enterprises that can shape the economy)—not lifestyle-based ventures. It uses an interactive and dynamic Web portal that assists in rigorously:

- Identifying attributes of the potential entrepreneur
- Quantifying the product's risk profile and venture opportunity
- Assessing the quality of the business plan from an investor's perspective
- Prioritizing commercialization strategies
- Creating valuation model scenarios to assist entrepreneurs in negotiating with investors at each stage of investment (preseed; A,B,C rounds; mezzanine)

"Entrepreneurs need all the tools at their disposal to successfully commercialize high-risk, high-performance ventures," says Goldsmith, who has employed the toolkit at several incubators where he has worked, including the Oklahoma Technology Commercialization Center and the Mississippi Technology Alliance. "Entrepreneurs who can successfully navigate the process of moving from concept to market with the fewest number of missteps are the ones most likely to succeed."

Using the toolkit, Goldsmith creates an independent and objective snapshot of each venture's strong and weak points; potential stumbling blocks in its development and financing; and insights into the coaching, mentoring, and product development path for the venture's technology platform. But the tool is only as good as the data entered into it, Goldsmith warns. "The more honest the entrepreneur and his/her team can be in their answers and in the thinking process leading up to their answers, the more valuable the tool," he says.

The toolkit also is the start of an ongoing discussion of the company's potential and how the incubator can help. "At the same time, we often assess the venture and compare our readiness assessment to theirs," Goldsmith says. "This facilitates a rich conversation about what it is going to take to move the venture forward in a significant way."

The intensive nature of the toolkit is key to its success, Goldsmith says. While the odds of funding a venture in the United States average around 2 percent (one in seventy-two), those completing the toolkit "stand a 50 percent chance of getting funded," he says. When he employed the toolkit as head of the Oklahoma Technology Commercialization Center in the early 2000s, he says, companies were averaging about $300,000 per funded deal.

Sharing Space with University Technology Commercialization Office
Northeast Indiana Innovation Center, Fort Wayne, IN
Karl LaPan, president and CEO
www.niic.net

The Northeast Indiana Innovation Center is a partner with Indiana University–Purdue University Fort Wayne's Office of Engagement. Since its launch in 2006, the Office of Engagement has become an integral component of NIIC's efforts to facilitate relationships between higher education and northeast Indiana industry.

"The Office of Engagement is really the portal to university research, projects, and resources," says Karl LaPan, president and CEO of NIIC. And it's a big portal, opening doors at Purdue University in West Lafayette, Indiana University in Bloomington, and Indiana University–Purdue University Fort

Wayne. Among the resources available through the Office of Engagement are interns, cooperative education students, research faculty, and specialized equipment and facilities.

The office is located at NIIC, which also provides financial support (through local grants) and has a seat on the office's advisory board. The primary benefit to NIIC, LaPan says, is access. "It gives us a portfolio of value-added services that makes companies want to locate here, because otherwise they would have to go out and find all this themselves," he says. Some of the companies that have sought assistance through the Office of Engagement have become incubator clients.

"The goal is to marry research available in the university's intellectual property portfolio to entrepreneurs who want to start companies," LaPan says. He notes that a study by the Association of University Technology Managers found that only 1 percent of university-developed technology has been commercialized. "We're trying to take all those wonderful technologies being developed in university buildings and labs and get them out to create jobs and payroll by getting IP to people who will start a company."

The office also facilitates the Indiana branches of federal small business programs such as the Technical Assistance Program, which connects companies with Purdue resources and assists them in implementing state-of-the art technologies, and the Manufacturing Extension Partnership. Those programs also benefit NIIC. For example, in 2006, the IPFW Division of Continuing Studies partnered with the Purdue MEP to offer MEP courses to the public at NIIC. The first classes, offered in spring 2007, drew 117 participants for seven courses—all at the incubator, further raising awareness among potential clients.

Perhaps the highest-profile example of the partnership is the IU-Purdue Technology Showcase, an annual event that highlights new intellectual property developed at the university. Since 2006, each showcase has drawn faculty researchers and commercialization specialists from Purdue and Indiana University to meet with business leaders and venture capitalists. Each year, several companies wind up pursuing licensing of the IP they have seen at the showcase, LaPan says.

The showcase is held at NIIC, which also cosponsors the event with IU and Purdue. Again, the payoff is visibility: "Rather than having an open house, we get people who are really interested in technology to come to our campus," LaPan says. "It gives us a chance to get people from all along the spectrum of innovation and commercialization on campus, all at the same time."

- Expand business and technical services available to incubator clients
- Offer access to pro bono and low-cost consulting and employees
- Provide a pool of future employees for client firms
- Provide incubator clients with access to specialized facilities and equipment
- Reduce the development costs of the incubator facility and its clients

university and federal laboratory linkages

Universities and federal laboratories can be valuable allies in helping incubation programs achieve best practice status. In addition to new technologies for commercialization, these institutions can provide other valuable services and unique resources to both the incubator and its clients, such as:

- Technical and managerial consulting
- Student interns and employees
- Technical facilities and equipment
- Specialized databases and researchers
- Research and development financing
- Patent knowledge
- Alumni advisors, business contacts, and investors
- Access to laboratories and expertise
- University foundation investments

Although these linkages are a potentially valuable asset for any incubation program, a number of factors can affect an incubator's ability to capitalize on these opportunities:

- The university's or laboratory's view of the incubator's role in helping it attain its mission and goals
- The attitudes of administrators and technology commercialization offices toward commercialization via new venture formation and growth
- The entrepreneurial culture of faculty and researchers
- The impact (rewards and penalties) on tenure-track faculty
- The integration of entrepreneurship curriculum into nonbusiness departments (e.g., engineering, sciences)
- The institution's interest in entrepreneurship and applied research
- Institutional policies on non-academic-related consulting

- The ability of the client to manage and utilize the expertise of the faculty/technologist (more often than not, this requires an intermediary who can manage the relationship and expectations between the client and the faculty/technologist)
- The fee structure for equipment or lab use
- The ability of the faculty/technologist to work in a private market environment

Best practice programs have strong support from the institution's administrators and faculty, who view the incubator as an integral part of their offering to faculty, students, and the community. Regardless of the situation, incubator management and staff must monitor these services closely to ensure that all parties involved benefit from the experience.

BEST PRACTICES IN ACTION

Leveraging Relationships with National Laboratories
Santa Fe Business Incubator, Santa Fe, NM
Marie Longserre, president and CEO
www.sfbi.net

Marie Longserre, president and CEO of the Sante Fe Business Incubator in New Mexico, knows both the benefits and challenges of having linkages to a research laboratory.

Her incubator is near two of the biggest federally funded labs in the country—Sandia National Laboratory and Los Alamos National Laboratory—which together account for one of the highest concentrations of scientific brainpower in one spot anywhere on the planet.

Both labs have agreements with the state of New Mexico to provide technical help to small businesses in the interests of economic development. An incubator can help entrepreneurs connect with the labs, but making the linkages to the labs themselves is the tricky part.

"It's important that the incubator manager has individual contacts at the appropriate laboratory departments and has knowledge of various programs that may help clients," Longserre says.

Clients in the Santa Fe Business Incubator can request technical consulting services (such as computer modeling or equipment testing) from the labs' scientists—but it's up to an individual researcher to choose to fill the request.

"It has to be picked up by a willing participant in the labs," Longserre says. "But a number of our clients have made use of the program and received valuable assistance."

As with any federal program—especially one involving high-security research—getting help from the big national labs involves a certain amount of red tape. For example, the labs can't offer services if by doing so they cut out a private-sector supplier.

"The labs can't [act on a request] if there is a commercial vendor or other source available," Longserre explains.

Los Alamos has a program called the Venture Acceleration Fund, which can provide two to three $100,000 grants to help area small businesses commercialize technology developed in the lab. Three-quarters of the businesses that have received the grants since the mid-2000s have been Santa Fe Business Incubator clients. Longserre attributes her clients' success in obtaining the grants to the strength of her program.

The labs offer entrepreneur-in-residence programs and will sometimes let small businesses use their equipment. Sandia also offers an internship program, which can provide companies management assistance from MBA candidates from area universities. The industry sectors and eligibility criteria depend on the lab, not the incubator, Longserre says.

No matter what the program or request, Longserre helps clients make the appropriate connections and processes referrals from the labs themselves.

In addition, Longserre says, sometimes researchers from the labs will themselves start a business venture to commercialize their technology, which is where her incubator can help. She admits that while some in the national labs "get" the idea of entrepreneurship, for others it's a learning process.

"It is a bit of a culture shock," she says. "It is a challenge for scientists coming out of a lab." She added that this makes the Santa Fe Business Incubator "the perfect halfway house [for start-ups] coming out of the labs."

But in dealing with the byzantine rules of a federal bureaucracy, she stresses, having personal contacts inside who appreciate the commercialization mission and knowing who knows what are absolutely essential.

"One of the keys to working with the national labs is building relationships with people in the various departments up there," she says. Longserre regularly attends events and

meetings at the labs, and she works her network of contacts to wrangle introductions as needed. With an entity the size of Los Alamos or Sandia, she adds, knowing who you need to talk with to solve a particular problem, before you pick up the phone, is a necessity.

"Absolutely," she says. "You don't just ring up the labs unless you know specifically what department you want, what the person's title is, and what their extension is. And you do have to have people who help make the connections."

A Joint Operation
Technology 2020, Oak Ridge, TN
Shawn Carson, director, operations
www.tech2020.org

Shawn Carson of Technology 2020—a technology-based economic development organization—says that from his incubator, he can "toss a rock and hit the front gate of the Oak Ridge National Laboratory." Also nearby is the University of Tennessee in Knoxville.

Both sponsor the Center for Entrepreneurial Growth, an entrepreneurial support organization operating within Technology 2020 and providing, in Carson's words, "hands-on entrepreneurial support for companies that have an intellectual property relationship with one or both of the institutions."

The lab and the university both benefit financially from the relationship in multiple ways, he says. Typically there is a royalty-based agreement for the technologies licensed to start-ups based on sales of the products using the licensed technology. Royalties go to UT or the ORNL, which use them to fund CEG programs but don't share revenue numbers with the incubator.

In some cases, the lab or university may even take an equity stake in a company. Cash from a CEG seed fund can be issued as debt convertible to equity, though the incubator does this rarely—it currently holds what Carson calls "a very minor equity stake" in four companies.

"Another type of payoff for the lab and university is positive publicity when a company creates jobs and local economic development with the help of the CEG program."

– Shawn Carson, director, operations, Technology 2020

Another type of payoff for the lab and the university, he says, is positive publicity when a company creates jobs and local economic development with the help of the CEG program. For example, when TrakLok Corp., a company that makes a high-tech device that keeps valuable products locked up while in transit, won Technology 2020's "pitch competition" in 2009, it earned itself a big, glowing write-up in the Knoxville *News Sentinel*.

For its part, the incubator is paid directly to run the CEG program, collecting $200,000 annually from the Oak Ridge lab and $125,000 from UT.

Technology 2020 enjoys what Carson calls a "very close relationship" with the UT business college, which provides teams of MBA candidates to help selected client companies fulfill "some sort of strategic need."

Through a track of courses in the MBA program focused on entrepreneurship—whose requirements include two projects—the university typically provides three to four interns each summer. The incubator submits a short list of client needs to the program advisor, who matches student teams with companies based on backgrounds, interests, and skill sets.

Typically the client company will pay these interns; the university does not.

Both the lab and the university will sometimes sign on to cooperative research development agreements with incubator client companies, providing reduced-cost access to lab facilities and technical assistance, especially if the project holds out a strong promise of economic development potential for the region.

"A lot of our time is spent tracking down the resources and making those agreements happen," Carson says. When such an agreement can be arranged—it happens only on a case-by-case basis—the discount can range from 30 percent to 60 percent.

UT, Carson noted, has been ranked eleventh among U.S. universities for the rate at which technology developed by its researchers is funneled to small businesses for commercialization.

And Oak Ridge, he says, is "just cranking out IP like you can't imagine," some of which may be snapped up by corporate giants like GE before a small company could get anywhere near it. But some of it, he says, "might be better in the hands of a start-up." He cited, for example, a hybrid solar lighting technology, that not only produces outdoor lighting from sun power, but even generates electricity. (This company is a CEG client using licensed technology.)

Metrics of CEG's success include job creation and salary numbers, as well as total equity raised; for 2009, the incubator claims an impact of 2,169 total jobs at an average salary of $66,226. Incubator companies have raised $60 million in equity since 2002.

Lab Linkages as a Revenue Stream
Mississippi Enterprise for Technology
Stennis Space Center, MS
Charles Beasley, president
www.mset.org

The Mississippi Enterprise for Technology incubator has working relationships with two labs: the NASA Stennis Space Center (where MsET is located) and the University of Southern Mississippi Center of Higher Learning's High-Performance Scientific Visualization Center. In both cases, it serves as a matchmaker between companies and the labs to fill specialized business needs.

Through an agreement with the NASA Stennis Space Center and the state of Mississippi, MsET identifies business needs and requests specific SSC lab and shop services on the companies' behalf. (MsET also is the state's official technology transfer office.) In a single year, according to MsET President and CEO Charles Beasley, the incubator may provide this service for fewer than ten companies; most will submit twenty to thirty such requests annually.

"Basically, we are a conduit for industry and other organizations to access services of the labs," he says. These include help in such technical areas as organics, gas and material sciences, environmental, measurement standards and calibration, instrument cleaning, electronics and instrumentation, and GIS services. The "other organizations" can include universities or government agencies. The requests must include a particular reason to use the NASA lab, because SSC is barred from providing services that could be arranged with a private company.

For the most part, Beasley notes, MsET arranges services for mature companies—mostly nuclear power and some environmental firms—from all around the country rather than for incubator clients. But although the incubator's client companies don't typically use the service, the funding it brings in helps keep the incubator in operation and thus benefits them indirectly.

"A company pays MsET for the costs of service," Beasley explains. "MsET, in turn, pays NASA. We take a small percentage fee from each transaction."

Benefits for the lab include an avenue to fulfill NASA's technology transfer mission and a way to keep its personnel's skills sharpened and revenue coming in during down times.

"We keep their labs busy when NASA use of the lab is not so busy," Beasley says. "This keeps their talent in place at the lab and it keeps their cash-flow going."

The incubator's relationship with the visualization lab, like that with NASA/SCC, caters mainly to companies outside the incubator, which partner with the Center of Higher Learning to create computer applications for high-performance scientific and engineering visuals.

One example is the lab's agreement with the Atlanta-based education firm CORE-ESC, whose parent company is based in India. In a program that began in 2008, the Center of Higher Learning trains Indian students in all aspects of immersive visualization, including software programming and development, design of graphic applications, and procurement of visualization equipment.

The payoff of the arrangement for the visualization lab, according to Beasley, stems from the fact that it's an entrepreneurial organization interested in commercializing its technology—for which the lab needs partners to help create applications and attract funding. In hooking up these partnerships, MsET is merely a facilitator, not involved contractually. Any financial agreements are between the CHL and the company.

An Entrepreneur Ecosystem
University of Central Florida Business Incubator Network
Orlando, FL
Tom O'Neal, director
www.incubator.ucf.edu

The University of Central Florida Business Incubator Network is integrated into an overall entrepreneurship ecosystem at UCF. Incubator and university staff aggressively support and promote incubator client–university partnerships to leverage available intellectual capital and promote technology transfer and economic development. As a result, numerous client companies of the UCF Business Incubator Network license UCF intellectual property, conduct joint research with UCF faculty, and hire UCF students. The UCF incubation program is part of the UCF Office of Research and Commercialization. This structure enables strong support for such partnerships.

University-company partnerships are encouraged through a matching grants program that provides up to a 1:1 match for companies funding university research. Additional incentives are provided to help companies secure Small Business Innovation Research (SBIR) and Small Business Technology Transfer (STTR) grants by leveraging university faculty, students, and research labs to make their grant proposals more competitive.

UCF is home to one of the top research facilities in the world in optics and photonics, the Center for Research and Education in Optics and Lasers. Some successful incubator clients were established based on technology developed at CREOL. Leveraging this, the UCF incubation program has provided space for companies that would benefit from being in CREOL to facilitate more effective tech transfer during their early stages.

UCF's College of Business also supports the UCF incubation program by providing access to MBA interns; hosting numerous activities, including business plan competitions (winners gain access to incubation support); and delivering cutting-edge technology commercialization and entrepreneurship curricula targeted at students serious about entrepreneurship.

The latest UCF incubation program internal survey indicates that more than fifty UCF faculty and one hundred students and former students are working with incubator client companies in some capacity. To date, UCF incubator clients have conducted more than $10 million in research projects with UCF faculty. At one point, UCF faculty and incubator clients were collaborating on more than fifteen SBIR contracts simultaneously.

The UCF Technology Incubator, the first of the UCF incubation programs, is located in the Central Florida Research Park (CFRP) adjacent to UCF. The 1,100-acre research park is home to over one hundred companies, ten thousand employees, and several university departments and projects.

Incubator graduates who choose to locate their companies at the CFRP have the opportunity to maintain their close relationship with the university and continued access to postincubation entrepreneurial support.

- Improves program performance
- Enhances value proposition
- Streamlines program management

■ leveraging innovation to further program effectiveness

Business growth and its long-term success can be enhanced by integrating innovations into operations, whether it be adopting an automated accounting and inventory control system using a program such as QuickBooks, adding social networking to a company's marketing strategies, or inserting RFID (radio frequency identification) technologies into business practices. Best practice programs keep abreast of innovations that support the industry sectors they serve and adopt those that enhance their value proposition or increase the effectiveness of their operations.

BEST PRACTICES IN ACTION

Online Performance Evaluations
Northeast Indiana Innovation Center, Fort Wayne, IN
Karl LaPan, president and CEO
www.niic.net

The Northeast Indiana Innovation Center has developed a comprehensive approach to training and development of its twelve team members. Using the online program Success Factors (www.successfactors.com), NIIC has automated and customized elements of its performance reviews, including employee goal setting and performance tracking, to facilitate more regular and timely employee performance reviews and feedback from leadership.

President and CEO Karl LaPan chose Success Factors because it is Web-based, giving anyone access from anywhere, at any time, to complete their performance review and update their goals. Similarly, managers can log in and access their employees' self-reviews and deliver their own feedback to complete the process. "In a small organization like ours, making it easy to complete the forms is important," LaPan says.

The system routes the reviews to the appropriate leaders electronically and notifies individuals automatically when they need to complete forms. In addition, NIIC can customize the performance review form, determine the rating system and values to be measured, and establish the criteria for evaluation.

Mobile Business Incubation Services
Louisiana Business & Technology Center, Baton Rouge, LA
Charles D'Agostino, executive director
www.bus.lsu.edu/lbtc

Small business owners and entrepreneurs in rural Louisiana lacked access to the resources and networks necessary to develop successful businesses. The Louisiana Business & Technology Center at Louisiana State University in Baton Rouge recognized the need to help potential clients whose locations prevented them from taking advantage of LBTC's services.

LBTC implemented the Incubator on Wheels program in 2005 to bring business development services to residents of rural Louisiana. Known as the Driving Louisiana's Economy initiative, the Incubator on Wheels is an eighteen-wheel mobile classroom, replete with state-of-the-art audio/visual capabilities, a large plasma screen monitor, and broadband wireless Internet connection. The mobile incubator has focused on business recovery and development in areas devastated by hurricanes Katrina and Rita in 2005 and Gustav and Ike in 2008. In the aftermath of these storms, the Incubator on Wheels reached disaster areas before telephone and Internet lines were repaired and offered Internet access to businesses through satellite connections and laptop computers.

The classroom seats up to twenty-four people for workshops on topics such as how to start a business, leadership development, entrepreneurship training, business planning, marketing, and access to capital. In conjunction with local partners—including chambers of commerce, Small Business Development Centers, and incubators—LBTC schedules workshops and seminars over three or four days in each town it visits. "This program brings services to entrepreneurs who normally don't have access to quality incubation programs and counseling," says Charles D'Agostino, LBTC executive director. "Once the Incubator on Wheels whets their appetite, LBTC offers quality follow-up services and places entrepreneurs in its incubator or in other incubators located closer to the entrepreneur."

A "Smart" Building
William M. Factory Small Business Incubator, Tacoma, WA
Tim Strege, executive director
www.williamfactory.com

In 2003, the William M. Factory Small Business Incubator moved into a new facility that was "technologically the most sophisticated small office building in the Puget Sound region," says Executive Director Tim Strege. In late 2009, Strege opened a second building comprising an incubator campus that now totals 42,000 square feet in both Phase I and Phase II construction. And as technology has leapt forward, so has the William M. Factory Incubator.

Technological improvements to the original facility have ensured that the incubator maintained its reputation for sophisticated technology. The additions also will serve to make the incubator itself more efficient and ensure its clients have access to the tools that can better serve their businesses.

The technology upgrades include:

- IT hardware systems

- Cisco Voice-Over-Internet-Protocol (VOIP) devices

- Telephones with built-in Web and video conference solutions and upgradable cameras

- Combined voice and data networks

- Expanded video monitoring of the facility

- Four telecommunications rooms

- Enhanced meeting room facilities with built-in multimedia presentation equipment

"We have given our clients the same high-tech office telephonic and Web and videoconferencing capabilities you would expect to see at Boeing, IBM, or the White House," Strege says. These and other amenities make the incubator even more attractive to potential clients, who already pay above market rate.

The sophisticated hardware includes Cisco phones that are "really computers with phone handsets," Strege says. The system's applications allow clients to access their phones and databases remotely via the Web, as well as use other applications such as programs that allow employees to track customer records using their telephones or punch a virtual timeclock.

The incubator's traditional clients are in specialty construction trades, and the incubator has expanded its programming to attract to new clients in clean energy, information technology, and transportation logistics sectors. The enhanced technologies are designed to give clients a leg up over their competitors and ensure the incubator stays far ahead of other available facilities in the region.

We have given our clients the same high-tech telephonic, Web, and videoconferencing capabilities as Boeing, IBM, or the White House.

– Tim Strege, executive director, William M. Factory Small Business Incubator

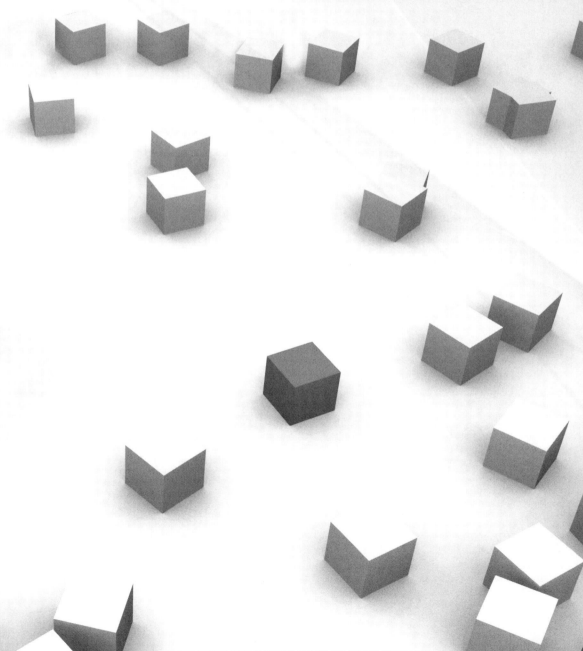

client services

Incubation professionals who seek excellence in their programs put clien
services first. They know that offering start-up and emerging businesse
the services they need to grow and succeed is the main goal of incubatio
programs and is what separates them from simple real estate operations

Management and boards of incubators should strive to

- Prioritize management time to place the greatest emphasis on client assistance, including proactive advising and guidance that results in company success and wealth creation

Preincubation Services

- Develop a pipeline of viable incubator clients
- Offer an additional revenue stream
- Extend the incubator's community outreach

Client services have evolved as the incubation industry has developed. In the industry's early years, shared equipment and services such as fax, copying, conference rooms, and the like were a significant focus: "Shared office services" was its own category in NBIA's *1989 State of the Business Incubation Industry* report. That publication also listed only sixteen types of "management and technical assistance," what we today consider true incubator services. Compare that with the *2006 State of the Business Incubation Industry* report, which lists thirty-three distinct types of services offered by incubation programs.

To become a best practice incubator, however, a program must do more than offer a menu of client services. It must customize and effectively implement these services as part of a comprehensive business assistance program that meets the incubator's mission and goals—whether it focuses on low-income clients, kitchen entrepreneurs, or biotechnology firms—and that aligns with the community's economic development strategy.

■■ preincubation services

Entrepreneurs who may not yet have developed their ideas or businesses enough for residency in an incubator are candidates for preincubation programs. These programs assist entrepreneurs who may never need incubator space, as well as those who may eventually become resident clients. In addition, they offer an opportunity to increase revenues and expand an incubator's visibility and impact in a community.

According to NBIA's *2006 State of the Business Incubation Industry* report, 16 percent of North American incubation programs offer preincubation services alone, while half offer both pre- and postincubation services. In some cases, incubators provide affiliate clients with a "hot desk" in the incubator for a certain period of time, during which the incubator management may provide advice on developing a business plan required for acceptance. In other instances, the incubator may offer access to certain resources—a desk or cubicle, Internet, and basic advisory services—until the company can meet the requirements for full client status. Still other programs offer entrepreneurship training as a preincubation service.

BEST PRACTICES IN ACTION

Preincubation as a Taste of Incubation
San Juan College Enterprise Center, Farmington, NM
Jasper Welch, director
www.sanjuancollege.edu/gcb

There was a time when the San Juan College Enterprise Center treated not-quite-ready-for-incubation clients rather passively. "We used to have the approach of 'Here's some information, here's the tour, here's an application, work on your business plan, get back to us,'" says Director Jasper Welch. "It wasn't very engaging."

Several years ago, Welch decided to make his program more welcoming to would-be clients in hope of turning them into paying customers. They still get the tour, but they get access to a lot more now—at no charge—including:

- A temporary office space with a telephone, a computer, and a desk

- A lending library stocked with resources for entrepreneurs, such as books on business planning, marketing, business development, and accounting

- Small Business Development Center resources and staff (co-located with SJCEC) for business plan development, loan preparation, and one-on-one consulting

- Help from incubator staff for ideas on business models, application questions, and one-on-one consulting for initial business development

- Enrollment in monthly Starting Your Business workshops (cosponsored by the SBDC) to address business questions and challenges

"We want them to hang around the Enterprise Center and get used to the services," Welch says. "It's essentially selling by doing, not telling."

Usually, there are one or two clients in the preincubation phase at any given time; about half of them become clients. One recent convert was a woodworker who wanted to start a business making custom, high-end doors. "He'd been in business awhile but had never really run it as a company," Welch says. With the preincubation program, the would-be entrepreneur "got immersed" and eventually became an EC client.

Although giving services away may seem counterintuitive, Welch knows it won't last forever. Those who come to realize the value of what they're getting will eventually ask what it costs, and Welch knows they're in "when they're asking to pay for it."

Preincubation for High-Potential Companies
Boston University Business Incubation Program, Boston, MA
Clifford Robinson, former director
www.bu.edu/otd/about/incubation

The Boston University Business Incubation Program provides a limited amount (1,200 square feet) of preincubation space for student- or faculty-founded companies that show promise but that may not have fully developed their business propositions yet.

Space is offered—on a shared basis and at low cost—to entrepreneurs who have formed companies and are in the process of writing business plans and working toward raising their first institutional funding. Some may have received small amounts of seed-stage funding, been awarded SBIR/STTR grants, or raised preseed funding from one of several

sources within the university. In addition, they may have licensed BU-owned intellectual property. These preincubation companies receive full access to incubator resources and the opportunity to develop their technologies into successful business ventures.

Companies in the preincubation stage that are successful in raising capital or building viable businesses may later transfer from the shared space into fully equipped, private incubator suites dedicated to their needs. Some may use other technical resources provided by the university's core facilities. Others may choose to locate off-site or find commercial real estate if incubator space is unavailable.

"The advantage of preincubation space is that early-stage, conceptual companies can be given a chance to succeed," says Clifford Robinson, who retired as BU's director of business incubation in fall 2009. "The odds may sometimes be long, but experimental, high-risk technologies or new markets may be explored for companies that are only just emerging from the research laboratory. This is in keeping with the technology commercialization mission of a major research university engaged in translational research programs. In some cases, companies in the preincubation stage may not be held to the same high standards of business due diligence that are expected of the external companies admitted to the incubator," he explains. However, in all cases, the founders will gain educational value from networking and mentoring provided by the more established companies in the incubator and the affiliated entrepreneurial community.

The BU incubator is fortunate to be located at the center of a world-class research and entrepreneurial community. In addition to BU, the region includes many major universities (e.g., Harvard University, Massachusetts Institute of Technology, University of Massachusetts, Brown University); major medical research institutions (e.g., Massachusetts General Hospital, Dana Farber Cancer Institute, Whitehead Institute, Broad Institute); and government research laboratories (e.g., Draper Laboratories, Lincoln Laboratory). The region also has a well-established community of angel investors and venture capital firms, as well as a high population of successful serial entrepreneurs and founders of technology companies. As a result, most of the regular BU incubation participants have raised at least $1 million, many have raised $2 million to $3 million, and some have raised $4 million to $6 million before even entering the incubator.

Each new incubator client brings with it new technology, entrepreneurial leadership talent, investment capital, and the investment's professional backers. All of this contributes to the entrepreneurial business community and culture that complements the university's research and academic culture. By drawing from the surrounding community, funded companies in the incubator exhibit a high degree of professional due diligence and have high expectations of success. "They are exemplary of the industry standard for raising investment capital and represent the benchmark by which other emerging preincubator companies may be compared," says Robinson.

In addition to launching new companies, the preincubator facilitates the education of new entrepreneurs. "Even for companies that may ultimately be unsuccessful, the founders will nonetheless gain new skills and knowledge so they will become more qualified as entrepreneurs," says Robinson. The focus is on educating the individual rather than on the success of the company, since Robinson believes that an unsuccessful company may ultimately produce a successful entrepreneur.

The preincubation space is divided by partitions into smaller desk areas capable of serving two- and three-person companies and other desks for single founders. About six companies can be housed in the preincubator space. "Because it's shared space we don't charge as much, and it's good value considering what they gain. They essentially have desks, phones, and Internet access," Robinson explains, "but they also use the conference rooms and other incubator amenities. The real value comes from networking and support from all the other companies and from BU faculty who teach entrepreneurial management."

Impetus for the preincubation space arose because "there is a transitional period during which you think something that's come out of research might have value but you need to look at the market and address that," he says. "Additionally, BU's president intended the incubator system to serve the entire university so that new companies might emerge from all disciplines and departments. Thus in this space, any faculty member or student can take hold of the project, research the market, write a business plan, and present it to investors," Robinson says. Preincubated businesses may also survive temporarily on SBIRs. "Usually, in a year or two, they either make it or fail."

As an early-stage adjunct to the main incubator, the preincubator is home to a variety of companies tapping different financing mechanisms (e.g., angel, VC, seed funds, corporate partners), pursuing myriad business models, and developing different strategies and pathways to commercialization. "Whereas most eventually have institutional investors with expectations of value accretion and ROI, others may evolve as 'lifestyle' companies for the founders," Robinson explains. However, firms aren't expected to stay in preincubation more than about three years.

"In all cases however, the preincubator/incubator combination offers an ideal, almost perfect, teaching environment for any student with a desire to learn the complexities of entrepreneurship and technology commercialization. The preincubator might be considered a laboratory where the university and entrepreneurs alike may experiment with new business models and try out new ideas for business creation," he says. "By this definition, the preincubator is essentially a classroom or laboratory—no different from any other traditional classroom or laboratory within the university, still serving the university's core missions and providing value to society."

Coaching and Facilitation

- Expand clients' management expertise to include core competencies that are needed to build and grow a successful venture but that may not otherwise be affordable until the business reaches a certain size or secures sufficient capital

- Provide clients with outside perspectives on their businesses and allow for strategic thinking that owners might neglect because of the pressures of dealing with the daily operation of the business (working in their business instead of working on their business)

- Provide staff with a mechanism for continually assessing and fulfilling clients' needs

- Provide for the timely mobilizing of resources and client decision making

- Provide support and oversight to ensure that the full benefit is derived from each incubation service

■ ■ coaching and facilitation

Few incubator clients have experience in planning, launching, or operating a business; bringing a product or service to market; or securing capital. The task of an incubation professional is to guide them through each of these phases of venture development. Serial entrepreneurs, on the other hand, may want more in-depth assistance that enhances their business-building skills. Coaching and facilitation can serve both types of clients.

Telling them what to do or simply providing referrals to other experts is not coaching (see the section on Service Provider Network in chapter 2, "Staffing," and the section on Mentors, Entrepreneurs-in-Residence, and Advisory Boards later in this chapter). The true value of coaching and facilitation comes when incubation professionals can orchestrate the use of specialized resources or instruct clients on how to do something in such a way that they can then complete the task themselves. The idea is to engage entrepreneurs throughout the incubation process to ensure that the client company attains its desired outcomes.

Other ways to coach include serving as a sounding board and advocate for client businesses as they face the many challenges associated with starting and growing a new venture and helping identify issues before they become urgent or problematic.

Be careful, though. The role of a coach is to help clients through an issue, not solve it for them. Coaches should resist the temptation to complete tasks for clients, which can undermine the entrepreneur's ownership of the business and diminish the entrepreneurial spirit and drive needed to successfully launch a new venture. (A program that invests in its client companies or takes equity in them may have a different approach.)

Many first-time incubator managers say, "I've never coached a business before," or, "I don't know anything about this particular industry cluster or technology." That may be true, but coaching and facilitation can be learned with the proper training. If incubator management does not have a background in coaching and facilitation, these skills can be developed over time, and skilled advisors can supplement that knowledge. NBIA offers a number of resources on coaching and facilitation, including educational sessions and workshops at training events and newsletter articles. Visit www.nbia.org for more information.

It is important that the incubator protect itself from unforeseen issues by asking each client, at the time of entry to the incubator, to sign a waiver of liability for the advice sought and given during the incubation process. NBIA's book *Put It in Writing* (Athens, Ohio: NBIA Publications, 2002) includes several examples of leases with liability waivers.

BEST PRACTICES IN ACTION

Meytav Incubator
Kiryat Shmona, Israel
Orit Shaked, CTO
www.meytavti.co.il

Although the Meytav Incubator is privately owned and operated, its clients (after a rigorous screening process; see chapter 6, "Client Entrance and Exit") are approved and funded by Israel's Office of the Chief Scientist of the Ministry of Industry, Trade, and Labor. In a program unique to Israel (see chapter 9, "Case Studies," for an explanation of the Israeli Technological Incubators Program), the chief scientist's office invests up to 85 percent in total project budgets, ranging from $350,000 to $600,000, to support technology projects for up to two years; 15 percent of project budgets must be provided by private-sector investors. (The project budgets are developed by the technologist and the Israeli incubators and their investors, all of whom are involved in determining the resources necessary to get the company through major milestones.) For biotechnology projects, government funding of an additional $300,000 is available for a third year in the incubator, and the government will fund up to 80 percent of these projects. (The projects may raise additional, supplemental funding from the private sector for these efforts as well.) Funds invested by the government are provided as a grant or soft loan. The match for central government support may come from angel investors or Meytav backers, which include several investment firms, or others.

Meytav relies on its broad and deep connections with VC and strategic alliance partners to get the client company to subsequent stages of funding or to the point that it can succeed once it has graduated.

In addition to supplying work space, the incubator provides legal and accounting services, consulting, a computer network, maintenance, and general administrative services. A state-of-the-art laboratory offers access to shared equipment that would be too expensive for each project to acquire. It also offers fermentation, cell culture, molecular biology, and chemistry facilities. An in-house engineering unit helps clients develop prototypes quickly, a special need for medical device companies.

Postinvestment monitoring involves:

- Provision of daily access to the Meytav management team and to "continual scientific, financial, managerial, administrative, and marketing support and advice from a dedicated team of professionals"

- Assistance in structuring the company and setting up a board of directors

- Provision of a Meytav professional to the investee board of directors

- Assistance by Meytav in acquiring strategic alliances and investment that will contribute to the company's future success and maximize ROI

Company books are managed by the incubator's financial staff of three bookkeepers and a manager. Since virtually all of a client's initial funding comes from the chief scientist's office and private investors, the Meytav accounting department oversees all investments and company expenditures and ensures compliance with salary caps set during the screening process. Meytav also ensures that each company has a board of directors and a scientific advisory board, and it helps appoint those individuals.

Because of its rigorous screening process, Meytav is well aware of the state of each firm's intellectual property and the regulatory processes required for its companies. Meytav is also intimately involved in developing licensing agreements and ensuring an experienced CEO is in charge of the company before the client ever enters the incubator.

Once the business is inside, "We look for achieving major milestones while in the incubator," explains Meytav CTO Orit Shaked. These differ, depending on whether the product is a medical device or a new drug. In many cases, the incubator requires that the project already have at least one strategic partner or investor in place; then all parties will sit down to determine what milestones must be achieved.

Quarterly meetings are set with each company, but the number of other meetings is determined by the company's needs. While Meytav's CTO manages this process, both the CEO and CTO consult with the companies. Meetings are set up to deal with any problem on the scientific side. If the client "needs advice from pharma, we work with protocol and formulation experts," Shaked says. Each client can tap expert consultants on every topic with which the company needs help. While some individuals volunteer to assist companies, most consultants are paid from the budget agreed upon with the chief scientist's office.

"We believe in a method where if the company works well, you don't have to interfere too much," Shaked says. "The minute we identify a problem, we closely follow the company."

The incubator's assistance and coaching are tightly targeted and designed to help the firm achieve its milestones for success. The incubator requires a rigorous screening process. Other controls specify that bookkeeping is done by Meytav staff. In addition, a monthly report must go to the chief scientist's office; accredited investors, strategic alliance partners, and a CEO are already on board. And each firm's board of directors must include a Meytav professional.

The coaching clearly pays off. Graduates include Protalix Biotherapeutics, a biotechnology company traded on the American Stock Exchange. Protalix was rated a "best buy" by Marketwire in December 2009, when it also completed its new drug application filing with the U.S. Food and Drug Administration for a biotherapeutic product to treat Gaucher's disease. It recently entered into an agreement with Pfizer to develop and commercialize that product. Another graduate, Endogun Medical Systems, has achieved FDA approval for its medical devices used to treat pelvic organ prolapse and urinary incontinence. Endogun also has developed other products used by doctors in treating urinary and gynecological conditions.

Outsourcing Coaching
The Mississippi e-Business Innovation Center, Jackson, MS
DeAnna Adams, former executive director
www.innovationcenter.ms

The Mississippi e-Business Innovation Center, located in Jackson State University's e-Center complex, is dedicated to growing emerging technology companies to become independent, self-sustaining, long-term successes, thus providing higher-quality, higher-paying jobs in Mississippi.

Recognizing a need for "high-impact, high-quality" on-site coaching services, but acknowledging limited staff resources, MBIC partnered with The Growth Coach—a business-coaching franchise system with 155 locations in the United States, including one in Jackson—to provide coaching services to MBIC clients.

The relationship began when the Growth Coach advisor approached MBIC Executive Director DeAnna Adams about using the incubator's conference room for training. Adams quickly recognized an opportunity.

"Clients come to me with all kinds of questions, and I have to do a lot of research to find out what they should do next," Adams says. The local Growth Coach franchisee, however, was the retired owner of an international company and thus had lots of firsthand business experience.

Adams offered the advisor free office space in exchange for providing a specific number of hours of coaching to clients. At first, he provided four hours of open-office coaching each week; that segued into an hour of coaching per client per month, for a total of twenty-four hours. "It's turned out to be a lot more than that because he promotes his services," Adams says. "He really likes working with the incubator clients."

In addition, the advisor offers two of his Growth Coach workshops to the most promising incubator clients for free. Each workshop lasts a year, with an optional second year (which is not free). "It's supposed to help them work through business ownership and balance their lives," says Adams, who took the classes herself ("I don't take in anything I don't sit through myself"). "They're very high-end classes—it would cost the client a couple thousand dollars."

The partnership has worked well, although it has had some issues. "He would talk with clients and give them advice, and then they'd come to me and say, 'Well, he says such-and-such,'" Adams says. "I need to know what advice he's giving them." To make sure she stays in the loop, Adams set up weekly meetings with the advisor to go over his meetings with clients and discuss them. She also shares each client's monthly activity report to gain the advisor's insight into each company's progress and discuss possible solutions to common problems.

"He has been good for our clients," Adams says.

■■ entrepreneur education

Many incubators offer entrepreneurial training programs as a way to help existing clients grow their businesses and to attract potential clients into their facilities. In fact, some incubators specifically offer fundamental business training for nascent entrepreneurs who are not yet ready to become incubator clients. When they're successful, training programs can do more than bring new clients into the incubator; they even help open new doors for individuals who had not considered entrepreneurship a viable career option, including those who transition from public assistance and those with disabilities.

Educational programs also benefit incubators in other ways. Training events can raise awareness of an incubator's mission, attract sponsors, contribute to its bottom line, and help create a thriving business community.

At many incubators, training means short (one- to two-hour) sessions on business fundamentals: developing a business plan, attracting investors, marketing, hiring and evaluating employees, maintaining cash flow, and the like. Other programs take more in-depth approaches, offering classes and workshops that explore targeted topics within broader issues—for example, focusing on seed funding rather than the larger issue of investment capital.

While educational programs are valuable, they shouldn't be taken up lightly. Managing a training program takes time—choosing topics, recruiting instructors, marketing the events, and handling registration. And then there are the physical details—setting up the room, making sure audiovisual equipment is on hand and working, and buying refreshments and other supplies. The amount of time involved varies by the type of educational program. A brown-bag lunch might require an hour or two to pull together; organizing a multiweek seminar on marketing techniques with a series of speakers or a facilitator might require several days of a staff member's time.

Considering the amount of time involved, the incubator may wish to charge for the program. Fee-based programs demonstrate to clients the value of training; if they have to pay for it, then they commit to completing the training and learn from it. But money is tight for many entrepreneurs, and many service providers offer free or low-cost workshops to attract customers; so reality often outweighs theory when incubator managers face the question of charging fees for training programs. Many incubators charge just enough to cover their costs. Some get grants or sponsorships to cover their costs; others build the expense into their budgets and include the cost in client fees or charge only nominal fees for training.

CEO Strategy Forum
San Diego CONNECT, San Diego, CA
Camille Sobrian, chief operating officer
www.connect.org

San Diego CONNECT's CEO Strategy Forum provides "quality guidance from experienced CEOs," says CONNECT Chief Operating Officer Camille Sobrian. It is a "light" version of programs offered by the Entrepreneurs' Organization, formerly Young Entrepreneurs' Organization. The Strategy Forum is for start-ups, and unlike the older, international EO, it has no requirements for the age of the entrepreneur or the size or stage of the company. The CEO Strategy Forum involves monthly meetings, some in the morning and some in the late afternoon. Each meeting is limited to twenty-four people in order to ensure an intimate discussion. CONNECT brings in top CEOs like former Qualcomm Chairman and CEO Irwin Jacobs and Slacker CEO Dennis Mudd (who sold MusicMatch to Yahoo!), explains Sobrian. "We feature a highly successful CEO and discuss topics like turnarounds, working with a board of directors, high-speed innovation, branding on a budget, or other topics of interest to CEOs," she says. CONNECT looks at the experiences of the region's star CEOs and how they might share those in a manner that provides valuable insights to CONNECT clients. For example, a cofounder of Nintendo talked about the art of market domination, customer retention, and loyalty. "Weathering a Turbulent Economy" was a popular topic for 2009. "We're trying to help our companies be as virtual as possible to reduce their burn rate," Sobrian notes.

While business service providers sponsor each monthly meeting, only two representatives of the sponsoring organization are permitted to attend in order to keep the focus on the CEOs. CONNECT has one program manager who runs the CEO Strategy Forum and two other CONNECT programs: FrameWorks Workshops, half-day workshops held two to three times a month, and Frontiers in Science and Technology, a lecture series featuring groundbreaking research being conducted in the San Diego area.

In 2008, this program was ranked as very good or excellent by 4.5 out of 5 attendees, and its membership continued to grow.

Marketing through Education

Enterprise Center of Johnson County, Lenexa, KS
Joel Wiggins, CEO and president
www.ecjc.com

Until about 2006, the Enterprise Center of Johnson County approached entrepreneur education somewhat haphazardly. "Someone would call and say they wanted to do a workshop in something," says Joel Wiggins, the incubator's CEO and president.

Then, Wiggins decided it was time to get serious about workshops and raise the program's community profile. The staff created a slate of workshops covering six topic areas: finance, sales and marketing, technology, legal issues, governance and leadership, and human resources. And they gave the series a name: ECJC U.

"Now, we actually set a calendar at the beginning of the year, think through the tracks, and decide what we want to do," Wiggins says. About one-third of the twenty-eight or so workshops offered each year are developed in-house; the rest are created and presented by experts from the community.

Marketing is low-key: e-mailed notices to the 1,500 names in ECJC's mailing list and posts on the ECJC Web site. Copromotion is frequent, as presenters and sponsors step up to spread the word.

Each workshop costs $25 to $50 and includes a box lunch (clients receive a 50 percent discount). The incubator can accommodate up to twenty-five participants per workshop, most of whom are prospective clients. Workshops that draw less than ten registrations (advance registration is required) are cancelled. "If you get fewer than ten people, it's a downer," Wiggins says.

Feedback is very important. Every workshop ends with an evaluation and feedback form, and the incubator staff take those comments to heart. "We're much more organized and systematic in trying to figure out topics people need to know and what they are looking for," Wiggins says. For example, in response to feedback and its own observations of the market, ECJC added a series on social media to the 2009 ECJC U curriculum. "Not just the curiosity stuff, but how you can use Twitter, LinkedIn, and Facebook in your business," he says. Those classes sold out quickly, he notes.

In 2008, ECJC U had nearly five hundred participants and made about $7,000 for the incubator. "We don't make a lot of money on it, but we're getting known for this," Wiggins says. "It's a way for us to serve the community, and entrepreneurs love the workshops because they're designed for early-stage companies."

Industry-Specific Training

Rutgers Food Innovation Center, Bridgeton, NJ
Lou Cooperhouse, director
www.foodinnovation.rutgers.edu

For many incubators, entrepreneur education focuses on the basics: writing a marketing plan, protecting intellectual property, hiring good people. Few of their clients have to worry about U.S. Department of Agriculture inspections.

That is a concern for clients of the Rutgers Food Innovation Center, however. FIC does offer general business classes aimed at food entrepreneurs, but it also offers Hazard Analysis and Critical Control Point certification training.

Many food processors must comply with HACCP standards, which require them to identify potential hazards in their production and set up a way—a critical control point—to mitigate those hazards. For example, a canner of jams and jellies has to worry about mold in its products, so its critical control point could be the addition of an acidifier to kill mold spores. The USDA requires each processor to have at least one person trained in HACCP, and verification of that training is part of the inspection process.

Introduced in mid-2009, the certification classes had already drawn one hundred participants by early 2010, says Lou Cooperhouse, the incubator's director. Most of those were representatives of established food companies.

Private HACCP training courses can cost as much as $1,200 per person, Cooperhouse says. Because he has a full-time staff member dedicated to safety training and can offer the classes at FIC, Cooperhouse can train up to ten people from a single processor for $2,500. "I tell them, 'Send your whole quality control team, because it's in your best interest to train as many people as possible,'" he says.

Although the classes are rarely used by FIC client companies, the training does benefit the incubator because the mature companies that sign up for classes may later decide to use the incubator's state-of-the-art facilities to test new products or pay to have more of their staff take FIC training. "It's a great way for us to market the center and develop relationships with established food companies," Cooperhouse says.

There are commercial options when it comes to training programs for entrepreneurs. FastTrac, a product of the Ewing Marion Kauffman Foundation of Kansas City, Missouri, and NxLeveL, from the University of Colorado Center for Community Development, are comprehensive training programs designed to guide entrepreneurs through the business development process.

The commercial training programs are more extensive—and, in most cases, more expensive—than training workshops conducted by incubators, which often are topic-specific. But many incubator managers have found that the commercial programs can complement the training their incubators offer.

FastTrac offers nine distinct programs, and NxLeveL has five turnkey programs. The curricula are similar: business fundamentals, start-up options, understanding budgets and financials, and developing a business concept.

NxLeveL's Business Start-Ups program includes ten weeks of three-hour classes. Clients receive a textbook, workbook, resource guide, and support materials.

FastTrac's similar program, NewVentures, runs for eleven weeks, with weekly three-hour classes. Depending on the level of sponsorship by the community organization hosting the classes, participants in either program can expect to pay several hundred dollars to attend.

Both NxLeveL and FastTrac are administered through chambers of commerce, Small Business Development Centers, and other community development organizations—including business incubators—which act as local sponsors. Certified trainers, most of whom are experienced entrepreneurs (some are even incubator managers), conduct the trainings in communities throughout the world.

For more information about FastTrac and NxLeveL, visit www.fasttrac.org and www.nxlevel.org.

Client Networking

- Provides clients with psychological support, reducing stresses and the likelihood of failure due to burnout, depression, and other ills

- Provides instrumental benefits, including opportunities for sharing expertise, employees, and other resources, and co-bidding, among others

- Provides important contributions in preparing clients for learning and enhancing the learning experience

- Shifts some of the burden of counseling clients to others inside and outside the incubator, permitting management more time for monitoring and higher-level coaching

■■ client networking

If a program doesn't promote client networking in some way, it's in the minority. In NBIA's *2006 State of the Business Incubation Industry* report, 96 percent of North American incubation programs said they provided networking opportunities for their clients.

The reason for their popularity is simple: Who you know really can make a difference, especially for start-up businesses. Networking—whether with fellow incubator clients, representatives of the larger business community, or potential customers or funders—gives fledgling entrepreneurs a host of benefits, from helping them develop needed business skills and relationships to providing vital emotional support. Such help can mean the difference between success and failure.

But if networking is something nearly everyone promotes, the ways incubators try to make it happen and the benefits they see from it vary in important ways. Many incubators offer regularly scheduled brown-bag lunches aimed at keeping clients in touch with each other. Some go in for more ambitious public events that draw in the local business community or for tightly focused problem-solving sessions with selected clients. Others facilitate joint projects among several clients, which not only help these companies generate revenue but also give them experience in working with other small businesses.

Events can aim at making deals, attracting investors, and launching spin-off companies, or at giving entrepreneurs and experts a chance to swap news and tips. They can be big or small, formal or casual, indoors or out. Not surprisingly, given the Internet's power as a networking tool, they are moving online as well.

> "It's a more targeted form of networking than attending a chamber of commerce party."
>
> – Joel Wiggins, CEO and president, Enterprise Center of Johnson County

BEST PRACTICES IN ACTION

Entrepreneurs Happy Hour
Enterprise Center of Johnson County, Lenexa, KS
Joel Wiggins, CEO and president
www.ecjc.com

In Kansas City, entrepreneurs in the life sciences and technology network the old-fashioned way: over a drink.

Since 2006, the Enterprise Center of Johnson County—located in suburban Kansas City on the Kansas side—has hosted a quarterly Entrepreneurs Happy Hour for KC Sourcelink, a group of about one hundred entrepreneur-support organizations. "They needed a partner on the Kansas side and asked us to host it here," says Joel Wiggins, ECJC CEO and president.

Each two-hour event (always from 5 p.m. to 7 p.m. on a Thursday) includes hors d'oeuvres and drinks—that's it. No program, no speaker, maybe some giveaways. Those attending simply eat, drink, and talk. And talk they do: "Every once in a while we have to kick people out" at the end, Wiggins says.

The happy hours have a core participant group of ten to twenty people, Wiggins says; the events average about sixty attendees. It's a more targeted form of networking than attending a chamber of commerce party, he adds. "This focuses on life science and growth-oriented companies," he says. But it's not a hard-core business setting, either. "It tends to be a good time, but there aren't a lot of outcomes from it that are specific to the event itself," he says. "They just get to meet."

Each happy hour costs ECJC $300 to $400 "depending on how much wine they drink," Wiggins says. (He's joking; that cost and the danger of overindulging are controlled by distribution of drink tickets.)

Wiggins considers the cost a form of marketing. "It gives us good visibility—we get people in our building," he says. "And it ties us in with other [like-minded] organizations."

Miniature Golf Tournament
Emerging Technology Centers, Baltimore, MD
Ann Lansinger, president
www.etcbaltimore.com

In 2006, Ann Lansinger, executive director of Baltimore's Emerging Technology Centers, wanted to offer a fun event to encourage clients from ETC's two facilities to interact. A colleague who often planned social events suggested an indoor nine-hole miniature golf tournament as a way to bring representatives of different companies together.

Lansinger assigned each participating client a hole to design. "We had graphic artists and engineers involved, and they really got into creating and decorating their part of the course," Lansinger says. "The event started at 5:30 p.m., and many of them spent the day designing and setting up the course, which wound through the center's wide hallways, conference rooms, and offices."

One group produced a Halloween-themed hole that featured wet noodles in a witches' cauldron positioned just under the edge of a conference table for unsuspecting players retrieving their golf ball. At a hole designed by a group of electrical engineers, LEDs lined each side of the putting surface.

Each four-person golf team included representatives from different companies to allow them to interact with other clients in a fun atmosphere. "Clients enjoyed the creative aspect of the event as well as the competition," Lansinger says. "Having them construct the course allowed them to utilize their skills and enjoy themselves in the process. The camaraderie lasts much longer than just one day."

Lansinger says the first event cost ETC next to nothing and attracted some seventy-five participants and onlookers. A local Italian restaurant provided food trays, and retailers from nearby outlets supplied drinks, snacks, and prizes.

The event has been so popular that the center offers the golf tournament each year; Lansinger held the third annual tournament in fall 2009. "It's really incredible," Lansinger says. "During the tournament, the teams cheer and root for each other. Afterward they joke and tease each other for months. It's a lot of fun and the clients absolutely love it."

CEO Roundtable

Boston University Business Incubation Program, Boston, MA
Peter R. Russo, Boston University School of Management
www.bu.edu/otd/about/incubation

The facilitator of the Boston University Business Incubation Program's CEO Roundtable has a long history of participating in such resources. Peter R. Russo, former CEO of Data Instruments (eventually acquired by Honeywell), participated for ten years in a CEO roundtable initially organized by the American Electronics Association. In 2007, Russo, who is now senior lecturer in Strategy and Innovation in BU's School of Management, volunteered to create a CEO roundtable for the incubator.

"We found that we could share things with our fellow CEOs that we wouldn't even share with our own board of directors," says Russo. Using his own experience, Russo was able to convince the incubator client CEOs that participation was a good idea.

Of course, incubator firms are headed up by busy people, as every incubator manager knows. "At our initial meetings, some CEOs would ask, 'What's in it for me? How will this help?' The fact that I could speak from my own experience about how a similar roundtable was important to me was helpful," he explains.

Approximately ten incubator clients participate regularly in each roundtable, normally held monthly for an hour-and-a-half at noon on a Friday. The incubator provides sack lunches and bottled water. In approximately two-thirds of the meetings, only the CEOs meet to share issues and concerns. About four times a year, Russo brings in an outside expert. In those cases, the outsider doesn't give a presentation, but he or she and the CEOs simply sit around the table and discuss the issue.

"They are all at a similar stage of development," explains Russo. "Topics are, 'How do you find the right kind of person to be CFO or somebody to manage the IT (information technology) for your company?' or, 'How do you hire your first business development person?' 'How do we compensate people we're bringing into the company after the founding team?' The CEOs will bring to the discussion prior experiences or what they've learned from business service providers," says Russo.

Participants decide on the agenda but often add to it as new issues come up. As facilitator, Russo's role is "to make sure the air time is evenly split among people in the room. Sometimes I have to say, 'We've explored this as far as we can today, and there are more things we want to get on the table,'" he says. Good facilitation is critical since some participants will always think their own issue is most important.

First-time participants tend to be quiet until they get to know the group, but getting them involved is also part of the facilitator's role. "We discuss the rules and the importance of playing by the rules," says Russo. "First, everything shared in the roundtable is confidential and has to stay in the room. That's the biggest thing of all. Second, it's important to put things on the table. We say we don't want anybody to leave the room without talking about something that is important to them."

Russo believes the ideal size is about ten or twelve and the maximum size for participation is fifteen. "If people are missing and the group is too small, you can't have a good meeting, but if you don't have enough air time people never get to talk about the things that are important to them." The CEO roundtables have been so popular that at least one BU incubator graduate still returns on a regular basis.

> Providing help with marketing can help firms generate sales; the resulting cash flow will support business operations and improve the client's ability to secure capital.

■■ marketing assistance

In-house expertise, mentors, and a professional services network can help your clients progress from idea and proof of concept (i.e., whether it is feasible to produce or provide the product or service) to market readiness. But at some point, the clients actually have to make a sale. Providing help with marketing can help firms generate sales; the resulting cash flow will support business operations and improve the client's ability to secure capital.

Marketing assistance can take a number of forms. The most obvious is publicity—news releases, advertising, and so on. But incubators also can help their clients by giving them access to markets by sharing trade-show booths, helping them connect to potential customers, or offering marketing training.

BEST PRACTICES IN ACTION

Joint Publicity Program
Purdue Technology Center–West Lafayette
West Lafayette, IN
Tim Peoples, director
www.purdueresearchpark.org

The Purdue Technology Center–West Lafayette—one of five incubators located within Purdue Research Parks throughout Indiana—recognizes that a key component of its success is its credibility gained over decades of success. And it also recognizes that clients want to leverage that credibility to attract investors, seasoned management, and partners. To help clients achieve that goal, PTC has offered comarketing services to clients since 2000. These services include writing and editing news releases, coordinating news conferences, offering media training, and distributing news releases directly for free or, for a fee, through the BusinessWire subscription service.

The program leverages the resources of Purdue University and gives clients marketing reach they otherwise could not afford. For example, the university's public relations department sometimes purchases advertising on the back page of regional magazines to showcase an incubator client or graduate. Research park successes—including incubator clients and graduates—make frequent appearances on the JumboTron screens during home football games. Even something as simple as an open house for a new client company can make an impact and save money for a fledgling business.

"Feedback from our client firms suggests that much of their success would not have occurred had it not been for the exposure they received, and they are proud to advertise their affiliation with Purdue and the benefits they obtain as a client of the Purdue Technology Center," says John Hanak, statewide director of the PTC system.

The most frequently used service, however, is the writing and distribution of press releases. Purdue PR staff will publicize clients' product releases, significant milestones, significant hires, closings on a significant funding round, or other newsworthy events. And because the press release comes from Purdue, the university, research parks, and incubators get some of the glory, too.

Although some incubators leave press releases to interns, Tim Peoples, director of PTC-West Lafayette, advises against it. "You need to have seasoned, knowledgeable people with a newsperson-type background working on this effort," he says. "It is more heavy-lifting than an intern or a co-op student can be assigned to if you expect to achieve extraordinary results."

Government Relationships for Construction Bids
William M. Factory Small Business Incubator, Tacoma, WA
Tim Strege, executive director
www.williamfactory.com

Although marketing has changed dramatically in the Internet age, William M. Factory Executive Director Tim Strege notes that clients can draw on a wealth of resources on Web 2.0 marketing. He and his staff focus on helping clients use three traditional communications strategies:

- **Outreach.** The incubator staff take strong steps to represent their clients when neither the entrepreneur nor anyone else with the company is present, whether in the incubator building or during external outreach activities. Incubator personnel become familiar with client companies' areas of expertise, the equipment used, the owner's capabilities, special certifications obtained, previous contracts, and lines of credit. "This enables incubator staff to speak up during project-specific meetings and offer consideration of an incubator firm," Strege says. The staff's detailed knowledge of client capabilities was put to good use in the $200 million Salishan residential development in East Tacoma. Launched in 2000 as a project of the Tacoma Housing Authority, the ongoing project entailed construction of a combination of 1,200 units, including subsidized, market-rate rental, and owner-occupied housing. Incubator staff presented client firm competencies to the general contractor, Walsh Construction, and encouraged the contractor to include locally based and minority companies as a corporate objective. As a direct result, a total of twelve incubator clients participated in the construction effort, bringing in over $10 million to incubator companies alone. Since then, the incubator has recommended Walsh to two other cities for similar projects—increasing the likelihood that incubator clients and graduates will continue to subcontract with Walsh.

- **Networking.** The incubator conducts commercial matchmaking events in which clients meet informally in small groups and one-on-one sessions with larger corporations to discuss projects in which contracting opportunities are available. For example, the incubator regularly organizes events that bring the largest Pacific Northwest construction companies (including Hoffman, Skanska, Kiewit Pacific, and Turner Construction) to the incubator facilities to discuss contracting opportunities on major investment projects, such as constructing an underground light rail tunnel in Seattle; building a second Tacoma Narrows Bridge; and creating new facilities at nearby Fort Lewis and naval shipyard military bases. During the three years of the Tacoma Narrows Bridge

project, for example, all subcontractor work meetings were held at the incubator, giving clients visibility and better access to subcontract work on this $630 million construction effort. "The incubator initiates direct communications with contracting decision makers and discussions regarding the scope and size of feasible work that could be performed by incubator firms," Strege explains.

- **Advocacy.** The incubator opens the doors of the commercial marketplace to new entrants (especially minorities, women, and other disadvantaged business owners) by pushing larger companies and public agencies to consider the small firm as a contracting partner. For example, incubator staff promoted the credentials of client Mike Monteleone of SCS Consulting (a structural project management company) for a relatively small contract on a prominent underground utility project in the vicinity of the Tacoma Municipal Building. Following his successful completion of this work, the incubator introduced SCS to both the city of Seattle and the Seattle office of global engineering giant URS and endorsed inclusion of SCS as a small disadvantaged firm in the large Spokane Street Viaduct rebuild. SCS was awarded a $300,000 contract for three years of project management related to footings and foundations on construction work that will tie into the multibillion-dollar Alaska Way Viaduct and Seattle Seawall improvements. "Introducing talented entrepreneurs to large contractors for involvement in component parts of a significant project can propel the incubator firm to obtain greater participation in upcoming endeavors," says Strege.

As Gregory Stewart, president of Allaura, an incubator IT company that has proprietary RFID technologies, including his Orbitor product, explains, "I was able to get two contracts from the city of Seattle and the Port of Tacoma" because of the incubator's important regional contacts, the credibility the program offers clients, and the fact that "procurement people know if they're having trouble with a contractor, they can come back to the incubator staff, who can step in and help." The incubator's advocacy and networking efforts mean that contractors are "more willing to consider an unknown vendor."

"The program opens doors to meet the big guys," explains Danny Farrow, president of Farrow Concrete Services. "It allows for relationship building that serves as a stepping stone to bigger independent contracts."

Marketing for Smarties

San Juan College Enterprise Center, Farmington, NM
Jasper Welch, director
www.sanjuancollege.edu/gcb

To help his clients get a grasp on marketing, Jasper Welch—director of the San Juan College Enterprise Center in Farmington, New Mexico—has forged a strategic partnership with the author of Marketing for Smarties, a marketing training program developed by a New York–based marketing consultant.

Around 2004, M4S author Don Warner did a presentation on marketing at the Small Business Development Center at SJCEC. Welch was so impressed that he invited Warner to use his training center to train M4S coaches.

That relationship has continued, with Welch helping to train M4S coaches and publishing materials for M4S courses. The course, developed jointly by SJCEC and Warner, comprises three workshops that lead participants through a fourteen-step process to identify, hone, and communicate messages while creating a marketing plan.

The key to the M4S method is the active participation of the entrepreneur, Welch says. "It's a process, versus a show-and-tell session with a presenter," he says. "Companies come out with a platform that helps them better communicate their message, a database to manage customers, a series of marketing projects, and a plan to put them all together."

Welch charges participants $100 to $150 for the course, plus $50 for the materials—well under the $300 or so that similar business development courses may cost. And it teaches entrepreneurs to do the work themselves, a skill especially critical for a start-up that probably can't afford to hire a marketing firm.

"Most companies suffer from failure to implement," Welch says. For example, they may want to publish a newsletter but falter because they become overwhelmed by what's involved: getting pictures, writing copy, hiring a designer, finding a printer. "If they don't have a process, they won't follow through," Welch says.

Welch also is working with Warner on an online learning portal for M4S. When it's finished, the site will offer interactive instruction, a blog, and a calendar, among other functions.

The M4S course has caught the interest of other incubators and SBDCs, Welch says. He hopes to begin licensing the content, which will help recoup some of the $10,000 he's invested in the project. "I want it to be self-supporting, not make a lot of money from it," he says.

Weekly Newspaper Stories on Clients

Business Incubator Center, Grand Junction, CO
Christina Reddin, executive director
www.gjincubator.org

A reporter's interest in the people behind local businesses has turned into an opportunity for readers of the Grand Junction Free Press in Grand Junction, Colorado, to get to know clients of the Business Incubation Center.

Sharon Sullivan, a reporter with the newspaper, has been featuring stories about the incubator's clients—one client per week—since July 2008.

Among the entrepreneurs who have been featured are a former chef who now does business as The Computer Lady; two longtime friends who decided to start their own tool supply company after they lost their jobs; and a woman who worked as a waitress, bartender, and dental assistant, all the while dreaming of opening a women's clothing store.

According to incubator Executive Director Christina Reddin, the articles are a hit because "they are about the people, not so much the businesses."

Reddin says the articles started after Sullivan attended an incubator event at a local coffeehouse. There, Sullivan met several entrepreneurs and wrote a human-interest piece for the paper. She asked Reddin to let her know if she had other potential human-interest stories.

"I told her we had fifty-two in-house clients alone and that I could easily supply her a story a week," Reddin says. Sullivan agreed to continue the series as long as Reddin could supply newsworthy stories.

Reddin provides Sullivan a draft lineup and contact information a month in advance. "And I tell my clients to make it as easy as possible for Sullivan to do the interview," Reddin says.

According to Reddin, the articles have generated interest in individual clients and the incubation program. "It's better than people just becoming more aware of our logo or our name," she says. "They're gaining an understanding of what we do."

For example, Reddin says the articles have helped local readers better understand what business consulting can mean. "Some people think consultants are expensive people who prepare fancy reports about things you already know," Reddin says. "This helps people understand what type of business consulting [we] do, and how it might be helpful to their business."

> "Almost everyone has some investments, but most are in things far away. If people just invested a very small part of their investments in local businesses, it would make a gigantic impact."
> – Craig Scharton, former CEO, Central Valley Business Incubator

Made in the Central Valley
Central Valley Business Incubator, Fresno, CA
Craig Scharton, former CEO
www.cvbi.org

The Central Valley Business Incubator in Fresno, California, raised money for its operating fund and promoted its clients' businesses at the same time through Made in the Central Valley, a fundraiser featuring local businesses, food, and entertainment. Approximately three hundred people paid $50 each to attend the fall 2007 event, which raised $70,000 for the incubator's operating fund.

As entertainment and to promote its clients, CVBI gave each guest $1 million in CVBI bucks to invest in one or more of twenty-eight participating businesses from CVBI's two incubator facilities, the mixed-use Launching Pad and the Claude Laval Water and Energy Technology Incubator. Clients who received the most investment in this mock Central Valley Stock Exchange won weekend getaways donated by local bed-and-breakfast establishments.

Throughout the evening, a local band entertained guests, who sipped locally produced wines, and a local restaurant catered a meal prepared with locally produced foods.

The Made in the Central Valley theme helped the incubator accomplish its goal of keeping the spotlight on the clients rather than the event itself, says former CEO Craig Scharton.

"Each business set up displays that were creative and energetic to attract 'investors,'" he says. "Unlike other trade shows, our guests wanted to go to booths to decide where to invest."

Scharton says the event showed the valley is growing new businesses—and local crops—and it encouraged guests to buy and invest locally. "We want people to think about that with their investments," he says. "Almost everyone has some investments, but most are in things far away. If people just invested a very small part of their investments in local businesses, it would make a gigantic impact."

Access to Professional Market Intelligence
TECH Fort Worth, Fort Worth, TX
Darlene Ryan, executive director
www.TECHFortWorth.org

Through a partnership with the University of North Texas Health Science Center, TECH Fort Worth offers its clients access to market intelligence data from Frost & Sullivan. Each client must sign an individual agreement with Frost & Sullivan (at no charge to the client) and is issued its own ID and password for the system. At that point, they get unlimited market intelligence reports in any of the three industries to which the incubator subscribes; in 2009, those industries were life sciences, food and chemicals, and environment and energy.

About half of TECH Fort Worth's clients take advantage of the offer, which is included in the $5,000 service fee they pay to be a part of the incubation program (in addition to rent, if they reside in the facility). In 2009, clients accessed 955 reports from Frost & Sullivan with a total retail value of $281,620.

"Some of them, before becoming clients, priced out these reports on their own and found that they would cost them up to $50,000, so this is a tremendous benefit of being one of our clients," says Executive Director Darlene Ryan.

The service costs TECH Fort Worth about $7,500 annually— half of the university's total bill for it. "I don't know what the cost would be on our own, but it would be significantly more," Ryan says.

The reports are a major asset to TFW companies, says Brent Sorrells, the incubator's operations manager. "Many of the reports have assisted clients in identifying new markets for their products," he says. "In addition, this data becomes invaluable to them as they prepare investor pitches to outline the potential market revenues, market growth, existing competition in the market, market drivers, market segmentation, and so on."

■ mentors, entrepreneurs-in-residence, and advisory boards

cubator clients can benefit from interacting with seasoned
usiness owners and senior managers who have successfully
loted a new venture, introduced a new product or a new
vision for an established company, obtained equity funding,
successfully developed a new sales channel, and who
ave been in circumstances similar to theirs. Although the
cubator can provide some of this support through its own
aching, it may not have the breadth of experience needed
y a diverse client base or the time to be responsive when
ents want a viewpoint right away. Besides, an outside,
ird-party perspective can enhance the effectiveness of the
idance provided.

cubation programs have several ways to offer that
utside perspective.

Mentors

- Give clients access to practical, real-world experience in dealing with the formation and growth of a new venture
- Expand the level of service and breadth of expertise offered to clients
- Lend credibility to the incubation program
- Provide the incubator manager with a pool of individuals to help expand their own coaching and technical skills
- Expand the number of stakeholders interested in supporting the incubator

Mentors

Typical mentoring programs draw on a pool of experienced entrepreneurs or senior executives—even incubator graduates—who have been successful with their own ventures and who wish to share this experience with others. Because their interactions with clients are one-on-one, mentors learn the intricacies of the client's business operations and develop trust at a level that may not be feasible for client advisory board members or incubator staff. Mentors also give clients what they may perceive to be a more realistic approach to handling an issue or to making a business decision.

Mentoring can be especially valuable to clients in specific industries (e.g., life sciences, advanced manufacturing, food processing) in which senior executives may bring technical information related to product development or product rollout in specific markets.

Mentoring programs can take different forms. There may be one mentor, an advisory board of three to five mentors (see below), or both. They may meet once a month, once a quarter, or even on the phone. But the goal of these meetings remains the same. The entrepreneur discusses whatever business-related problems he or she may be experiencing. The mentor offers advice, assistance, and sometimes the most important thing of all, a sympathetic ear.

Managing mentor relationships, however, can be tricky. Mentors generally expect that clients will heed their advice (or at least strongly consider it). If a client ignores or dismisses the mentor's guidance, incubator staff may need to step in to resolve the issue. And because mentors are privy to client secrets, it may be advisable to have them sign confidentiality agreements.

Most importantly, mentors must understand that they cannot take control of the business away from the entrepreneur. A dominant mentor can undermine the commitment of an entrepreneur going through challenging times, putting the venture at a higher risk of failure. Mentors may take a more active role in the business as an investor or board member, but mentors should be monitored carefully to ensure that they maintain their role as guides, not as principals.

BEST PRACTICES IN ACTION

Springboard
San Diego CONNECT, San Diego, CA
Camille Sobrian, chief operating officer
www.connect.org

Springboard is San Diego CONNECT's flagship program. It offers free mentoring for one to six months to companies in all stages of development, from concept to start-ups to firms that have reached a significant point in their growth and strategy development. CONNECT says that in 2008 "more than one hundred scientific and technological breakthroughs [were] guided by CONNECT through the process of innovation to commercialization" in high technology, including semiconductors, software, e-commerce/Web 2.0, and communications technology; wireless health, cyber security, and autonomous robotics; clean technology; action and sport innovation; biopharma, medical devices, and diagnostics; and outsourcing.

Via Springboard, CONNECT works with 180 entrepreneurs-in-residence and two hundred "domain experts." The former have experience growing companies and raising equity investments, while the latter have expertise in a specific field such as intellectual property law or an industry sector. Two EIRs and relevant domain experts work with each company during the mentoring period. "The coaching process is focused on the development of a compelling business proposition that can be presented to investors," CONNECT's Web site explains. The process ends with a company presentation to a panel of investors, business service providers, and industry experts.

Camille Sobrian, CONNECT's chief operating officer, says that more than twenty-five hundred companies have gone through CONNECT's mentoring programs in its twenty-five years of operation. Some fifty graduate each year from the Springboard program, out of up to two hundred applicants. All applicants receive guidance for moving their companies forward.

Successful applicants must plan a significant presence in San Diego and have a science- or technology-based innovation or business. Once it's determined that the application meets CONNECT's criteria, a team of staff and EIRs contacts the applicant for an initial meeting to assess whether the project is viable and whether Springboard can help the applicant and how.

ith Springboard, "a huge part of what we do is help
trepreneurs prepare their presentations," says Sobrian,
her to attract equity investment or to vie for one of
ONNECT's awards, which bring attention and recognition to
e winners. As with incubator clients the world over, many
trepreneurs can describe their technology but not the
portance of the innovation breakthrough or its commercial
lue, she says.

aking a presentation to the panel of experts, including
vestors, business service providers, and industry specialists,
designed to produce candid advice for the entrepreneur
out how to further refine his or her plan and implement next
eps and to provide an initial Rolodex of valuable contacts.
ter the panel presentation, the entrepreneur meets with his
her assigned EIRs to plan how to incorporate the panel's
vice and move forward for the following six-month period.

cording to the CONNECT Web site, potential outcomes of
e Springboard program may include:

Getting feedback on the commercial potential
of technology

Developing a compelling business presentation

Constructing a cohesive financial model

Evaluating the management team

Creating a go-to-market strategy

Developing a stronger strategic plan

Developing a realistic funding strategy and readiness
for investment

Getting feedback on a specific business challenge

Expanding the company's network of prospective advisors
and potential clients

itrepreneurs may complete an application for Springboard
line, and a resource section of the Web site offers example
ecutive summaries, business model presentations, and
usiness plans. Two CONNECT Springboard staff administer
e program.

utcomes are individualized according to the specific
eeds of each client. Success for one company might mean
lidation of the technology and acquisition of grant funding,
hile another might successfully raise venture capital or spin
ut an innovation as a separate company. CONNECT reports
at virtually all 2008 Springboard graduates landed funding,
d similar results were expected for 2009. Approximately
percent of Springboard graduates from the last five years
chieved funding.

Entrepreneurs-in-Residence

- Give clients an in-house source of firsthand expertise
  in starting a new venture

- Lend credibility to the incubation program and
  differentiate it from real estate operations

- Offer experienced entrepreneurs an opportunity to
  give back to the community

Entrepreneurs-in-Residence

Unlike mentors, entrepreneurs-in-residence have a more
immediate relationship with the incubator. Usually current
or former CEOs of start-up companies, EIRs spend a set
number of hours or days in the incubator. Most stay a year,
although some residencies last longer, depending on the EIR's
availability. Some are paid stipends or full salaries. Some work
with a very limited group of clients, while others take on a
larger workload. Some incubators have only one EIR at a time;
others have as many as five at once.

Although a rags-to-riches story may be appealing to clients,
success shouldn't be the only factor in choosing an EIR. In
fact, entrepreneurs who have experienced failure may be
more valuable because they can share lessons learned. Even
if his or her company was a success, the EIR should be able
to speak with authority about dealing with real challenges and
failures. He or she should be good at interacting with young
or inexperienced entrepreneurs. And, of course, the EIR's
business background should mesh with the fields in which
your clients operate.

BEST PRACTICES IN ACTION

An Entrepreneur-in-Residence Program
Lennox Tech Enterprise Center, West Henrietta, NY
Terry Gronwall, manager
http://htr.org/incubator.asp

Terry Gronwall of the Lennox Tech Enterprise Center in West
Henrietta, New York, knows the value of an entrepreneur-in-
residence to an incubator manager. He should; he has served
in both roles.

Opened in 1997, Lennox started its EIR program in 2002. After
a successful career in the software industry, Gronwall became
the first EIR for the 50,000-square-foot high-tech incubator,
which hosts from twenty to twenty-five client companies.
He got a free office in exchange for sharing expertise with
incubator clients on a part-time basis.

"Basically, it gave me a place to [use] as home base, and in
exchange for that, I did coaching and mentoring for a day-
and-a-half a week," he recalls.

Gronwall has since become incubator manager at Lennox, but the EIR program continues. It has had from two to five EIRs on board at any given time (it's currently at five). They don't contract to serve for any specified period of time and are not incubator employees; according to Gronwall, the arrangement is "open-ended; it's more of an understanding."

The number of EIRs has fluctuated with available funding; for example, some one-time grants from the U.S. Department of Labor allowed the incubator to get up to five EIRs by offering some the office-space-for-coaching deal and paying others to provide mentoring on a contract basis. "There are two models that work," Gronwall says, with the space-for-expertise swap as the default and the contractor model as a useful adjunct "when you have the budget for it."

Gronwall's basic definition of a good EIR is a serial entrepreneur who's either in retirement and looking to stay active and give back to the community or in the preretirement stage, but still interested in new business opportunities. The second type, he says, may end up focusing on a particular incubator client and even taking an executive position with the company, while the first is more likely to serve multiple clients. "An EIR who's looking for the next CEO assignment is different from an EIR who's coaching and mentoring four or five clients," but both can add value to the incubator, Gronwall says.

He cited a successful Silicon Valley entrepreneur who, having achieved financial independence, wanted to move back to the upstate New York region with his new family but was still seeking new business opportunities. Within six months at the incubator, he was interim CEO of a start-up specializing in microchips for consumer electronics.

Finding qualified EIRs—at least for a high-tech incubator— is not difficult, according to Gronwall. "There's a constant stream of people trying to network to get appointed to opportunities," he says. "You don't have to recruit—there's a constant flow of potential EIR candidates."

EIRs are chosen by the incubator president, and it's Gronwall's job to hook up client firms with the EIRs who can help them with their business challenges. Gronwall says that general business savvy is more important than experience in a particular industry; thus the same EIR can help a software firm or an optics company, even if he or she comes from a different tech field.

Gronwall says having one or more EIRs on staff is definitely a credibility boost. "What I've learned is, when an aspiring client approaches an incubator manager to try and see if this is the right place to put their business, they're evaluating that person," he says. Having an experienced serial entrepreneur at the interview table sends the message that the incubator offers more than low-rent space. "We use EIRs as part of the recruitment process," Gronwall says.

Entrepreneurs-in-Residence
Oregon Technology Business Center, Beaverton, OR
Steve Morris, executive director
www.otbc.org

With a slim staff (currently only an executive director and a receptionist), Oregon Technology Business Center Executive Director Steve Morris makes constant use of entrepreneurs-in-residence as coaches. OTBC has about ten EIRs at any time, and one is assigned as "point" EIR to each firm. The point EIRs (who have a significant relationship with their assigned firms) are responsible for keeping in touch with their clients, providing mentoring, and making connections with others who can help. They also work with OTBC clients on needs identification, using a checklist provided by the incubator to chart progress in each firm's growth. (See the section on Monitoring Client Progress in chapter 6, "Client Entrance and Exit," for more on the checklist.) Other EIRs with domain expertise in human resources and angel investing are called in as needed.

"We like our coaches to touch base with clients every couple of weeks at least, to serve as a sounding board, and make introductions to other coaches and resources as needed," Morris says. Coaches also serve as members of a vetting committee when new applicants are reviewed.

EIRs include current and former CEOs, a longtime management consultant, angel investors, and technology and sales experts, as well as individuals with medical device, software, and open source technology expertise. These individuals don't come primarily from Morris's Rolodex. "Most of them find us through community board interactions and let us know they are interested in volunteering," Morris says.

Each EIR signs an agreement drawn up by Morris that requires him or her to:

- Make a reasonable effort to provide three to four hours of volunteer coaching time each week to OTBC ventures

- Potentially serve as a "point coach" for one or two member ventures (based on mutual agreement of the coach and OTBC)

- Make reasonable efforts to attend OTBC coaches' team-building meetings that are scheduled from time to time to update coaches and give them an opportunity to network

In return, the incubator makes guest offices and meeting rooms available to EIRs. The agreement also permits either party to terminate upon written notice to the other party.

Former EIR Mark Paul, a very experienced management consultant, helped companies orchestrate pricing analyses. "He helped them determine value-based pricing," Morris explains. "Many people screw this up; they guess on pricing or look at their competition. The companies Paul worked with invariably found their pricing was either far too high or far too low." Paul also helped companies with market validation, determining whether, in fact, "If you build it, they will come," Morris explains.

TBC doesn't require its coaches to serve a set term; it mes down to how long they stay interested and have fficient time. Morris schedules a conversation if he rceives that they are "ratcheting down their time. I think important to cull them when they're not contributing," he ys. The OTBC executive director also checks with clients to ake sure the relationships are working.

ice some EIRs also have consulting businesses, Morris akes sure that if a client company desires to develop a ntractual relationship with a coach, he sits down with both rties. "I want to make sure they both understand these are parate things," he says. "I have learned through experience at it's good to separate what coaches do for the incubator a volunteer from having a paid consulting relationship."

Entrepreneurs-in-Residence Program
mpStart, Inc., Cleveland, OH
ris Mather, president, JumpStart TechLift Advisors
vid Nestic, entrepreneur-in-residence
ww.jumpstartinc.org

virtual business incubation program without a physical cility, JumpStart strives to create community wealth and a ore prosperous future" for twenty-one counties in northeast io by accelerating the progress of the region's high-growth, rly-stage companies. Additionally, it works closely with the ents and management of incubators in Akron, Cleveland, rain, Mansfield, and Youngstown; the health-care incubator Enterprise; and other entrepreneurial support organizations ross the region.

mpStart, which began operations in 2004, provides ensive guidance and advice to innovative, high-potential mpanies and invests risk capital in the most promising of ose. It also has a special focus on women and minority trepreneurs.

hough JumpStart offers many educational seminars and ents, publishes newsletters, offers podcasts, and hosts online community, its major programs rely on skilled trepreneurs-in-residence—former entrepreneurs and start- company CEOs who serve clients. Eleven people act as Rs in JumpStart's various programs.

- JumpStart Ventures, a seed investment and technical assistance program, has five EIRs.

- JumpStart TechLift Advisors, which provides guidance and assistance in business development and fundraising to high-growth–potential technology companies, has five EIRs focused on different technologies. JSTLA also incorporates access to regional entrepreneurial specialists and industry experts at five regional incubators.

- JumpStart Inclusion Advisors has one dedicated EIR who works with women- and minority-owned firms that are not eligible for JSV or JSTLA services.

All eleven EIRs have cofounded technology companies, made venture presentations, and raised capital, and they are intimately familiar with the start-up process. Additionally, the EIRs are aware of local, regional, and federal (e.g., SBIR) funding opportunities and are connected to important regional institutions. (For additional information on JumpStart Ventures and JumpStart Inclusion Advisors, see www.jumpstartinc.org.)

Initiated in 2007, JumpStart TechLift Advisors focuses its activities in five technology sectors including:

- Advanced materials
- Biosciences
- Instrumentation, controls, and electronics
- Information and communications technologies
- Advanced energy, power, and propulsion

These sectors represent the strengths of the region's manufacturing communities and research-rich universities and colleges, as well as existing and evolving industry sectors.

JumpStart TechLift Advisors resulted when NorTech, a regional technology advocate devoted to invigorating growth of the northeast Ohio technology economy, applied for and received funding from Ohio's Third Frontier Project Entrepreneurial Signature Program. The Third Frontier is a ten-year, $1.6 billion initiative devoted to expanding high-tech research and technology commercialization and building technology-based businesses, thus generating high-paying jobs.

"We work with companies or entrepreneurs as early as conceptual stages of the business," says Chris Mather, president of JumpStart TechLift Advisors. Eligible companies are located within the twenty-one-county region, have breakthrough technologies, and have less than $10 million in sales. Most clients are prerevenue and are 'burning cash' when they come to JumpStart, Mather says. JumpStart TechLift Advisors prefers companies that are aimed at a $500 million to $1 billion market, are based on technology that is unique and protectable, and project sales of $30 million to $50 million within five to seven years—the "metrics of interest to funders."

The review of companies seeking assistance is based on both science and art. The disciplined, scientific approach considers the firm's management team, its IP or protectable technology, the size of the market, and the desire to grow beyond the present ability of the firm to fund itself (and, therefore, the need to raise capital). The art often lies in gauging the less obvious skills of entrepreneurs, such as whether they have been consistently excellent performers in past experiences (even if they weren't entrepreneurial experiences).

"All the EIRs have been involved with start-ups for a long time, and we can often recognize those entrepreneurs that can make it and those that will struggle," Mather says.

While any entrepreneur can put in an application for assistance, the EIRs typically ask the businesses to forward an executive summary of their business or idea. "Those that can't put together an executive summary or a concise description of their opportunity tend to go back to work on their own at that point. We typically communicate with somebody for an hour at least via phone or e-mail, and then if it looks like we can work with them, we go out and visit them," Mather says.

Most TechLift Advisors maintain active engagement with fifteen to twenty companies at any one time, "meaning that we've engaged with them in the past three weeks or will be engaged with them in the next three weeks," Mather says.

According to the JumpStart Web site, JumpStart TechLift Advisors engages with clients to help them:

- Create and articulate high-growth strategic and operational plans
- Access investment capital
- Plan and achieve key growth milestones
- Connect with potential customers, partners, and investors

Mather notes that the EIRs are equipped to handle multiple functional areas in a start-up situation; some are more experienced in finance, and others in marketing, business development, or other needs.

Work with clients can range from brainstorming on deal structure for license agreements to assessing executive talent needs or mediating disagreements between founders. Dave Nestic, a JSTLA EIR, recently connected a client company that has a unique design for gear boxes for wind turbines to two other clients: one with heavy equipment manufacturing capability and capacity, and another with a potential military application. "In a virtual incubator setting, it's important to have people that can make those connections that strengthen entrepreneurial companies," Nestic notes.

All JumpStart TechLift Advisor EIR activity is intended to better position the start-up for success in pursuing desired objectives, be they equity investment, grants, partnerships, or sales revenue. Mather says that JumpStart TechLift Advisors' major metric is follow-on funding. "At early stages when you put funds into a technology company, the objective is not as much direct job creation as it is to develop the technology and the business to the point where it is attractive to investors or customers," he says. "When it gets to those stages is when the really significant, high-quality job creation occurs. Supporting the very early development stage with funding and guidance is critical to achieve that follow-on funding where big job creation occurs."

From mid-2007, when JumpStart TechLift Advisors was initiated, through 2009, the program engaged with 819 entrepreneurs, which resulted in 461 client relationships. JSTLA clients have raised $26.1 million in follow-on funding from non-JumpStart sources, while all JSTLA clients (including those that were also successful in getting JSV funding) have attracted $48.3 million in total follow-on funding.

Client Advisory Boards

- Give clients an organizational framework for building the business early in the development process
- Provide a sounding board for client management
- Provide an extended Rolodex of additional resources through board members' own networks
- Expand the number of stakeholders interested in supporting the incubator

Client Advisory Boards

During the early stages of development, many new ventures lack an effective board of directors. An incubation program can provide value by helping clients form a temporary advisory or "shadow" board to serve in this function until the establish a formal board of directors.

Advisory boards can be a good, early substitute for a board directors. They are easier to recruit because such boards ha no fiduciary responsibility (see Board of Directors in chapter 1, "Governance") and are better suited for entrepreneurs wh have yet to establish a corporate structure. In addition to a management board, some clients may also benefit from mo specialized boards. For example, a customer advisory board can help with marketing, customer feedback, and customer image. A technical board can offer guidance on product development, market acceptance, or research.

The composition of the advisory board may change over time as the business develops, but for continuity's sake, it's good idea to get a core group of members—say, three or fo individuals—to commit to remain on the board over time.

The very thing that makes a client advisory board effective— the expertise and contacts of its constituent members—can also be a liability, however. Because the best advisory board members will tend to be active in the business community, they may be subject to conflicts of interest. For example, advisory board members may have access to information that they could (intentionally or not) use to the detriment of the client or other companies with whom they work. Advisory board members who are incubator staff members or otherwise involved with the incubation program may find themselves in uncomfortable situations as well. To protect everyone involved (the incubator, the client, and the advisory board members), you should consult with an attorney to dra a conflict-of-interest policy and a nondisclosure agreement that addresses such concerns before you launch an advisor board program for your clients. (For a detailed discussion an examples of conflict-of-interest policies and nondisclosure agreements, see *Put It in Writing* (Athens, Ohio: NBIA Publications, 2002).

Kitchen Cabinet

Virginia Biosciences Development Center, Richmond, VA
David Lohr, executive director
www.vabiotech.com/bioincubator

When David Lohr became head of the Virginia Biosciences Development Center in 2000, he brought everything—including the kitchen cabinet.

This cabinet, however, was an idea he had implemented at BIOSTART in Cincinnati, Ohio. Each client was paired with a targeted group of "eight really, really smart, experienced, senior-level people who had skill sets relevant to the business the entrepreneur is trying to start," Lohr says. It was dubbed the kitchen cabinet, after the nickname given to a group of unofficial advisors to President Andrew Jackson in the nineteenth century.

For Lohr, the kitchen cabinets are the centerpiece of his incubation program. From the moment he meets a prospective client, Lohr starts thinking of the skill sets that start-up will need. He keeps mulling it over through the selection and admission process; by the time a company becomes a VBDC client, Lohr has a pretty good idea of what the company needs.

After the client's first month, Lohr meets with the entrepreneur to discuss the kitchen cabinet and how it will apply to this particular company. Lohr lists what he thinks the company needs; if the client wants something else or something additional, they talk that over, too.

In the following month, Lohr combs his database of contacts to create a list of about twelve people—by name, position, and company—who might be on the kitchen cabinet. (Lohr constantly keeps an eye out for potential kitchen cabinet members to add to his Rolodex.) He then goes over that list with the client to make sure the suggestions are satisfactory, both professionally and personally. "If I have someone on there who's a former brother-in-law, that's a problem," Lohr says. "Or someone they did business with before and it didn't work out well, we don't want that."

Usually, though, the client doesn't know most of the people on the list personally, but knows the names. With the client's approval, Lohr sets out to recruit members of the kitchen cabinet from that list, starting with a potential chair. He keeps working until he has eight people signed up. "With fewer than eight, you don't get critical mass," Lohr says. "More than nine gets unwieldy."

It doesn't take long, because few people turn down the opportunity. "Everybody wants to be cool and have their own little company that they've 'invested' in," Lohr says. "Most people don't have the guts to roll money out, but everyone has the guts to put a little time into it." Once someone has

participated in a cabinet, they're an even easier sell. "They get hooked on it," Lohr says. "It's addicting, because it's fun."

Once Lohr has assembled the cabinet, Lohr's assistant takes over, setting up two initial meetings within a four-week period. The first is a get-acquainted meeting and an opportunity for the client to introduce his or her company. Lohr facilitates the meeting to ensure that cabinet members don't give advice, but only ask questions.

At the second meeting, the company updates the cabinet on developments, and then Lohr facilitates what may be the most important discussion of the process: asking cabinet members what they like about the company, what they don't like, and how the cabinet can help.

After those two meetings, Lohr steps back and lets the cabinet and the client take the lead. His assistant coordinates the meetings. Clients are encouraged to provide some kind of refreshments to show their appreciation for the free mentoring.

The kitchen cabinet model benefits everyone involved, Lohr says. The incubator manager gets free coaching and a bevy of engaged stakeholders, many of whom either have been or will be kitchen cabinet members. The cabinet members get to give back to the business community and, in the case of service providers, a steady pipeline of new customers. And the clients get a network of high-level connections they wouldn't otherwise have met.

"When you bring that many bright people with the right perspectives together, you get great outcomes," Lohr says.

Client Advisory Committee

La Cocina Business Incubator, San Francisco, CA
Caleb Zigas, acting executive director
www.lacocinasf.org

San Francisco's La Cocina cultivates low-income food entrepreneurs as they launch, formalize, and expand their businesses. Contributing to this effort are thirty-five food industry experts who serve as advisors to clients and help with the incubator's educational programming.

The incubator staff of five includes experienced chefs knowledgeable about many facets of the food industry. However, La Cocina leverages its offerings by tapping the thirty-five advisors, who include restaurant owners and consultants, individuals with marketing and branding experience in the luxury food industry, financial professionals, and experts in food testing and specialty food products, among others.

Members of the Client Advisory Committee are expected to work up to three years as La Cocina volunteers if possible, explains Caleb Zigas, acting executive director. "We want to capture their knowledge without significantly impacting their lives," he says.

"You have to deliver what you say that you'll deliver," he explains. "A lot of people get into the food industry because they love food . . . . and the impetus to give back to the industry is very strong."
– Caleb Zigas, acting executive director, La Cocina

Client Advisory Committee members serve in three main capacities:

- Screening client companies and, if necessary, helping them identify and meet benchmarks during a preincubation period that will lead to their acceptance as full clients

- Assist in designing and refining La Cocina's curriculum for training client businesses

- Serving as ad hoc advisors, when needed, to assist a client in solving a problem

Each application from would-be incubator clients is reviewed by a three-person team chosen from the Client Advisory Committee, plus a staff person and someone with financial expertise. The team looks at elements of the applicant's business plan, including market, operations, and production, as well as the applicant's entrepreneurial spirit and level of commitment. They identify holes in client business plans and benchmarks the food entrepreneur needs to meet—and determine whether the prospective client has met the benchmarks.

The period from application to acceptance in the incubator typically is three months. Companies meet with their teams of advisors once in the third month, then take time to address concerns the team might raise. Companies identified as having weak areas may be accepted into a preincubation phase. During this period, these clients will work with incubator staff and their advisory committee team to correct deficiencies so that they can be accepted as full clients. Some technical assistance is also provided to groups of clients in the preincubation phase so they can help each other.

Generally, applicants are given no more than six months to address concerns raised by their advisory teams. If they are admitted to La Cocina as full clients, they work more closely with incubator staff and, when needed, volunteer advisors from the Client Advisory Committee and business experts La Cocina accesses from the San Francisco community. In some cases, the initial team from the advisory committee may continue to work with the clients as they are incubated.

La Cocina also has developed technical assistance protocols and curricula as well as a complementary set of twelve workshops it conducts each year. The workshops are free to clients; nonclients pay a fee. Members of the Client Advisory Committee assist staff in developing, reviewing, and refining La Cocina workshops and technical assistance protocols, and they offer a valuable perspective from the food industry. "We have a small staff, so it is useful to have outside eyes looking in," says Zigas. "The value is that they can say, 'We run a kitchen and what you're doing or saying is wrong.'"

La Cocina doesn't have a system for vetting potential members of the Client Advisory Committee. "We do personal vetting, build personal relationships, and work to keep members invested," he says. How does La Cocina keep advisors invested?

"You have to deliver what you say that you'll deliver," he explains. "A lot of people get into the food industry because they love food . . . . and the impetus to give back to the industry is very strong."

Client Advisory Board
Springfield Business Incubator, Springfield, MA
Deborah King, former executive director
www.stcc.edu/sbi

Deborah King is no longer the director of the Springfield Business Incubator, whose home is in the Scibelli Enterprise Center at Springfield Technical Community College in Massachusetts. But during her time running the center, King relied heavily on the SEC's volunteer advisory board to give intense, hands-on assistance to client companies in the incubator.

Just as important, she expected—in fact, demanded—that the incubator's clients take full advantage of the advisory board's talents.

As a condition of the lease, for example, client companies are required to attend quarterly team development meetings. Each company is matched with an advisor team, carefully chosen to help meet its particular needs. The client sets the agenda and provides financial reports.

We'd tell prospective tenants that we are an incubator," King says. "'If you're not willing to meet with advisors to share your challenges and financial information, then we can't help you.'"

The incubator has relationships with three different boards: the college's board of trustees; the trustees that oversee the 65,000-square-foot technology park of which the SEC is a part; and its own advisory board. The incubator's advisory board has no fiduciary responsibility but does have, inevitably, some input into incubator policy. When King was hired as director, for example, among those she interviewed with was the chairperson of the advisory board.

The board's main purpose, however, is to "work directly with the clients," she says.

The board usually has around twenty-eight members. Criteria for selection include diversity, King says. "We want individuals from all business disciplines: marketing, operations, law, accounting, insurance, and most importantly, entrepreneurs," she says.

When clients talk about what they want from their advisors, she notes, they confirm this priority. "The one thing they would say to us is, 'We want people who have actually been in our shoes, business owners who know what it's like to struggle to meet the weekly payroll,'" she says.

In the mixed-use incubator, which typically has around ten clients, companies run into different problems, but certain needs arise frequently.

"Sales training is a good example," King says. "Some of them don't really like to sell, or don't have a sales process in place." To help such companies, the advisory board has offered sales seminars provided by member Kate Kane, managing director of the Northwest Mutual Financial Network.

Advisory board members may not themselves solicit business from the companies they assist, but if the client makes the approach, a board member's company can enter a business relationship. That incentive to grow companies is one reason that King never had trouble finding volunteers for the board.

"I had qualified people asking to be part of the board," she says.

■■ access to capital

Access to capital is one of the most valuable services an incubation program can offer as part of its comprehensive business assistance services. Helping clients establish a sound management team, develop a viable product or service, identify market potential, and myriad other factors will influence their chances of success—but even if everything else is in place, lack of capital can force the most promising new ventures to stumble. Missed opportunities caused by delays in bringing their product or service to market or an inability to buy materials or hire staff to meet sales demands can take the competitive advantage away from an early-stage venture, particularly in the fast-paced technology marketplace.

Capital can come in the form of equity, debt, grants, or some hybrid of these (each alternative is explored below). Regardless of the source, incubator management must understand—and facilitate access to—all sources that are available within the area by using personal contacts, venture forums, or other vehicles, such as business plan or state and federal grant competitions. In addition, it is important to understand and maintain information on each source (such as the approval process, information requirements, allowable uses of funds, amounts available, and time until the release of funds) and be prepared to assist clients in securing the capital they need at various stages of their development.

Incubation programs can secure equity and debt capital for clients through a number of approaches. Some incubators have been able to establish relationships with traditional equity and debt sources by extending incubator board seats to venture capitalists, angel investors, and bankers. Others have accessed outside resources and state funding programs or taken steps to establish their own in-house capital pools. (Note: Establishing incubator-specific capital programs is time-consuming and complicated and should be undertaken only if the program has sufficient expertise and support to manage them.)

Client Capitalization and Financing

- Provide alternatives to conventional bank lending
- Contribute to a fast-growth venture's chance of success, since few can finance growth solely from revenue generated from sales
- Add to the overall success of client companies and, in turn, the success of an incubation program
- Attract entrepreneurs to the incubation program

While it isn't necessary to have client capitalization and financing services in place before a program opens, they should be established soon so the first clients can get funding at the appropriate stages of their development. The ability to help clients get funding is a strong marketing tool. Best practice programs have found that this capacity has increased both the quantity and quality of deal flow for the incubator.

Equity Capital

Equity is the most important form of capital for new, high-growth ventures. Consequently, an incubator's ability to fully understand and provide access to various stages of equity capital will be essential to the long-term success of programs serving these types of clients.

Early-stage seed capital from an established fund or angel investors is the most likely initial source of equity for companies. Start-up and emerging companies require specific expertise to help them through the application process (e.g., term sheet review, negotiations, and legal review of final agreements). Although acquisition of seed capital is an important first step, it is also important for the incubator to provide access to additional sources that can supply subsequent rounds of equity investment so the business does not stall for lack of funds as it reaches new milestones.

In all cases, incubator staff should consider how best to support the client so that initial and subsequent investors have an exit strategy through stock repurchase, initial public offering, or sale. Subsequent rounds of capital may not be available locally, but best practice programs recognize the need to establish relationships with investors from outside the area that may be interested in investing in their clients.

Sources of equity capital include, but are not limited to:

- The entrepreneurs themselves
- Venture capitalists
- Angel investors
- Corporate investors
- Federal and state equity funds
- In-house incubator venture funds

BEST PRACTICES IN ACTION

Mid-America Angels
Enterprise Center of Johnson County, Lenexa, KS
Joel Wiggins, CEO and president
www.ecjc.com

Lawrence Regional Technology Center, Lawrence, KS
Matt McClorey, president and CEO
www.ltrc.biz

Mid-America Angels is a regional network of angel investors dedicated to identifying and funding the most promising start-up business opportunities in the Kansas City area. Founded in 2006 by the Enterprise Center of Johnson County and the Lawrence Regional Technology Center, the fund has 102 members who have invested almost $3.8 million in sixteen companies. The fund's investments range from $250,000 to $2 million.

The fund was born when Joel Wiggins, ECJC CEO and president, and Matt McClorey, president of LRTC, attended a 2005 event on angel investing sponsored by the Ewing Marion Kauffman Foundation. Realizing that there were no angel investment organizations in eastern Kansas, the two decided to put one together. Drawing on various sources—the Kauffman Foundation, former investors in a defunct angel group, the Kansas City Business Journal, and so on—Wiggins and McClorey amassed a list of 425 potential investors. Of those, twenty-four became the founding investors.

The two incubators share administrative and operational duties for the fund. "We run the Web site, we source the companies, we interview the companies, we select the companies that are going to present to the angels, and we help them prepare for that presentation," Wiggins says. "We run all the logistics of the companies' interactions with the angels." The incubators also perform due diligence on companies selected for investment and may even lead negotiations of the terms and conditions of the deal.

Each angel pays $1,000 annually to be part of the network, which helps cover the costs of running the fund, Wiggins says. The incubators pay for Wiggins's and McClorey's time, as well as that of Rick Vaughn, ECJC's vice president for business development, who once worked in mergers and acquisitions for Hallmark. About half of Vaughn's time is devoted to MAA, Wiggins says.

Although deals can be completed in as little as forty-five days, most require about ninety days, Wiggins says. It's a grueling process, not only for the incubators, but also for the companies. Of 367 companies that had applied to the network by early 2010, only 97—just 26 percent—were asked to present their companies to the angels.

he angels meet monthly, usually with two or three ompanies ready to present. (The angels receive PowerPoint resentations and biographies of the company principals head of time.) Each presentation lasts about fifteen minutes. any of the twelve to twenty angels at the meeting express nterest in the company, Wiggins, McClorey, and Vaughn et up a separate meeting between the angels and the ntrepreneurs to further discuss the opportunity. At least three f the angels have to agree to a tentative deal for the process o continue. (The individual angel investors can pick and hoose their opportunities; not all one hundred investors put heir money into a company at the same time.)

Once three angels have stepped up as potential investors, 's time for due diligence. "We'll work with companies after here's real interest," Wiggins says, saving time in research hat might be wasted if the angels choose not to proceed.

Of the ninety-seven companies that have presented to the ngels, only twenty-seven had gone to due diligence as of his writing. But by that point in the process, the odds of unding are considerably better: Sixteen of those twenty-even were funded. And of those sixteen, six have been pproved for second rounds of funding. MAA experienced its rst exit in November 2009, when an ECJC graduate that was unded in 2007 sold for "single-digit millions," Wiggins says, dding, "They stayed intact and are staying local." None of he funded companies has failed or closed as of this writing.

Even better, MAA has a spin-off. The Kansas Women's Business Center (which is located in the ECJC facility) developed its own angel group from among MAA investors. ts thirty-four members, all women, invest in high-end companies led by women; at this writing, they had invested in hree companies.

Creative Venture Capital Matching
Ben Franklin TechVentures, Bethlehem, PA
Wayne Barz, manager of entrepreneurial services
www.bftechventures.org

From dot-coms to green technologies, venture investment is subject to trends. Ben Franklin TechVentures capitalizes on hat fact to create annual venture capital events for its clients hat reflect trends in popular culture.

n 2005, the incubator offered a venture capital speed-dating event in which sixteen of its clients made five-minute pitches o individual investors. A gong sounded when it was time for each client to move to the next investor. Each company got to pitch to at least six investors, and the audience of economic developers, BFTV service providers, and other BFTV clients got to listen in and mingle.

"Just from that one night, there had to be hundreds of ntroductions, given the number of companies and the number of VCs present," says Wayne Barz, BFTV's manager of entrepreneurial services.

For the last several years, the event has followed the American Idol format. At Lehigh Valley Venture Idol, a group of BFTV clients (preselected and coached on their presentations by BFTV staff) makes eight-minute pitches to a panel of four area venture capitalists. The panel gives feedback on the pitch. The whole process takes place before an audience of economic developers, service providers, mentors, clients, and other investors who eventually vote on the best company. "Half of the audience has no idea of the components to build a company, so they vote for what they like," Barz says. The winning company receives $5,000.

The event is held on the campus of Lehigh University, where the incubator is located. The cost of the event (including food) and the prize money is underwritten by twelve to fifteen corporate sponsors, who pay $500 each. The audience of two hundred or more pays $25 per person.

Planning doesn't take long: the incubator has a deep bench of venture capital contacts thanks to its proximity to Philadelphia and a dedicated effort to recruit VCs as partners (see chapter 2's section on Service Provider Network for details). Most of the staff's involvement, Barz says, is in coaching the companies.

The work is well worth it, he says. "It's important for us to get companies in front of VCs," he says. "Most of our companies need venture capital, and it's been a great awareness-raiser for us among VCs."

Nova Scotia First Fund and HPI Microfund
Innovacorp, Halifax, Nova Scotia, Canada
Dan MacDonald, former president and CEO
www.innovacorp.ca

Capital is the fuel for the knowledge economy, yet Canadian knowledge-based businesses garner less than half the amount of capital invested in similar U.S. ventures. The situation is even worse in Atlantic provinces, such as Nova Scotia: Atlantic Canadian investment rounds are half the Canadian average.

To bridge the gap in private sector venture capital funds, Innovacorp—a program of Nova Scotia Economic Development—manages several investment funds to help provincial companies grow and succeed.

The first vehicle was the Nova Scotia First Fund, established by the provincial government in 1989. Since then, it has invested over C$30 million in Nova Scotia knowledge-based businesses under Innovacorp's management. One of Innovacorp's key objectives is to work with the province of Nova Scotia to ensure the fund's long-term viability and capitalization.

NSFF considers investments in the range of C$100,000 to C$3 million. The fund's goal is to achieve a ratio of 1:3; in other words, for every dollar invested by NSFF, $3 would be invested by strategic investors, financial institutions, and venture capital funds. In 2008–9, NSFF leveraged over C$32 million of invested capital in syndication with other investors.

Innovacorp performs due diligence, offers mentoring and incubation services (if appropriate), and goes with the company to meet with syndicate investors. Investment decisions are made by an independent, twelve-person board. Innovacorp manages the investments but does not receive any additional compensation for providing services.

In 2004, Innovacorp introduced the HPI Microfund, which makes investments of less than C$250,000 in high-potential early-stage companies. This fund recognized the need for a continuum of capital throughout the life of a business. Innovacorp staff selects the portfolio companies and consummates the investments.

NSFF has invested C$101.3 million from inception through FY2008–9, an increase of 20 percent over FY2005–6. About 20 percent of Innovacorp's client companies have received NSFF funding. Overall, the amount of venture capital financing received by Nova Scotia companies has risen from C$7 million in 2004 to C$17 million in 2008. Peak investment was C$24 million in 2006.

Debt Capital

Debt capital sources include both conventional lending institutions and nonconventional lenders. Conventional lenders such as banks are less likely to lend money to start-ups and early-stage clients, while leasing companies may be willing to take the risk with specific types of equipment purchases (e.g., copy machines and production equipment), although at a higher cost to the business.

Nonconventional lenders such as nonprofit and government-operated community-based lending programs and venture leasing may be better suited to the needs of incubator clients, since many are established to leverage equity investments or focused on broader economic activity in a specific geographic area. These programs vary in size and complexity; some have specific requirements related to job creation, type of activity

funded, and loan size. Clients supported by a nonconventional source of debt financing can use it as a stepping stone to build their businesses and establish credit histories that will make them more attractive to conventional lenders.

In addition to these sources, there are also U.S. government loan guarantee programs. For example, debt funding is available through participating lenders in the U.S. Small Business Administration's 7(a) Loan Program and Capital Access Programs (CAP), which guarantee a portion of the loan as a way to encourage conventional bank lenders to make loans with slightly higher risks. Program lending criteria, allowable uses, and acceptable levels of risk will vary by source and require individuals with sufficient expertise to determine the best program(s) to meet client needs and assist with the application process.

Because of limitations imposed by conventional lenders or other restrictions of nonconventional lenders, some incubators have established focused lending programs that are available only to their clients. These programs have modified typical lending criteria by shortening the required time in business, the level of collateral needed to secure the loan, the term or length of time for repayment, and the interest rate charged. In addition, these programs have provided different lending products such as contract or purchase order financing (e.g., financing secured by revenues to be generated from an identified contract or purchase order) as a means of supporting early-stage ventures.

Regardless of the source, debt obligations can be tricky for a start-up or early-stage venture because of the need to repay the obligation. As a result, it is be important to provide a sufficient level of postloan support to ensure the clients are generating and managing their cash flows to meet these obligations.

> "One of the keys to its success is that we operate it just like a bank. We're very serious and formal about it"
>
> – Christina Reddin, executive director, Business Incubator Center

BEST PRACTICES IN ACTION

In-House Loan Fund
Business Incubator Center, Grand Junction, CO
Christina Reddin, executive director
www.gjincubator.org

The Business Incubator Center in Grand Junction, Colorado, administers a business loan fund under a grant from the state's Office of Economic Development and International Trade. Available since the mid-1980s, the fund is one of fifteen statewide. Since its inception, BIC's fund has loaned more than $13 million to more than 250 Mesa County businesses, of which 95 percent are still open. About 20 percent of those loans are made to companies while they are BIC clients.

"One of the keys to its success is that we operate it just like a bank," says Executive Director Christina Reddin. "We're very serious and formal about it."

A loan fund committee comprising bankers, CPAs, and entrepreneurs reviews and evaluates every loan application. Applicants must provide a business plan; financial statements and tax returns from the past three years for the business and its investors; a three-year cash flow projection; and schedules of collateral, among other documents. The owner must retain at least a 20 percent equity stake in the company.

Loans range from $8,000 to $500,000 and may be used as operating capital, to fund building improvements, or to buy equipment, real estate, or inventory. The repayment period is three to seven years, and interest rates range from prime to prime plus four percent, depending on risk.

BIC earns interest on the unused portion of the fund, as well as the interest from loan payments and loan fees. The salary of the full-time BIC staff member who runs the fund is underwritten by the state.

The fund is especially vital, says Reddin, because companies in her region don't generally have access to venture capital. "Most growth businesses here are debt-financed," she says.

Most loans are made to fill gaps between the firm's need and what a commercial bank will lend to that company. Although the fund has been perennially popular, it sees increasing demand when the economy is slow. For example, in the mid-2000s, many entrepreneurs could tap home equity loans or other credit to bootstrap their businesses. As credit has tightened, though, BIC has seen an increase in loan applications.

"When credit was pretty loose, we generally saw people who didn't have personal or business collateral to get a loan, even in a fairly favorable credit environment," Reddin says. "Now we're also seeing people with a healthier credit rating and more collateral who still can't get funding from the banks."

BIC maintains its relationships with local banks to ensure that they refer customers who need additional funding to the loan fund. "It's all about our relationships with the banks and making sure that when they run into something they're not interested in, they refer those people to us," Reddin says.

■■ coaching for investor presentations

When clients are ready to make a pitch to investors, incubator staff can give them a leg up on the competition by helping them perfect the presentation that investors will see. However, the initial investor presentation and elevator pitch—most often a hard-hitting, pithy PowerPoint—is only the show that grabs the investor's attention. The client must have a solid business proposal and the skills to explain its potential clearly and compellingly.

BEST PRACTICES IN ACTION

Investment Readiness Assessment
Emerging Technology Centers, Baltimore, MD
Ann Lansinger, president
www.etcbaltimore.com

All growth-focused entrepreneurs want investment capital. But are they ready to get it? To make sure the answer to the second question is "yes," the Emerging Technology Centers in Baltimore, Maryland, requires its clients to complete a four-step Investment Readiness Assessment before introducing them to angel and venture investors.

The first step is a self-assessment in which clients use a scale of 1 to 5 to rate their performance in management, market, technology, traction, and business model. An accompanying sheet lists the criteria needed to achieve a given rating level for each item. Under traction, for example, clients are asked to rate whether their product or service is ready to sell. If the product or service is still just a concept, the client scores 1 point. Clients that are using or testing presale versions can give themselves 4 points. Those with something ready to sell get 5 points. In the second step, clients total their scores to see how many points they earn out of a possible 100 for all five areas.

In step three, clients must review their scores in each area and consider whether their venture is truly investment-ready. "In a comparison of an investment in your business against the model investment opportunity, no score guarantees an investment," the evaluation instructions read. "A score of less than 3 for any individual criterion indicates a weakness in the investment opportunity, which requires further consideration." The client also must consider each area individually; scoring well in management but poorly in market doesn't indicate readiness.

Finally, the assessment directs clients back to their individual venture coach, who also has completed the assessment on the company. The clients and their coaches compare their assessments to see where they agreed, where they disagreed, and how to address any issues revealed in the assessment.

The process ensures that ETC is bringing only the most viable and attractive companies to the attention of its network of investors. And it works: Using this process, eighty-four ETC clients received $2.1 million in funding between 1999 and 2009.

CapVenture
Advanced Technology Development Center, Atlanta, GA
Charles Ross, general manager
David Sung, venture catalyst
www.atdc.org

Every start-up business needs money. But as venture capitalists have moved away from seed-stage investing toward later-stage companies—and as investment capital in general has become scarce in a weak economy—getting money for a new venture has become a greater challenge than ever.

Since 2006, the Advanced Technology Development Center in Atlanta, Georgia, has been trying to even the odds for some promising companies through its CapVenture program. Each summer, a carefully screened group of about thirty entrepreneurs undergoes a five-week intensive course in business capital and how to position a company to get it.

Applicants submit an executive summary of their business or idea; a group of ATDC staff reviews the applications to decide which would benefit most from participation.

"We look for technology companies that have the most potential to move the needle in learning and raising capital," says David Sung, an ATDC venture catalyst who took over the CapVenture program in 2009.

Once accepted, the CapVenture companies are matched with individual coaches—current or former entrepreneurs themselves—who donate their time to work side-by-side with the entrepreneur throughout the five-week curriculum of lectures and workshops. Those coaches give participants the benefit of their experience, combining classroom education with real-world smarts. (CapVenture participants also are automatically accepted as ATDC client companies.)

The program culminates in a graduation celebration that features three-minute pitch presentations from each participating company. The idea is not to get money then and there, but rather to practice the presentation and get feedback. "Honing your story down to three minutes and no more than six to eight slides is greatly helpful," Sung says. "At the end of the day, lots of these early-stage companies may be working on something fantastic, but they don't know how to tell that story."

Past classes have used their CapVenture training well: Sung estimates that about one-third of each previous class has gone on to raise real money. He's not sure how well the 2009 class will do, but he knows they will be able to capitalize on any opportunities that come their way.

"We're not only helping these companies [get capital], but also educating them about the kinds of capital they can raise," he says.

Venture Roundtable
San Diego CONNECT, San Diego, CA
Camille Sobrian, chief operating officer
www.connect.org

San Diego CONNECT puts significant effort into connecting high-quality start-ups to formal venture capitalists and angel investors and to raising San Diego's profile among VCs as a source of innovative technology deal flow opportunities.

CONNECT works with these groups of investors via its Venture Roundtable series. It hosts four Venture Roundtables a year, each focused on a different area: life sciences, clean technology, high technology, and software and Web 2.0 (new in 2009). Each roundtable features six or more prescreened companies. Entrepreneurs-in-residence sit on screening committees and review applications; industry experts sit on judging panels to select companies that will be presented to potential funders. Formal venture capitalists and angels review the finalists in a half-day program from 10 a.m. to 2 p.m., a time frame that allows out-of-towners to attend easily. Only accredited capital providers may attend, and these may include fifteen to twenty-five VCs at each roundtable.

Entrepreneurs' applications must include an executive summary. A maximum twenty-slide PowerPoint presentation and a spreadsheet providing sales projections for three to five years are optional. Information and examples are available at www.connect.org/programs/venture-roundtable/.

The summary is intended to tell potential investors why this company has a market advantage. In addition to a brief description of the business, entrepreneurs are asked to include information on:

- The management team and the executive team's experience

- The product itself, including its technical readiness and how it outstrips any competition

- The type, size, and growth potential of the product's market niche

- The target market and how the company will reach prospective customers

- The company's core competency or competitive advantage

- Capital efficiency, or how investors will make money

- The company's financial plan and financing strategy, including capital needed and company valuation preinvestment

A screening committee of EIRs ranks applicants on both quantitative and qualitative criteria. A dry run presented before a panel of industry judges narrows the list to the top six presenters; then a one-hour orientation with an experienced entrepreneur-in-residence and sector experts is held prior to the formal Venture Roundtable, which includes a networking luncheon following the presentations.

In addition, CONNECT provides program support for a formal angel capital network, San Diego Tech Coast Angels. The angels make investments of $50,000 to $500,000 and may play a hands-on role in advising their investees. Tech Coast Angels includes five regional networks in San Diego, Orange County, Los Angeles, Westlake Village/Santa Barbara, and the Inland Empire.

TCA offers a full-day seminar on angel investing licensed from the Ewing Marion Kauffman Foundation. The session compares angels with VCs and addresses the myths about angel funding; whether angel investing is the right strategy for a company; angel portfolio strategy; due diligence; structuring the deal; valuation; and the postinvestment relationship.

The angel network features one quick-pitch session each year during which applicant companies make two-minute elevator pitches. Fifteen finalists are chosen from among the applicants present. The event is preceded by a reception and after awards are announced, is followed by dessert and coffee. Attendance is free to TCA members, and a fee is asked of nonmembers. Admission is open to investors, TCA members and potential members, and anyone who is interested in learning about angel investing, including entrepreneurs. However, the quick-pitch sessions are not open to the public.

Recognizing that the number of formal venture capital deals slid during the economic turmoil of late 2008 and 2009, CONNECT also boosted its work with high-net-worth angel investors, debuting a new program called Deal Network, in which "scrubbed" (vetted and mentored) companies are put before individual investors. "Individual investors were continuing to invest and looking for a place to put their money after the capital markets disintegrated," CONNECT Chief Operating Officer Camille Sobrian explains.

CONNECT organizes Deal Network meetings every six weeks. The meetings are open to investors who aren't looking for the commitment required by Tech Coast Angels. During the first six months of 2009, twenty-two investors saw sixteen companies, resulting in five investments and others in the offing. "We anticipate at least half of them will get investments," Sobrian explains, "with perhaps all achieving investments by the end of the year through the VC Roundtable, Deal Network, and individual introductions."

Presentations are no more than three to four minutes, after which the presenters are expected to "ask for the money," says Sobrian. Presenters must have been Most Innovative New Product award winners, Springboard graduates, or Venture Roundtable presenters. Events are by invitation only. More information on Deal Network is available at www.connect.org/programs/deal-network/.

About seventy companies apply for each CONNECT-related investment program, and around 420 apply for the Venture Roundtable, the Deal Network, and Tech Coast Angels. Six or more prescreened companies are chosen to participate in each Venture Roundtable, and approximately fifteen finalists present at TCA Quick Pitches; sixteen companies presented at Deal Network meetings during the first six months of 2009, or four per event. About twenty to thirty VCs participate in each Venture Roundtable, and twenty-two investors participated in Deal Network meetings during the first six months of 2009. The number of companies that receive funding varies from year to year.

Affiliate Programs

- Extend incubator services to home-based or other nonresident client companies
- Help incubator management focus on the value of services versus the value of the building
- Provide an additional revenue stream to the incubator
- Raise the incubator's profile in the larger business community
- Create a pipeline of qualified ventures that may need incubation space as they grow and gain traction

■■ affiliate programs

Many incubators offer services to affiliate clients, who pay fees to use the incubator's services and participate in its activities without taking up space in the incubation facility. Commonly referred to as an affiliate program, this service is used by many incubators to:

- Groom clients who aren't quite ready for admission to the full incubation program
- Reach out to clients who meet incubator eligibility criteria but already have premises elsewhere
- Serve clients when the incubator is fully occupied
- Ease graduates' transition to life outside the incubator

Affiliate programs can meet the needs of the marketplace while generating additional revenue. Program pricing varies around the world; the price depends on the market and the perceived value of the services being offered. As with any service, it is necessary to weigh the actual cost of supporting affiliates against the revenue and other benefits generated to determine the viability of such a program.

BEST PRACTICES IN ACTION

Gaining Affiliates through Contracts
Louisiana Business & Technology Center, Baton Rouge, LA
Charles D'Agostino, executive director
www.bus.lsu.edu/lbtc

The Louisiana Business & Technology Center has about three hundred affiliate clients—a number Executive Director Charles D'Agostino is quick to credit not to his incubator per se, but to its business model. In addition to running an incubation facility on the campus of Louisiana State University, LBTC manages the local Small Business Development Center and administers the Small Business Innovation Research program that gives entrepreneurs federal funds to test the feasibility of intellectual property for federal agencies—in this case, the NASA Stennis Space Center.

AFFILIATE PROGRAM OR VIRTUAL INCUBATION?

Affiliate programs are sometimes referred to as "virtual incubation." The term first gained popularity in the late 1990s and early 2000s, when a number of Web-based incubation programs sprang up. The idea was to provide incubation services via an online interface. Those types of incubation programs remain rare, although many incubators use social networking tools such as Facebook, Twitter, and YouTube to deliver services electronically. In general, however, NBIA recognizes that many in the incubation industry use "affiliate program" and "virtual incubation" interchangeably.

"My incubator is much more far-reaching than the typical incubator," D'Agostino admits. (For more on LBTC's business model, see chapter 3, "Finances.")

D'Agostino uses these programs as a kind of preincubation for prospective in-house clients, giving those entrepreneurs a glimpse of the services they could receive as LBTC facility residents. For example, entrepreneurs who take an SBDC class on writing a business plan may meet with some of the MBA students who help LBTC clients with their business plans (see chapter 2, "Staffing"). Entrepreneurs who successfully complete the SBIR application process also come to realize the value of LBTC membership.

"It's kind of a farm system—it's how I grow my clients," D'Agostino says. He estimates that more than a quarter of his current in-house clients started out as SBDC customers or SBIR applicants.

A Tiered Affiliate Program
Enterprise Center of Johnson County, Lenexa, KS
Joel Wiggins, president and CEO
www.ecjc.com

The Enterprise Center of Johnson County offers a tiered arrangement for affiliate clients with a corresponding schedule of available services and perks.

At the most basic level, clients pay $100 a month to maintain a mailing address and fax number at the ECJC facility. They also can use the copier, postage meter, break room, and wireless Internet access at the incubator; use of the conference room, administrative support, and business assistance services cost extra.

For $50 more a month, clients can maintain a virtual office at the incubator, including access to the conference rooms and a shared office space, as well as voice mail and personalized telephone answering.

Those choosing the Virtual Office Plus or Virtual Office Deluxe pay $225 or $325 per month, respectively; for the additional money, they get all of the services available to Mail Box or Virtual Office affiliates, plus the use of a private office for sixteen (VOP) or forty (VOD) hours per month.

No matter which option they choose, affiliates are charged a
75 setup fee and a security deposit equal to one month's fees.

The Mail Box option is popular with ECJC companies that
are transitioning to their own space, says Joel Wiggins, the
incubator's president and CEO. The other choices are good
for businesses that aren't quite ready to become full-fledged
clients. "They aren't ready to take the plunge for a real office,
but they want to take advantage of the things going on here,"
Wiggins says. "When they get funded or are a little more
secure, they come in as clients."

Revamping an Affiliate Program
Nussbaum Center for Entrepreneurship, Greensboro, NC
Sam Funchess, president and CEO
www.nussbaumcfe.com

While some incubators approach affiliate programs as
"incubation lite," charging less for affiliates than in-house
clients, the Nussbaum Center for Entrepreneurship takes
the opposite tack. Members of its Incubator without Walls
program pay up to twice as much as on-site clients.

The idea, Funchess says, is to weed out those who aren't
serious about using Nussbaum services. "We used to charge
90 a quarter," he says. "We found that people would pay for
one or two quarters and never come back in, never pay us
again. It became a more laborious project than we wanted to
expend energy on for the return we received."

So in 2009, Funchess revamped the IWOW program, adding
services and increasing the price tag accordingly. IWOW
companies pay $1,200 a year just to enter the program
(on-site clients pay $600 a year). Other services—such as
business counseling, market research and analysis, and
accounting help—are priced à la carte at rates that are $100
to $200 higher than those charged for on-site clients. Use of
the conference room is free, and IWOW clients can meet with
Nussbaum staff or service providers for a certain number of
hours per quarter at no charge.

The amended program also reflected new realities in
Nussbaum's market. The old IWOW also had been a de facto
waiting list for suitable companies wanting to enter Nussbaum
but were unable to because all the offices were full. But in
2001, the incubator doubled its space from 40,000 square
feet to 80,000 square feet. Suddenly, what had been a fairly
lengthy waiting list dropped to nothing.

With more space and a revamped IWOW, Funchess can target
companies that don't fit into his incubator's target market of
high-growth companies in industries such as transportation
and logistics, aviation, advanced materials, nanotechnology,
and biotechnology. "There are tons of lifestyle businesses
or even high-growth companies that fall outside our target,"
Funchess says. "They still need assistance, and we can offer
it at a reasonably affordable price point."

Postincubation Services

- Help retain graduates in the community
- Offer an additional revenue stream
- Enhance graduates' long-term viability

■■ postincubation services

Most postincubation programs focus on retaining graduate
companies and jobs in an incubator's community and/or
helping graduate companies survive and grow once they're
on their own. These programs can take the form of continuing
services targeted to graduates or an incubator-owned or
managed facility that's made available to graduates.

BEST PRACTICES IN ACTION

Creating Graduate Space
Ben Franklin TechVentures, Bethlehem, PA
Wayne Barz, manager of entrepreneurial services
www.bftechventures.org

By the early 1990s, the Ben Franklin Business Incubator
Center (now Ben Franklin TechVentures) had been operating
for a decade and was turning out graduate companies. The
trouble was, those graduates didn't always remain in the city of
Bethlehem, Pennsylvania, but located elsewhere in the region.

To keep incubator graduates in the city limits (and on city tax
rolls), the incubator partnered with the Bethlehem Economic
Development Corporation, the Lehigh Valley Economic
Development Corporation, and Lehigh Valley Industrial
Park to secure financing for two postincubator facilities.
Each partner contributed to a pool of money that was used
as collateral for a construction loan. The four partners
maintained individual equity stakes in the property, which
included a first building that opened in 1993 and a second
that opened in 2000.

The investment paid off in spades. The first building, called
Beth Tech 1, originally housed two incubator graduates plus
one local company. The second, called (surprise!) Beth Tech
2, originally was occupied by three incubator graduates.

In each case, one of the companies in the buildings grew
spectacularly and needed more space. In the case of Beth
Tech 1, IQE (now the world's largest independent producer of
semiconductor wafers) "squeezed out the other companies
and eventually bought the building," says Wayne Barz, BFTV's
manager of entrepreneurial services. The same pattern
developed in Beth Tech 2 with OraSure, a leading developer
of health-care diagnostic tests. In fact, OraSure eventually
bought two adjacent plots of land and constructed a facility
on one of them, leaving the other for future development.

The partnership not only kept high-potential companies
in the area but also yielded a literal payoff. When IQE and
OraSure purchased their buildings, the partners made a tidy

profit on the sales. BFTV used its share to buy and renovate a new 62,000-square-foot incubator facility that opened in 2007. The other partners loaned their proceeds to help in that venture, thus plowing their investments back into the incubator program.

Meanwhile, the area where Beth Tech 1 and Beth Tech 2 were built has become a hotbed of development. Back in 1993, it was a blighted area left empty by the closure of Bethlehem Steel factories in 1991. Today, Barz says, the area is undergoing a renaissance with trendy restaurants and apartments with "really cool architecture."

"It's really worked out beautifully, what's happened there," he says.

Clients for Life
Louisiana Business & Technology Center, Baton Rouge, LA
Charles D'Agostino, executive director
www.bus.lsu.edu/lbtc

Every year, the Louisiana Business & Technology Center holds a big graduation ceremony, complete with speeches. And the message of Executive Director Charles D'Agostino's speech is always the same: "You are clients for life."

"We consider our graduates to be affiliates of LBTC," he says.

Those aren't empty words. D'Agostino makes sure that all graduates know they can continue to call on him and his staff for advice and guidance as needed. "The first year, we see a lot of them," he says. "I get calls from some of them monthly saying, 'I need help doing this.'" As time goes on, the calls come less frequently, but they still come. D'Agostino has had companies that were out of the incubator for more than ten years call him for advice on a new product line or ask for an introduction. Recent graduates also are frequent participants in LBTC seminars and workshops.

"Recent graduates especially feel the need to be part of the program and to still need our help," D'Agostino says.

There is no charge for those services. LBTC's business model, which derives 85 percent of revenues from government and NGO contracts, allows D'Agostino to handle simple calls and such for free. However, if a graduate wants more extensive help, that's a different story. One graduate asked for an extensive analysis of its operations that required input from a Louisiana State University faculty member, several graduate students, and some LBTC staff. "They were willing to pay because it was above and beyond the call of duty," D'Agostino says.

LBTC takes such strong measures not only out of a feeling of responsibility toward its graduates but also because it wants something back. Every year, D'Agostino contacts every graduate to collect economic impact information for his annual report to stakeholders. Maintaining a helpful and friendly relationship with graduates makes them more willing to participate in the survey, D'Agostino says.

In addition, a network of happy and successful graduates is a source of potential support for LBTC. D'Agostino has had graduates on his board of directors, and many sign on to sponsor the incubator's programs and events. "By staying close to the ones that have been successful, we open up sponsorship and funding opportunities for the incubator," he says.

"By staying close to graduates that have been successful, we open up sponsorship and funding opportunities for the incubator."

– Charles D'Agostino, executive director, Louisiana Business & Technology Center

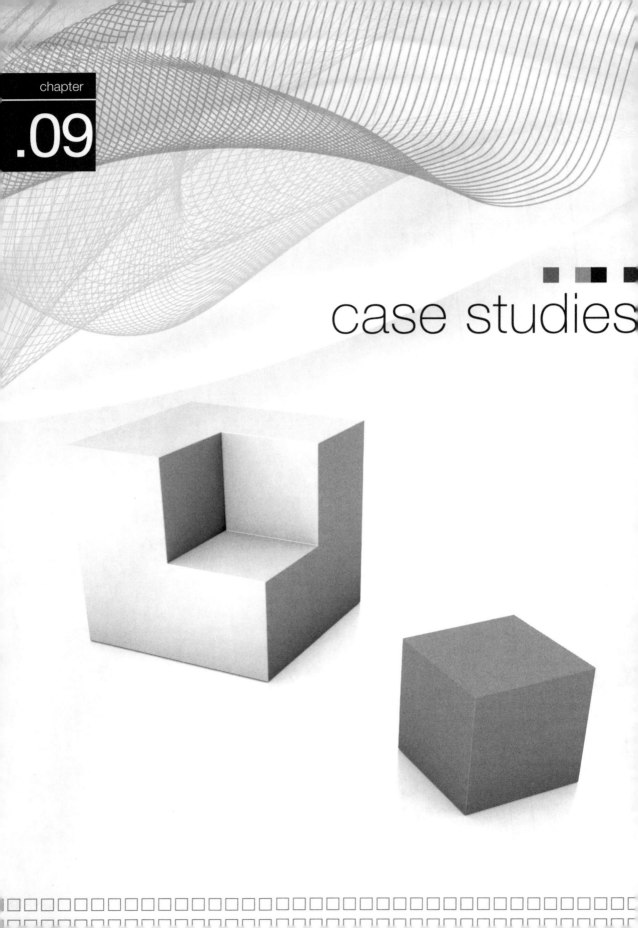

case studies

■ the innovation depot

Birmingham, Alabama
Susan Matlock, president and CEO
www.innovationdepot.net

The Innovation Depot opened in 2007 to become the new home of two incubation programs that combined operations: the Entrepreneurial Center, a longtime Birmingham incubator that originated in 1987 as the Birmingham Business Assistance Network, and the University of Alabama at Birmingham's Office for the Advancement of Developing Industries. Though both programs had operated under the Entrepreneurial Center's management since 2001, the incubator facilities were physically separated by more than ten miles until Susan Matlock, president and CEO of the Innovation Depot, brought them together. The programs now reside in a former Sears store that had stood vacant for twenty years. The facility, which is adjacent to Birmingham's downtown core and just three blocks from the UAB campus, has won regional and national architectural recognition.

Merging the two programs in one facility reduced operating costs and assisted in leveraging public and private assets. Because it sited the incubator next to the UAB campus, clients came within easy reach of research laboratories, researchers and equipment, and the community's large health science complexes. The merger placed entrepreneurs and researchers cheek by jowl with the Birmingham business community and experienced mentors, company growers, and serial entrepreneurs.

The Innovation Depot serves primarily technology clients and specializes in biotechnology and life sciences, engineering technologies, IT and software, and business services. According to incubator management, more than 90 percent of companies emerging from UAB have located in the incubator. Industry associations such as the Birmingham Business Resource Center, the Alabama Biotechnology Association, the Birmingham Venture Club, and TechBirmingham also are headquartered in the Innovation Depot and contribute to making the incubator well-known in the community and state.

At 140,000 square feet, the renovation was designed to provide appropriate space for its clients and to encourage networking. It features large plate glass windows in meeting rooms and staff offices, wide open spaces between the building's two floors, a large atrium, and the Culinard Café, where community residents, start-up companies, and staff gather. A "Main Street" corridor extends from the parking lot entry through the "Town Center" to administrative offices and conference rooms. Centralized offices, training rooms, break rooms, a copy center, and the café surround the two-story, sky-lit "Town Center." A courtyard green space with a boules court and a rooftop deck with tables and chairs also attract client company staff for informal meetings.

The premises are well-lit, with twenty-four–hour security and access to shared equipment, including microscopes, ultracentrifuges, autoclaves, and other equipment needed by life science start-ups.

While the Innovation Depot's facility is spectacular, management is the key to its success. In addition to a strong board of directors, Matlock possesses the interpersonal, technical, and managerial skills to bring together diverse stakeholders to work toward a common vision. Matlock's resume reads like a listing in *Who's Who in Corporate America*, showing that leaders of highly successful incubators could just as easily be the CEOs of major corporations. She also has hired highly qualified and effective staff. Current staff include the president and CEO, chief financial officer, chief operating officer, director of IT services, director of facility operations, and administrative staff. The incubator's chief operating officer, Devon Laney, previously was an analyst with Accenture LLP in Atlanta, Georgia, where he worked on a broad range of marketing, IT, and strategic organizational projects with various Fortune 500 companies. All senior staff are engaged and supportive of the incubator's mission of creating community wealth and commercializing new technologies through entrepreneurship. Altogether, the Innovation Depot employs seven staff members.

The original UAB incubator, OADI, was an office of the university, managed and staffed by university employees. When the university contracted with the Entrepreneurial Center's Matlock to manage OADI, she was able to hire new staff with superior private sector experience, benefiting both incubation programs. Also, because she had worked in the industry since 1987, she brought a rare understanding and focus to Birmingham business incubation, shepherding the incubation program through increasingly larger facilities with expanded programming until it evolved into the community showplace and sophisticated institution it is today. Her vision, determination, and skills all contributed to current success.

A key strategy of the Innovation Depot has been to ensure that all senior-level staff also serve on the governing or advisory boards of a variety of business, technology, and community organizations to assist in integrating the Innovation Depot into the fabric of the region. This broad-based engagement makes a significant difference in terms of community integration and attracting Innovation Depot client companies, board members, and stakeholders, and it brings credibility to the program.

The Innovation Depot has a large board of directors (thirty members in 2009) representing a broad cross section of its stakeholders, including financial supporters, UAB, the city of Birmingham, the investment community, utility companies, and private corporations and foundations. Board members include organization CEOs and senior-level vice presidents. The board was structured strategically to include prominent individuals from both the public and private sectors with a primary focus on increasing the value to clients and the incubator (i.e., sustaining its role in the broader economy and validating stakeholder investments). Board members have assisted the incubator in gaining wider community support and raising $11 million of the $18 million required to renovate the new incubator structure. Additionally, they mentor clients and assist them by providing further contacts within their own networks.

The Innovation Depot is a partnership with UAB, in which the president of the UAB Research Foundation also is on the board. The incubator works with the foundation to identify technologies for commercialization and to place start-ups based on UAB research in the incubator facility and provide them with ongoing support. Examples of successful UABRF start-ups that are currently housed at or have graduated from the Innovation Depot (and OADI) are BioHorizons Implant Systems, Emageon, MedMined, Transmolecular, Vaxin, Vista Engineering, DiscoveryBioMed, Photonics Innovations, and Endomimetics.

The Innovation Depot offers regular training seminars and workshops aimed specifically at the biotech, life science, and engineering companies participating in the program, and it works closely with the UABRF to find relevant topics and market these events to the researchers at UAB. In addition, Innovation Depot staff meet regularly with UABRF staff to discuss potential new companies, help identify funding sources, and provide general business guidance to researchers as they move through the process of starting a company.

The Innovation Depot is "more than just a building," according to its Web site. Services it advertises include:

- On-site coaching on planning, strategy development, marketing, financial, and other business advice
- Technical support and consulting for computer software applications, networking issues, and hardware configurations through an on-site IT manager
- Contacts for strategic partnerships and business alliances
- Identification of financing sources, including angel and venture capital investors
- Setup of panel meetings with accountants, lawyers, and other professionals to discuss financial, legal, or other issues
- Help developing clients' networks of business contacts
- Assistance in identifying and developing clients' competitive advantages
- Help with public relations, press releases, brochures, newsletters, flyers, advertising copy, logos, photographs, art, and other image media
- Educational seminars
- Dedicated Internet access, e-mail, domain name registration, and Web site hosting services with a T–1 connection
- Help with Web site development and identification of e-commerce partners
- Flexible space so clients can add offices or move to a larger space
- Help in remodeling or expansion decisions for clients' offices
- Assistance in identifying qualified employees and management
- Technical assistance provider for U.S. Small Business Administration Express loans

The Innovation Depot sees more than one hundred applications a year and admits approximately 10 percent of applicants. The incubator has a diverse mix of clients, so coaching times vary for individual companies. Some have been founded by serial entrepreneurs who need fewer resources but contribute as mentors and role models. Incubator staff develop a different matrix of services for

> "The bottom line is we understand our clients and adjust accordingly to provide the most effective services."
>
> – Susan Matlock, president and CEO, the Innovation Depot

dividual companies, according to Matlock. "The bottom line we understand our clients and adjust accordingly to provide e most effective services," she says.

cubator senior staff have introduced technology specialists serial entrepreneurs who became client company CEOs d who have helped clients obtain funding. Atlas RFID olutions CEO and founder Robert Fuqua says the public lations and business planning assistance provided by the cubator, as well as the location, gave the company "a seal approval" before its investors. The company raised 100 ercent of a first investment round in the Birmingham area. he biggest value is that people here are cut from the same oth and can relate to each other," Fuqua says. "Employees el the energy as well and believe when you come in here, u can succeed."

arly-stage biotech company Vaxin (based on UAB-licensed chnology) recently needed to secure a small, short-term an to fund a specialized audit required by the National stitutes of Health in order to release grant funds. These ant funds were extremely important in bridging a funding ap until the company's latest investment round could be osed. Vaxin had no luck working with financial institutions ecause of the company's lack of revenue, and it appeared at the audit could not be completed because of a lack funds. Laney worked with Vaxin to explore all options nd reached out to the Birmingham Regional Planning ommission, which has a small loan program. Through is introduction, Vaxin received the loan, the audit was ompleted, and NIH released the grant funds. Because the success of this endeavor, the Regional Planning ommission's Small Loan Program now is another resource vailable to Innovation Depot clients.

2008, the Innovation Depot served fifty-five client ompanies, welcomed twelve new clients (based on 114 pplications), and graduated four companies. The incubator eceived 120 applications in 2009, fourteen of which joined the incubator in the last half of the year, bringing the current client total to sixty-five. The Innovation Depot also reports 2008 client and graduate results (including graduates who left the program in 2005 and later) at $141 million in sales. Using government-supplied multipliers for each client's or graduate's industry sector, the incubator estimates an additional $274 million in revenues accrued to the community, as the dollars generated by these firms rippled through other area businesses, creating further impacts. Clients frequently have included the fastest-growing private companies in Birmingham, the region, and the southeastern United States. Birmingham incubator clients and graduates also have been recognized with NBIA Client of the Year and Graduate of the Year awards, as well as awards from other institutions.

The Innovation Depot operates with an annual budget of $2.5 million—of which approximately 70 percent is self-generated through fees for rents and services. The balance of the operating budget is derived from various contracts for services with UAB, the city of Birmingham, and Jefferson County, as well as from support from the regional business community. Currently, the Innovation Depot maintains a $14 million New Markets Tax Credit Loan that in 2013 (at the end of seven total years) will be reduced to a $3 million loan that will be amortized over thirty years. At capacity (a maximum of seventy-five to eighty clients), the incubator will be completely self-sustaining, covering all operating expenses and defraying its mortgage from rental and service fees and contracts.

Although Matlock and her staff have been extremely successful, she notes, "It took more than twenty years to get to this point." There were many challenges along the way, but vision and commitment (from both Matlock and her board of directors), combined with quality staff, a "lot of negotiations, bridge building, and blood, sweat, and tears" were needed to become a premier best practice program.

■■ the israeli technological incubators program

Beginning in 1991, the Office of the Chief Scientist of the Israeli Ministry of Industry and Trade established twenty-six Israeli technological incubators; there are now twenty-three regular technological incubators in the program, including fifteen located in peripheral areas and the rest in major municipalities including Jerusalem, Tel Aviv, and Haifa. In addition, one incubator is devoted entirely to biotechnology and especially drug development, and two "technology-based industrial incubators" accept incubator graduates and other more mature projects. The purpose of the incubators is supporting fledgling entrepreneurs in developing innovative technological ideas and setting up new companies to commercialize them.

In a program unique to Israel, the ministry financed the projects (i.e., new firms) the incubators supported as well as the incubators themselves. Today, the projects are the primary target of the ministry's financial support, and only seven incubation programs in remote peripheral areas continue to receive operating funds. While there was some concern both inside and outside Israel that privatizing the incubators would result in their demise, contrariwise, in the unique environment of the country, the privatization effort was successful in leveraging more funds—both per incubator and per company—than had been possible before the privatizations.

According to the chief scientist's office, by the end of 2008, approximately two hundred projects in various stages were being hosted by technological incubators at any one time, and 1,150 projects had matured and left the incubators. Of the graduates, around 60 percent had attracted private investment, and more than 55 percent had been active for more than five years. According to the CSO, 40 percent of all graduates since the inception of the program also were still in operation at the end of 2008.

By the end of 2008, the government's cumulative annual investment in incubator companies had risen to $500 million dollars, but cumulative private investments in these firms were a huge $2.5 billion. Annual private investment in incubated firms had "tracked" government investment for many years, and it began to surpass the government funds in about 1998. However, after the privatization process was launched in 2002, the growth of private funding became explosive. In 2007 alone, the government invested nearly $33 million in incubated companies, but private investment in graduates stood at nearly $440 million. Of this amount, $75 million represented series A investments (private money provided after graduation) in 2007 graduates of the incubator programs.

Total budgets for the projects in the technological incubators range between $350,000 to $600,000 and provide support for two years, except for biotechnology projects that are eligible for additional funds—up to $300,000 for a third year. Funds invested by the government represent up to 85 percent of the project's budget and are provided as a grant or soft loan. Government funding must be matched by an investment of 15 percent from the private sector. Projects in the biotechnology-focused incubator are eligible for greater amounts, and those focused on more mature companies and projects receive somewhat less.

Rina Pridor, chief of the Incubators Authority within the chief scientist's office, who oversaw the program from its founding until she retired in February 2009, said that "without the government making the initial investments in these projects, they would never have been ignited," and the private investments they attracted would not have been made.

Pridor described the incubator program as "the number-one manufacturer of start-ups in Israel today, establishing over seventy new start-ups each year." The program "has positioned itself as an important source of deal flow for the venture capital industry," which is constantly searching for new technologies in which to invest, she says.

As noted, the mission of the incubators established by the chief scientist's office was "to promote the development of innovative technology ideas of individual entrepreneurs and set up new businesses for their commercialization." Pridor says they were established because the ministry was convinced that "Israel's economic independence is contingent to a large extent upon the development of its technology-based industry." The program was designed to accept projects based on an innovative, technological idea that would produce a product intended for export.

Company ownership distribution has evolved over the years, but currently up to 5 percent of each project is owned by the incubator in return for its assistance; 25 percent to 65 percent (based on negotiations) is owned by the incubator as the provider of the government investment; 15 percent is held by the initial provider of supplementary financing; and 30 percent to 70 percent (based on negotiations) of the project may be owned by the entrepreneur. Shareholders' equity ownership is diluted proportionally as additional investment is needed for the company. The government-sponsored incubation network is intended only for individual entrepreneurs, not for commercially active existing companies, and a new small company is formed around each approved proposal. This too was unique, as incubators in most of the world accept existing fledgling companies as well as new ones.

While the government funding for incubator clients ceases at the end of the two-year or three-year period, with well-controlled cash flow this funding can be stretched for several more months, after which the company must stand on its own. Although the entrepreneur commits intellectual property and invests labor in project development against salary drawn from the funding, he or she is not required to make financial outlays. The entrepreneur may, however, bring along additional nongovernmental funding in exchange for an additional percentage of the initial shares. The combined government and private funding covers the project's salaries, supplies, equipment, subcontract services, preliminary intellectual property protection, regulatory procedures, basic marketing, and overhead.

Prior to the privatization of incubators in the Technological Incubators Program, client companies repaid the government loan through a 3 percent annual royalty on sales until the loan was recouped. Later, the privately owned incubator became responsible for repaying the loan in full within six to nine years from its equity earnings. If a project fails, the government will forgive the loan. The CSO's office considers repayment of the loan a good indicator of success, as it fulfills national economic goals for industry and business creation, job formation, increasing exports, improving the trade balance, and increasing tax revenues, among others.

The incubators' staff and a resource network of experts assist each client company. The incubator manager reviews monthly financial statements prepared by the incubator staff before forwarding them for approval by the Incubators Authority financial controller. The goal is for all projects to leave the program with financing or strategic alliances that can continue to carry them forward. In other words, the task of the incubators is to support technological ideas and proposals up to a level that will raise external investment interest.

Each entrepreneur must file an application to the incubator within which he or she wishes to operate the project. The project is first examined by the incubator, and if it is found suitable, the incubator will submit an application to Incubators Program Management at the Office of the Chief Scientist. The project is examined by that office before it is brought to a special committee headed by the chief scientist. If approved, it may then operate in the incubator and is eligible for government funding.

Before privatization, all government-supported technological incubators were organized as nonprofit companies that had volunteer boards and committees and supportive relationships with universities, research institutions, and the high-tech industry. They were owned by nonprofit organizations and municipalities. Now, except for those in remote peripheral areas, they are organized as for-profit companies and are owned by private investors such as venture capital funds, large investor groups, and holding companies. Since Israel is a small country (500 kilometers by 100 kilometers at its widest), the incubators all are located in relatively close proximity. An additional important feature of the Technological Incubators Program is the "fraternity-like" network of incubator managers who meet every two months, each time in a different incubator, for updating of procedures, exchanging of experience, and discussion of issues of common interest.

In the first years of the chief scientist's program, 75 percent of participants were Russian immigrants, as Israel sought to develop technology-based companies with assistance of a huge influx of scientists from the former USSR (more than 700,000 Russians immigrated over less than four years, many coming from research institutes and other elite institutions). Now, however, 90 percent of participants are non-Russian. However, the program was seen as a "technology absorption program, not a job creation program," according to Shmuel Yerushalmi, a former incubator manager who worked during those early years. Yerushalmi explains that the Israeli government was convinced that if it were unable to help the Russians create their businesses in Israel, the immigrants would create companies elsewhere, and then the Israelis would have to compete with them.

Generally speaking, the incubators are open to any field of research and development, though a few are specialized or have clusters in life sciences, medical devices, ICT, clean technology, water technologies, and homeland security. The largest cluster is medical devices (40 percent). Other technology fields are biotechnology (20 percent), software (15 percent), communications (8 percent), and environment (8 percent).

The incubators program management at the Office of the Chief Scientist holds a conference every four months, bringing together projects from the incubators in a specific field such as life sciences, medical devices, ICT, homeland security, or clean technology. During each conference, approximately fifteen start-up companies have the opportunity to showcase their innovative projects before entrepreneurs, managers, potential strategic partners, and private investors from that industry. The goal is to create collaborations between incubator companies, strategic partners, and investors.

With proper financial backing, and expert nurturing, Meytav aims to bring real technologies to fruition, with real products that are needed, and [that] will sell in real markets.

■■ meytav
technological incubator

Kiryat Shmona, Israel
Orit Shaked, CTO
www.meytavti.co.il

The Meytav Technological Incubator was founded by the chief scientist's office of the Israeli Ministry of Industry, Trade, and Labor. A highly respected Israeli incubator, it opened in 1991 in the north of Israel in Kiryat Shmona, near the Lebanese border. Meytav is one of Israel's largest incubators, which is somewhat surprising since Kiryat Shmona has little more than 22,000 inhabitants, and the city's economy is based primarily on light industry and tourism. The Economic Corporation of Kiryat Shmona, which manages real estate, tourism, commercial, and other projects for the city, also was a party to founding the incubator.

Meytav was privatized by several investor groups and VCs, including a major drug development company, in July 2003. In 2005, in consideration of a controlling interest in Meytav, the incubator secured a major investment from a public company traded on the Tel Aviv Stock Exchange. This company, Biomedix Incubator Ltd., is a holding company. Several investment groups are large shareholders of Biomedix, including Pontifax, a venture capital firm that has developed an agreement with Roche Holding AG to jointly invest in Israeli companies. A majority of Meytav directors represent BioMedix.

According to the Meytav Web site, the management team "consists of professionals and dedicated experts experienced in all areas" of biopharma and medical device technologies "geared toward achieving excellence in the field of life sciences." The CEO, Ido Agmon, holds an undergraduate degree in life sciences and management from Tel Aviv University and an MBA in marketing and finance from the Hebrew University of Jerusalem. The chief technology officer, Orit Shaked, previously worked for Teva Pharmaceuticals, which she describes as the world's largest generic drug manufacturer, and UBT Medical, a medical device start-up

company. She also holds R&D and board positions in sever biotechnology start-ups.

Meytav boasts impressive strategic alliances with organizations including the Weizmann Institute of Science; t Technion; and Hebrew, Tel Aviv, and Ben Gurion universities.

The incubator sources its deal flow from companies that are co-owners of Meytav; the institutions named above and other universities; hospitals; corporate spin-offs; independer entrepreneurs; and other local entities. A preinvestment "filtration system" identifies projects that:

- Represent the highest quality of scientific research and ensure solid proof of concept, IP protection, clea regulatory path, and commercial potential
- Are spin-offs of "existing industrial entities that are willing to assist in R&D, as well as the launching and marketing of the final product"
- Clearly identify an unfulfilled gap in the market
- Show potential to create beneficial alliances with strategic partners
- Can achieve a major milestone during their incubation period
- Are operated by experienced entrepreneurs with strong business (as well as scientific) backgrounds

Projects go through a "strict and comprehensive screening process" prior to investment. The Meytav CEO, CTO, and consultants review personal and business matters and conduct due diligence on the technology, "fit" with the incubator, and the project's work plan and budget. The personal review of the founder or managing director and his team involves examining the individuals' track records, ability to execute, and credibility. The business review includes examination of the possible business model and accessibility of potential partners (strategic and investment).

When the project has passed all these hurdles, Meytav negotiates the terms of its investment, and the company must be approved by the Meytav board of directors and the Office of the Chief Scientist. In concert with this, agreements and the work plan are finalized. The entire process takes, on average, three to five months.

cceptance of companies in the incubator is "conditional pon the recruitment of a CEO who will complement the kills" of the founding scientist or entrepreneur. Meytav then ppoints experienced entrepreneurs, industry experts, and cademics to the company's board of directors and scientific dvisory board. Meytav places "paramount emphasis on the ssembly of a well-balanced, professional, and experienced nanagement team for each of the portfolio companies."

he Meytav incubator is small—slightly less than 4,500 quare feet. Space is utilized efficiently because much of , including the incubator's laboratories, is shared—an rrangement that Shaked says does not bother individual rms or researchers. Companies using the state-of-the-art iological and chemical laboratory facility have access to their wn benches and desks but share equipment that would be 0o expensive for individual projects to acquire. The incubator ilso offers fermentation, cell culture, molecular biology, and hemistry facilities.

n addition to supplying work space, the incubator provides egal and accounting services, consulting, a computer etwork, maintenance, and general administrative services. An in-house engineering unit assists portfolio companies with ingineering required to quickly develop prototypes, a special ieed for medical device companies.

ostinvestment monitoring and consulting involves:

- Provision of daily access to the Meytav management team and access to "continual scientific, financial, managerial, administrative, and marketing support and advice from a dedicated team of professionals"

- Assistance in structuring the company and setting up a board of directors

- Provision of a Meytav professional to the investee board of directors

- Assistance by Meytav in acquiring strategic alliances and investment that will contribute to the company's future success and maximize ROI

Graduates retain a Meytav director on their own boards.

The incubator describes its investment philosophy as one that has "allowed it to build on investments in portfolio companies made by the state" [Israel] and achieve fast and consistent results. This occurs via identifying deal flow with strong potential, conducting rigorous due diligence, providing strong and strategic investments" and "working toward [a] rapid, effective, and commercially viable market launch." Its Web site notes, "Meytav does not believe that it should serve as a 'hotel' for its portfolio companies, providing merely space and secretaries. Indeed, we see our work as really beginning once financial investment has been secured for a portfolio company."

"With proper financial backing, and expert nurturing, Meytav aims to bring real technologies to fruition, with real products that are needed, and [that] will sell in real markets."

Significant graduates include Protalix Biotherapeutics, a biotechnology company traded on the American Stock Exchange. Protalix was rated a "best buy" by Marketwire in December 2009, when it also completed its new drug application filing with the U.S. Food and Drug Administration for a biotherapeutic product to treat Gaucher's Disease. It recently entered into an agreement with Pfizer to develop and commercialize that product. Another graduate, Endogun Medical Systems, has achieved FDA approval for its medical devices used to treat pelvic organ prolapse and urinary incontinence. Endogun also has developed other products used by doctors treating urinary and gynecological conditions.

Seventeen firms have graduated from Meytav in five years, including six that graduated in the last six months. Twenty-five firms are current portfolio companies of Meytav. They have attracted $16.25 million in investment from Meytav, the Office of the Chief Scientist, and supplemental sources, which has leveraged an additional $19.4 million in external investments.

■■ san diego CONNECT

San Diego, California
Camille Sobrian, chief operating officer
www.connect.org

San Diego CONNECT is very likely the world's most famous virtual incubator for technology ventures, with an impact far beyond its own activities. The organization's 2008 annual report notes that San Diego's "innovation economy [results] are spectacular by any measure. San Diego is now home to more than 1,100 communications technology companies and more than five hundred biotech companies. [In 2008], 367 new technology companies were launched [in San Diego]." San Diego's life science industry alone garnered $3.2 billion in venture capital investments from 2004 to 2007, according to PricewaterhouseCoopers *Money Tree Report*. Much of that success, many believe, can be traced directly or indirectly to CONNECT.

CONNECT was founded in 1985 by the University of California, San Diego, at the urging of the San Diego business community to link high technology and biotechnology entrepreneurs with the resources they need for success: money, markets, management, partners, support services, technology, and government. For many years part of the Division of Extended Studies and Public Service at UCSD, CONNECT served as an economic catalyst by bringing together the nascent technology industry in the region. The program inspired competitors and innovators alike to pull together in order to benefit the innovation community in a unique "culture of collaboration."

CONNECT is now recognized as the region's go-to organization for accelerating the commercialization of innovation. Industry groups such as Biocom, the world's largest regional life science association, and CommNexus—which together represent more than seven hundred member companies in Southern California—were established as a result of earlier work initiated by CONNECT. In order to become more responsive to its industry partners, which now include fifty research institutions, CONNECT established a foundation and a 501(c)(6) trade organization in 2005 and became independent of the university.

CONNECT has stimulated and supported an innovation economy that drives the creation of high-paying jobs and economic diversification, thereby sheltering San Diego from the impacts of economic downturns. This has led to the creation of CONNECT-like organizations by almost forty other communities across the globe in Australia, Canada, New Zealand, Norway, Sweden, Taiwan, and the UK. Global CONNECT, still a part of UCSD, acts as a consultant to help regions set up a CONNECT model appropriate for their geographic and economic needs.

CONNECT accomplishes its goals through mentoring, educational, and networking programs; practical business seminars; technology lectures and demonstrations; and financing forums. In 2009, CONNECT organized 330 events, or almost one a day. CONNECT's programs assist investors, serial entrepreneurs, and business service providers—attorneys, accountants, and marketing specialists—by providing them with knowledge about emerging technologies and access to new business opportunities. The entrepreneurs get to hone their ideas, develop alliances, and gain investment. CONNECT functions as a catalyst for entrepreneurial growth by providing a forum for exchanging ideas and opportunities to network with peers. As a virtual incubator, CONNECT provides programs but not space for its clients.

According to its annual report, in 2008 the organization mobilized 1,200 volunteers to collaborate in "mentoring, coaching, advising, and evaluating more than one thousand companies." Between 2005 and 2008, CONNECT doubled the number of its programs to twenty-six; the organization held three hundred events in 2008, with ten thousand participants.

CONNECT works with 180 entrepreneurs-in-residence—successful CEOs who have grown companies and raised equity investments—and two hundred domain experts with special knowledge, such as intellectual property or industry sector expertise. The EIRs and domain experts assist in CONNECT's well-recognized Springboard mentoring program in which two EIRs per company and relevant domain experts offer up to six months of free advice to entrepreneurs at all stages of development.

CONNECT raises operational funds through individual ticket and corporate table sales for events, along with sponsorships and member dues from 222 regional members such as venture capitalists, business service providers, research institutions, and corporations. CONNECT programs are administered by twenty full-time staff, including a new Washington, D.C., advocate who represents the unique needs of technology start-ups.

To track its progress, CONNECT partners with other organizations to gather and present quarterly data and trend analyses. Partners and their areas of expertise include the National University System Institute for Policy Research (technology-based business creation); UCSD Extension (patents, grants and research, wages and employment); Roth Capital (mergers and acquisitions); PricewaterhouseCoopers (venture capital); and Procopio, Cory, Hargreaves & Savitch LLP (bankruptcies).

CONNECT programs include technology discovery programs; technology transfer (including early business assessments); Springboard personalized assistance; an array of financing programs, including Venture Roundtable, Capital Forums, and Deal Network; business education programs; and recognition nd networking events such as the Most Innovative New roduct Awards and Entrepreneur Hall of Fame. Other gnificant programs are focused on cluster acceleration, ddressing each industry niche (wireless health, stem cells, ean tech, action and sports innovation, cyber technology, nd autonomous robotics) and policy and advocacy initiatives n regulation and trade, capital formation, state and federal &D funding, and other topics.

amille Sobrian, CONNECT's chief operating officer, notes at "a critical part of what we do is help entrepreneurs resent their business model," whether for one of the rganization's programs designed to attract equity vestment in entrepreneurial firms or in competition for one f CONNECT's awards, which attract great recognition and terest in winning firms. As in incubators the world over, any entrepreneurs can describe their technology but not the nportance of the innovation breakthrough or its commercial alue, she says.

partial list of CONNECT's programs and brief escriptions follows:

- **Springboard.** Springboard is a one-week to six-month program of mentoring conducted by entrepreneurs-in-residence to help innovators at all stages of development—from assessing the commercial potential of inventions to advising on the commercial potential of spin-outs.

- **Deal Network.** Twenty-two high-net-worth individuals meet for dinner and review CONNECT's "scrubbed" (vetted) deals. A new effort started by CONNECT in 2009, Deal Network is scheduled about every six weeks. Investments generally range from $50,000 to $500,000, and investors include individuals who are not members of the formal angel investing group, Tech Coast Angels.

- **Venture Roundtable.** Entrepreneurs chosen via a selection process that includes CONNECT's mentor volunteers and industry representatives present their businesses to venture capitalists in hope of attracting investments as well as advice and feedback. Each midday presentation focuses on an industry vertical such as life sciences, clean technology, software analytics, unmanned vehicles, cyber, and so on. The program is scheduled to permit VCs to fly in and fly out conveniently the same day.

- **Tech Coast Angels.** A network of private investors in early-stage companies meets monthly and hears pitches from vetted companies. Tech Coast Angels also sends selected investees to Deal Network meetings. CONNECT provides administrative support for this angel network.

- **FrameWorks Workshops.** Half-day workshops offering in-depth information on practical business skills are held two to three times a month.

- **Frontiers in Science and Technology.** This lecture series showcases groundbreaking research efforts from area research institutions, designed to alert both investors and entrepreneurs to new and potentially revolutionary technologies and how these might be used.

- **CEO Strategy Forum.** An exclusive community of CEOs, board members, and VCs shares success strategies at forums that feature a well-known CEO or company founder, with the goal of giving insights to the founders of entrepreneurial companies that are CONNECT clients. (See p. 104)

- **Connect with CONNECT.** Up to three hundred technology executives meet twice a year to network and learn from each other.

- **Most Innovative New Product Awards.** This program recognizes the best new area disruptive technologies, with awards described as the local Oscars of regional innovation. According to Sobrian, most winners will have global impacts in their sectors; the CONNECT imprimatur focuses attention on these new products and their companies.

- **Entrepreneur Hall of Fame Awards.** This awards program recognizes regional technology pioneers who had a major role in building the San Diego innovation economy. Luminaries such as Irwin Jacobs, founder of Qualcomm, and Bob Beyster, founder of SAIC, are past winners.

- **Public Policy Forum.** This program identifies legislative issues and advocates on behalf of innovation.

- **Cluster Development.** CONNECT participates in developing and supporting membership groups and forums for important clusters; these include CONNECT Sport Innovators, Innovation Support for Homeland Security, Stem Cell on the Mesa, and Wireless-Life Sciences Alliance.

- **The La Jolla Research and Innovation Summit.** In an effort to brand San Diego as a region that excels in both innovation and convergence technologies, CONNECT showcases researchers working on discoveries five to ten years out to venture capitalists from across the country. A recent summit attracted eighty VCs to hear four panels of researchers speak on clean technology, biotechnology, information and wireless technology, and convergence innovation—the latter including biofuels and other technologies that are converging, such as wireless health care.

■■ william m. factory small business incubator

Tacoma, Washington
Tim Strege, executive director
www.williamfactory.com

The William M. Factory Small Business Incubator was created in 1986 to help new businesses in East Tacoma as a means of improving living and working conditions in the neighborhood. The incubator is located within the boundaries of the Puyallup Indian Reservation and the area first settled by American pioneers in the mid-1850s. The neighborhood is adjacent to the Port of Tacoma, where industry has historically employed people with technical skills but only a high school education. During the 1980s, permanent closures of manufacturing plants in the port and nearby vicinities amounted to more than ten thousand job losses.

Lost jobs devastated the economics of the East Tacoma community. Decreased purchasing power among residents resulted in store closures along the Portland and McKinley avenue corridors, spreading further unemployment. As incubator Executive Director Tim Strege explains, "While Tacoma civic officials were 'smokestack chasing' to attract industrial operations to replace plant closures, East Tacoma neighborhood leaders decided to shape their economic destiny through the creation of a small business incubator in a building formerly used as a tavern on Portland Avenue."

It was entirely coincidental that previously out-of-work building repair, facility maintenance, and structural entrepreneurs were among the first incubator clients. However, this shaped the incubator's specialty construction trades focus. The William M. Factory Small Business Incubator now has seven staff who serve over thirty companies in construction specialty trades (e.g., electrical, painting, construction contracting); applied technologies (e.g., RFID, IT, clean technology, environmental remedies); and business services.

William M. Factory, a community activist who founded the incubator—known originally as the Tacoma–Pierce County Small Business Incubator—would be proud of the program's accomplishments, which include revitalizing the local economy, promoting job growth, and expanding the tax base of its neighborhood. The mixed-use incubator was renamed in Factory's honor after his death in 1996.

In 2005, the William M. Factory Small Business Incubator won NBIA's Incubator of the Year Award. This award recognizes the highest achievements among NBIA's member incubators. Since its inception, the incubator has graduated more than two hundred companies, employing over 1,200 workers. Approximately 80 percent of those firms remain in business or have successfully merged. According to incubator management, an economic analysis of current incubator clients identified thirty-three companies generating over $30 million in annual gross commercial revenues and providing over $7 million in federal, state, and local taxes.

Since its opening in 1994, jobs created by the incubator have cost about $1,400 each, according to the incubator's operating budget.

The William M. Factory incubator assists carefully selected businesses—many of which are owned by women, minorities, or low-income entrepreneurs. In 2009, clients at the incubator created nearly three hundred jobs, most of which benefit residents of the East Side—one of the area's poorest neighborhoods. "We haven't lost sight of our constituency," says Strege. "Many of our firms are managed by entrepreneurs who would otherwise be unemployed."

As part of their leases, all client companies sign first-source hiring agreements in which they agree to consider unemployed neighborhood residents for available job openings. These agreements create beneficial relationships between the businesses' growth and the residents' well-being. In effect, the employment clause helps incubator companies take ownership of the East Side and encourages desire to increase the quality of life in the neighborhood even after they graduate.

Santamaria Construction used both first-source hiring agreements and bootstrapping (growing from company-generated revenues) to expand the business and benefit the community. According to Strege, Jose Santamaria's first job after joining the incubator was a $500 side-sewer project on a public housing lot. Three years later—after he gradually acquired more sophisticated equipment, certifications, and experience—Santamaria completed a $300,000 contract for the foundation of the Health Service Building at the Universit of Washington's Tacoma campus, gaining great satisfaction in paying his underground utility workers an average of $26 per hour.

As required by federal HUBZone (historically underutilized business zone) regulations, WAKA, a road and bridge construction company and incubator graduate, must hire 35 percent or more of its workers from lower-income census tracts. WAKA President Andy Wilson explains, "The incubator's first-source hiring agreement permits us access to available workers as we grow our HUBZone enterprise." WAKA performed more than $2 million in economic stimulus work in late 2009, permitting HUBZone residents to earn an average of over $25 per hour.

Leaving behind its humble origins in a former tavern, the William M. Factory incubator moved into a $3.2 million, newly constructed building in 2003 with thirty offices and more than

...e hundred workstations (each capable of handling four data ...telecom connections). Another new building that is part ...an envisioned campus opened in late 2009, offering room ...thirty more firms, with plenty of windows and naturally ...corridors. The new 22,000-square-foot structure includes ...chnological upgrades that provide resident companies with ...deoconference-capable telecommunications; merger of ...ice and e-mail systems; an atrium exhibit and conference ...ea; a rooftop outdoor terrace with Commencement Bay in ...e foreground; and balcony views overlooking Mount Rainier. ...e two buildings are the most technologically advanced ...all office buildings in the Puget Sound region.

...ior to its move, the program was at a site where business ...vners stored trucks, cement mixers, and other equipment. ...ot only did the site become messy, but owners also ...ere distracted by equipment maintenance. Incubator ...anagement decided the new facility would provide ...fices rather than a secured yard for storage, allowing the ...trepreneurs to focus on the business components of their ...ms rather than operations. Clients now use other space ...ar the incubator to store their equipment.

...ich move helped the program reach more disadvantaged ...trepreneurs. "Every move was an upgrade," Strege ...ys. "And with every upgrade, our clients stepped up and ...erformed even better, both because people outside the ...cubator gave the companies more respect and because the ...mpanies held themselves to higher standards."

...erage annual revenues of incubator clients jumped from ...75,000 to $1 million after the program moved into its ...rpose-built facility 2003, as the companies responded by ...coming more professional and businesslike and as they ...ded bigger customers. "People got serious," says Strege, ...o hopes the new addition will have a similar effect of ...osting average client revenues.

...hen Strege assumed leadership of the incubator in 1994, it ...d passionate community support but needed an upgrade ...both its services and its clients. Firms included "pretend" ...sinesses and lots of part-time companies—many of which ...rege evicted to bring in firms whose founders had greater ...mmitment to their companies. "We practically had to start ...ain," he says. A significant upturn in construction between ...94 and 2008 also helped the incubator attract better clients ...d, in turn, helped clients increase their average annual sales.

...e William M. Factory Small Business Incubator's board ...directors gave Strege leeway to make many changes, ...cluding diversifying into other clusters such as applied ...chnologies, which has added to the original base of ...ecialty construction trades. Other changes Strege made ...clude:

- Developing a stringent selection process to ensure that the entrepreneurs' backgrounds match the products or services they hope to offer and that their business models are viable

- Structuring the incubator's books so that someone else could come in and understand what is going on and doing cross-training so that all incubator staff have the ability to take over other responsibilities

- Constructing the new buildings and an entrepreneurial campus

- Creating what Strege calls "premarketing efforts" to discover in advance what markets exist for road construction, port work, clean energy, and so on

Via these premarket activities, the incubator began to develop a vision of markets that would fulfill area needs and provide opportunities for sustainable businesses. "We're not saying to the businesses that they should figure all this out in advance," explains Strege. "We act as a facilitator and aggregator, and we're bringing together multiple players to identify opportunities and assist firms in bidding on larger contracts than they could on their own."

Incubator clients pay above-market rents, which include fees for all incubator services. These services include specialized assistance in accounting, human resources, engineering, and other business functions. The incubator has three staff—an executive director, a program manager, and an information technology engineer—and contracts for an on-site project management specialist and an economic cluster expert. Eight attorneys from three different law firms come to the incubator to provide pro bono advice to client firms. A Clover Park Technical College accounting instructor, a Bates Technical College civil engineering instructor, and eleven professional volunteer mentors skilled in Microsoft Project, construction management, human resources, and other important business fields also offer on-site assistance.

Because of the compatibility of the specialty construction trades and information technology sectors, incubator staff serve clients in both clusters. The incubator has recruited a part-time technology specialist to serve IT firms; engaged a pro bono legal team with expertise in entity formation, intellectual property protection, and media law; and formed partnerships with the Institute of Technology at the University of Washington and Devry University's computer engineering program to supply capable student interns.

Suzanne Hearring, the owner of incubator client Advanced Government Services, started her business with two employees (herself and her sister-in-law) and now has forty-two workers. The company provides support services to the construction industry (e.g., traffic control planning and staffing; job site setup and takedown; and rental of traffic control equipment such as warning panels and portable lights). Hearring discovered the incubator by going to the Tacoma Procurement Technical Assistance Center, which is now located in the incubator. Being a client of the incubator provided credibility to her business and gave her access to a business coach, Steve Rapkoch, who "opened doors to roads I'd never have travelled down without his questions." The experience also helped inspire her to undertake new business opportunities, she says. Formerly an incubator staff person, Rapkoch now is a professional mentor who serves incubator clients.

The incubator's exceptional facilities, state-of-the-art technology, and highly capable staff and volunteers have contributed to its success, but clients most frequently cite the opportunity to network with other entrepreneurs and to interact with visiting contracting agencies and corporations as the most beneficial aspect of their incubator experience, Strege says.

While lease-up of the new building is currently under way in a tough economic climate, Strege hopes they are "opening the doors of the economy to a lot of new entrants. . . . . Our first facility's clients employ nearly three hundred workers; an incubator campus could provide jobs for one thousand employees or more," he says.

The William M. Factory incubator example shows how a program that was initially underperforming can be turned around, attracting companies with the potential to be more successful and better serve the incubator's goals of providing jobs and increasing wealth in its neighborhood.

The incubation program also reveals the importance of identifying top-tier management to get the job done. Strege holds a master's degree in public administration from Harvard University and has undertaken advanced studies at the London School of Economics. He holds a bachelor's degree from Pacific Lutheran University. He has also been deputy mayor and a city council member for Tacoma; chairman of the Pierce County Law and Justice Commission; chairman of the Housing Policy Committee for the Growth Policy Commission; and president of the Washington Association of Small Business Incubators. This history and the strong contacts with these and other organizations have contributed to his success in building the William M. Factory program.

Should this be a surprise? Not really. NBIA has long noted that business incubators are highly dependent on the skills of their management and that incubator sponsors must provide compensation that will attract a manager with the skills both to grow the incubation program and to help client companies grow.

■ ■ la cocina

San Francisco, California
Caleb Zigas, acting executive director
www.lacocinasf.org

San Francisco's Mission District is an ethnically diverse and economically vulnerable neighborhood that thrives in part because of the many small informal businesses that serve the community. As in many cities, food lies at the heart of this community, and you don't have to look far to find hidden entrepreneurs in the kitchens of many homes.

La Cocina—which means "the kitchen" in Spanish—was founded to help low-income entrepreneurs launch, formalize or expand their food businesses. "We're focused on the transition from informal to formal, from income 'patching' to asset generation," says Acting Executive Director Caleb Zigas. "We turn bake sales into bakeries."

La Cocina was born out of the belief that a community of natural entrepreneurs, given the right resources, can create self-sufficient businesses that benefit themselves, their families, their community, and the whole city.

The incubator occupies only 4,400 square feet of space, mostly devoted to a full-service, shared-use commercial kitchen, of which approximately 2,000 square feet is dedicated to four complete prep stations. La Cocina provides a full range of kitchen equipment and rents the kitchen on an hourly basis. Dry storage, minimal offices for staff, and meeting rooms round out the facility.

Equipment includes fryers, mixers, a thirty-gallon tilting skillet, a steamer, convection ovens, broilers, ranges, stainless steel worktables and sinks, racks, ice machines, and more. The incubator boasts walk-in coolers and freezers and dry storage cases with lockable wire cages. Rental costs vary; incubator clients are charged $13 per hour, and nonclients are charged $35 per hour.

La Cocina opened in 2005 after six years of effort, from determining feasibility to conducting a capital campaign to opening the doors. Founders included the Women's Initiative for Self-Employment, the Women's Foundation of California, and a visionary anonymous donor. The partners raised $1 million to launch the project and obtained access to high-quality, low-cost space.

The incubator offers a good example of how a program can rely on excellent technical staff to support the incubator, its kitchen, and food processing activities but rely on outside organizations to support business-related training and advisory services. Among those who provide general business assistance services to La Cocina clients are the Renaissance Entrepreneurship Center, a San Francisco incubator for low- to moderate-income entrepreneurs, and the Women's Initiative for Self-Employment, which also offer entrepreneur training and education to high-potential, lower-income women.

Additionally, La Cocina has used its connections in the community to recruit high-quality partners in the food industry, including Mattson—the largest independent developer of new products for the food and beverage industry—and Bon Appétit Management Company, a restaurant company that provides on-site café and catering services to corporations, colleges and universities, and specialty venues, with over four hundred locations in twenty-eight states. Mattson offers nutrition testing, education, and training to La Cocina clients, while Bon Appétit provides advisory services and industry connections.

The incubator's staff of five—many of whom are multilingual in a combination of Spanish, Mandarin, French, and English—are experienced in many facets of the food industry and hold degrees in culinary arts and training from Le Cordon Bleu Paris. La Cocina also avails itself of nearly one hundred active volunteers who provide technical assistance, mentor, and assist the incubator with general volunteer duties, such as working with the La Cocina staff on events, farmers' markets, administration, and fundraising.

Each quarter, the incubator offers an orientation that attracts some fifty attendees and generally leads to twelve new applicants. The orientation includes a kitchen tour, a general introduction to the food industry, information about La Cocina and its operations, and a discussion of the application process. Each applicant is expected to have a business plan already to be selling products informally in some way (such at flea markets or street fairs) and must supply references.

Each application is reviewed by a separate three-person team from the incubator's thirty-five member Client Advisory Committee. Every team includes someone with financial experience, in addition to incubator staff. The advisory team looks at four key elements of the applicant's business plan: market, operations, production, and the applicant's entrepreneurial spirit and level of commitment. The review period takes about three months. Companies identified as having weak areas are accepted into a preincubation phase, which they work with the incubator staff to address the concerns. Once that happens, they join the incubation program in full. Generally, applicants are given no more than six months to take care of initial concerns raised by their advisory team. The incubation process itself is expected to take no more than five years, according to Zigas.

The incubator's marketing materials focus not only on the services offered but also on the incubator's value proposition to clients, asking, "Do you have a growing food business but can't fill big orders?" and "Would you like to get new clients or sell to stores but you don't have the proper insurance and permits?"

The incubator maintains a booth at the Ferry Plaza Farmers Market in San Francisco, where client products are sold, and the La Cocina Web site offers gift boxes made up of client products. Sales of the boxes introduce the public to client products and serve as a fundraiser for the incubator.

The incubator also offers twelve public classes each year, using clients and staff as chefs to raise revenues for the incubator. Classes and events described on the Web site in January 2010 included "Truffles, Chocolates, and How to Be a Better Lover"; "Day of the Dead: Celebrate with Traditional Breads"; "Masa Madness: Tortillas, Gorditas, and Pupusas" ("Do you know masa like we know masa?"); "Simply Salsa"; "Thanksgiving around the World"; "Updated Soul Food Classics"; and "Market Fresh Healthy Foods." Sessions normally attract between twenty and forty participants and include cooking classes, dinner, and a take-home box; the cost is $65 per person.

According to Zigas, La Cocina works from a $700,000 operating budget and is funded from self-generated revenues (30 percent), a Community Development Block Grant provided by the city of San Francisco (10 percent), and funds from individual donors, grants, and foundations (60 percent).

The La Cocina Web site offers a button on its home page permitting donors to give funds instantly via credit card—a unique feature among business incubators. The incubator also accepts stock donations. The incubator has 501(c)(3) tax status, permitting donations to be taken as tax deductions and is overseen by an eight-member governing board including representatives of the San Francisco Redevelopment Agency, IBM, a Mission District bakery and café, microbusiness support organizations, and foundations.

San Francisco 7X7, a Web magazine that covers local art, fashion, food, design, people, and culture, named incubator staff as winners of its SF Tastemakers recognition, noting that La Cocina organized the city's first-ever street food festival in August 2009, drawing 12,000 people to the event and raising nearly $40,000 for the incubator (and generating $125,000 in cash sales for the incubator's vendors). "While others harp on how unsustainable SF is for small businesses, La Cocina serves as a positive model for what's possible," *SF 7x7* notes.

SF 7x7 gave special kudos to two of the incubator's current twenty-seven clients, including "the excellent El Huarache Loco and Sabores Del Sur." Successful graduates of the incubator include Kika's Treats, a maker of chocolate-enrobed shortbreads, graham crackers, and other treats; and Peas of Mind, a frozen food company focusing on easily prepared organic frozen foods for children.

Zigas explains how working with people who are "making foods they love and struggling to make a living" is compelling. "It's not often that people get to make a living doing what they love. I do."

■■ san juan college enterprise center

Farmington, New Mexico
Jasper Welch, director
www.sanjuancollege.edu/qcb

In December 2009, the San Juan College Enterprise Center celebrated the tenth anniversary of the San Juan College Quality Center for Business, the facility that houses the incubator and other entities important to the economic development of Farmington, New Mexico.

With 43,600 residents, Farmington is the largest city in the scenic but largely rural Four Corners area, where Colorado, New Mexico, Utah, and Arizona meet. The area also includes the Navajo Nation, Southern Ute, Ute Mountain Ute, and Jicarilla Apache Indian reservations.

The culmination of a ten-year development process, the 43,000-square-foot structure houses the incubator, the San Juan Economic Development Organization, a Small Business Development Center, the Council of Governments, and the Center for Workforce Training, a college program that serves businesses and individuals throughout the region. Then-Mayor Tom Taylor (now New Mexico House minority leader) "dreamed the dream" in 1988 and ensured the SJEDO, city of Farmington, and San Juan College worked together to create the agreements that resulted in the Quality Center for Business. Initial funding of $4.2 million came from the U.S. Department of Commerce Economic Development Administration, state of New Mexico bonds, the city of Farmington, San Juan College, and private-sector funds.

Between January 2000, when the SJCEC signed its first client lease, and January 2010, the incubator served fifty companies; it normally hosts ten to fifteen clients at any one time. In early 2010, twelve firms were housed on-site,

and the incubator also served two affiliates (which are considered full clients). The incubator has graduated twenty-six companies; about ten companies overall have dropped out of the program. While many incubator clients remain small, current clients and graduates employ approximately 250 individuals. Success stories of note include graduate All American Technical Team, an industrial service and fabrication company that currently employs seventy, and PALS, a graduate company that provides home care and assisted living services.

The incubator offers 17,000 square feet of production space, 4,200 square feet of offices, and 5,000 square feet of administrative and shared space. Generally, the incubator will not lease more than 4,500 square feet of production space or more than three to four offices of up to 850 square feet to its largest client. Rent in early 2010 was about $12 per square foot per year for office space and $5 per square foot per year for production space. All clients—including Enterprise Center affiliates—also pay a service fee of $100 per month.

Director Jasper Welch has a wide range of business experience in the Four Corners area, and was formerly mayor of Durango, Colorado. He spends 80 percent of his time with the incubator, while maintaining a business consulting practice and serving on several corporate boards. Welch also previously managed the Center for Workforce Training and is himself a talented trainer. Other staff include Eileen Shelton, who handles facility management and program support for the incubator and provides support for the SJEDO and who works half-time for each organization. The SJCEC also has a part-time receptionist.

Lean incubator staff and shared facilities with the training center and the SBDC have led to close cooperation between these organizations. Currently the SBDC and the incubator provide referrals to each other and collaborate in working with clients and applicants to the incubator. The incubator requires that each applicant complete a business plan, and the SBDC

"Six billion people around the world woke up this morning with a good idea, but most don't do anything about it."

– Jasper Welch, director, San Juan College Enterprise Center

:lps with this. "We're business-plan ready," says Welch, who :plains that "six billion people around the world woke up this orning with a good idea, but most don't do anything about " Having client business plans in place before acceptance eans the incubator can "focus on implementation," he says.

; a division of the college, SJCEC does not have its own overning board but has a lease advisory committee that meets ice a quarter (at minimum) to review and approve applications commended by incubator staff (the board meets more equently, if necessary, to ensure speedy lease approvals).

ith Welch leading the way, the incubator also has solved cubation support problems by developing unique tools, cluding the 100 Point System. To encourage active articipation in his program, Welch requires clients to idertake activities or complete assignments that will help em grow their businesses. Over the year, clients accrue ints based on a weighted scoring system; those that score)0 points or less may find their leases aren't renewed. ients that score 400 to 450 points per year are eligible for vards. The forty activities are organized into categories, cluding business plan development, enterprise center ogram involvement, marketing plans and public relations, ofessional and skills development, and advisory board evelopment. For example, clients can get points for setting) advisory boards; attending incubator functions; taking asses, including NxLeveL workshops; updating business ans; and undertaking insurance and banking reviews and ssessments. (For more on the 100 Point System, see the ection on monitoring client progress in chapter 6, "Client ntrance and Exit.")

)ur 100 Point System is the magic," says Welch, who xplained that it was invented out of desperation due to ck of staff. "Essentially, we give them a Chinese menu of ings they need to do." The system is transparent; incubator articipants know exactly what is expected of them, and "we)n't need to bug them all the time," Welch says.

elch also has collaborated with a New York City–based arketing consultant to implement Marketing for Smarties,

a fourteen-step process that Welch has been using for five years and that is now being implemented by SBDCs in New Mexico and Colorado. (For more information, see the section on marketing assistance in chapter 8, "Client Services," and www.marketingforsmarties.com.) Welch has worked with author Don Warner to train coaches in using the process and to upgrade content.

SJCEC manages a preincubation program that provides services to potential clients that are not ready for full incubation—usually for no more than three months. This process assists in developing the incubator's pipeline, according to Welch. It also maintains a furnished office that includes a lending library of business publications and doubles as instant office space for affiliate clients, business consultants, and incubator staff to use in working with clients and applicants. "If they can see a physical space where we help them, it makes it a bit more real for them," Welch explains. (For more on the preincubation program, see that section in chapter 8, "Client Services.")

SJCEC and the SBDC jointly organize a workshop series. The incubator also holds monthly business development breakfasts facilitated by Welch on topics such as key performance indicators, and brown bag luncheons, at which outside speakers are invited to present. In addition, the incubator hosts a spring cookout and holiday potluck for staff, clients and their families, and invited stakeholders. It hosts its own annual open house and open houses organized by the local chamber of commerce. An annual Enterprise Center Luncheon serves to recognize stakeholders, clients that have graduated from the incubator, 100 Point System award winners, and winners of other awards, including recognition for both the individual and organization that have contributed the most that year to SJCEC.

In addition to being recognized in the community as an important contributor to regional economic development, the incubator has been certified by the New Mexico Department of Economic Development, a program that permits the incubator to receive state funding from the department.

■■ powerhouse ventures

Christchurch, New Zealand
Stephen Hampson, CEO
www.cii.co.nz

When speaking to staff of Powerhouse Ventures in Christchurch, New Zealand, two words come up repeatedly: expertise and capital. Providing expertise is fundamental to Powerhouse's business strategy, and underpinning companies with capital is something the organization does every step of the way.

Powerhouse is a venture development organization that combines business incubation and investment activities. It is funded in part by the New Zealand government and generates revenues from various venture development activities. Before exploring the Powerhouse Incubator's operations, it's helpful to step back and look at the organization, its partners, and its history.

Powerhouse's first incubator—formerly called the Canterbury Innovation Incubator—opened its doors in 2001 with the mission of supporting technology start-ups. Its primary goal was to provide advice and access to capital to turn high-value IP into profitable, growing companies.

According to Powerhouse CEO Stephen Hampson, "The Internet had just had its boom, and there was lots of talk of high-tech companies and rapid growth." Wanting to get involved with this prosperity, the city of Christchurch's economic development arm reviewed the strategies of other cities. "Canterbury Development Corporation looked around the world to see what we were missing, and as a city we were missing a business incubator," Hampson says.

The incubator's founding partners were Canterbury Development Corporation (the city's economic development and employment arm), Christchurch Polytechnic Institute of Technology, Lincoln University, Orion New Zealand (a public utility), and the University of Canterbury.

After CII had developed and refined techniques for facilitating technology commercialization, Hampson's next objective was to assist in the streamlining of investment into start-ups. Powerhouse was established in 2006, resulting in a public-private partnership between the original (public) funders and private investors (high-net-worth individuals). Powerhouse renamed CII the Powerhouse City Incubator, and all employment contracts shifted over to Powerhouse, which now has a contract to manage three incubators.

Powerhouse's operational budget is approximately NZ$2 million, half of which comes from New Zealand Trade and Enterprise (New Zealand's economic development agency). Powerhouse generates the balance of its income from the following programs and services:

- Interest on cash-out from equity in client firms
- Fees for new market and new technology opportunity assessments
- Technical and financial services to incubator clients and other external clients
- Training programs (workshops, corporate training)
- Rent
- Regional support and sponsorship

Powerhouse has a goal of reaching self-sustainability by 201 via these income streams.

Powerhouse now manages three incubators: the Powerhouse City Incubator, which focuses on ICT and general business ar has a capacity for up to twenty-four technology companies; the Powerhouse Lincoln Incubator at Lincoln University, which focuses on agriscience and biotechnology; and the Powerhouse Ilam Incubator, at the University of Canterbury, which focuses on clean technology and engineering.

Powerhouse Ventures also provides services to local Crown Research Institutes (CRIs), assessing technology for commercial potential, helping them shape opportunities, and providing seed funding. (CRIs are government research institutes that are charged with covering their own expenses They operate as corporations.)

Powerhouse employs fourteen individuals: a team of two on the University of Canterbury campus, a team of two at Linco University campus, four on-site at Powerhouse City Incubato and six specialists in the areas of IP and investment who are based out of the Christchurch incubator but spend time at al Powerhouse offices. Powerhouse's incubator activities are th focus of this case study.

Powerhouse has graduated forty-five companies since its inception, including seven between summer 2007 and summe 2008. The portfolio of those graduate companies alone is impressive: two university spin-outs, three student start-ups, and two serial entrepreneurs. Together they employ thirty-one individuals and have combined revenues of NZ $3.6 million.

Powerhouse has refined its model over the years to cultivate a pipeline of potential clients by engaging in the following activities: developing programs to work closely with universit researchers, creating a model for assessing potential opportunities, and creating sources of early-stage capital. These activities are detailed below.

Powerhouse takes a grassroots approach to growing companies, starting its process earlier than many incubators. it actually looks for technology that will result in the formation of companies.

With a mission of helping entrepreneurs to convert IP into profitable companies, Powerhouse needs a critical mass of commercializable IP. Powerhouse has found a successful way to work alongside the region's universities and research institutions to convert IP into start-up firms.

e incubator board and management recognized that to
nvert more IP successfully into local companies, they would
ed to encourage faculty and students at those universities
d research institutions to create more commercializable
in the first place. "This became a strategic imperative in
04," Hampson says.

any researchers in New Zealand are faced with the
allenge of creating the connection between research and
mmercialization," Hampson says. "They are driven by
e desire to create, but I think it is more the competitive
ment with other researchers—[to be the] first to find the
eakthrough."

counter this line of thinking, Powerhouse staff make it their
to get to know the region's researchers and to convince
m not only that Powerhouse can provide assistance with
hnology development but also that successful commercial-
tion can generate funds to advance their research.

lping get their feet into researchers' doors are formal
rtnerships between Powerhouse and the University
Canterbury, the Christchurch Polytechnic Institute of
hnology, and Lincoln University. These partnerships call
Powerhouse staff to provide commercial and financial
pertise and resources to the universities' technology
nsfer operations. "This provides the organizations with
ignificant scaling up of commercialization resources,"
mpson says. Additionally, Powerhouse has informal
reements with the local Crown Research Institutes, the
n der Veer Institute, and the Canterbury Development
rporation. Powerhouse staff visit these partners at least
arterly, and the partners pay for Powerhouse services on an
dividual project basis.

ving formal partnerships with the three universities
ows Powerhouse to have staff on campus all the time,
ilding relationships with researchers. "Early engagement
th researchers is necessary for spotting breakthrough
portunities," Hampson says, explaining that staff meet
gularly with industry leaders to discuss commercial
portunities for partners' IP. "Having selected those
ventions with significant commercial merit, the team's focus
to get those technologies through the proof-of-concept
age with input from customers." As ventures continue down
e commercialization path, Powerhouse's incubation facility
ovides business support to accelerate their growth.

etting to know the researchers on these campuses involves
th formal and informal interactions. Powerhouse offers
rmal training programs for researchers, designed to
peal to their philosophies of science and problem solving.
hrough such programs, we start with a broad overview
commercialization and move ultimately to one-on-one
ngagement on specific projects," Hampson says. "We
egin this process with presentations to research groups, to
w the seeds, and follow this up by individual visits to the
searcher where interest has been shown."

Powerhouse staff get to know individual researchers' areas
of expertise and current projects. Hampson says his staff
take the time to truly learn about research projects, doing
the background work necessary to be able to ask questions
and have in-depth conversations about the work. "If they
think you don't understand their technology, they believe you
can't appraise its commercial application," Hampson says.
"Understanding how truly clever their invention is becomes
a requirement to speak to them and for them to buy in to the
discussions and process that follows."

Hampson says building close working relationships with
researchers is by far the most important factor in successfully
identifying and commercializing IP. "The response from
researchers has been excellent," he says. "We have
uncovered IP that has never been identified as having value.
We have also helped to progress the IP that is more obvious.
Our ability to spot and enhance what may initially seem to be
limited opportunities has impressed many and enhanced our
reputation on campus."

Once Powerhouse has uncovered IP that has the potential to
make it to market, it uses various systematic methods to help
move the IP toward commercialization. These methods are
detailed in chapter 7, "Leveraging Innovation."

To help the region's research institutions and universities
maintain a constant flow of commercializable IP, the incubator
provides opportunity assessments of new markets and
new technologies. The assessments answer two important
questions:

- Who would use this technology, and for
  what purpose?

- What changes must be made to this technology to
  take it to market?

Using a systematic approach, incubator staff communicate
with industry experts, conduct focus groups, and talk to
potential customers to answer those questions. They focus on
how the new technology might be used to change the way a
particular job currently is being done.

The goal isn't necessarily to commercialize a technology as-is
but to influence further research toward commercialization.

As outlined above, Powerhouse operates incubation facilities
in central Christchurch and on the campuses of Canterbury
and Lincoln universities. Together the facilities have the
capacity to serve thirty-five companies. Between 50 percent
and 75 percent of resident clients come from research
institutions, and the remainder come from the private sector.
The incubator is increasingly recognized as the technology
hub of Canterbury, hosting networking events, clusters,
seminars, and guest speakers.

The incubator offers typical amenities, including office furniture, reception services, common areas, and high-speed Internet. Although Powerhouse offers a wide range of assistance, services, and facilities, it focuses its business assistance on five core areas:

- **Financial analysis.** Powerhouse helps clients determine when they need money and how much they need. During the early sales stage of a client's development, Powerhouse can provide bookkeeping so that accurate financials are available to manage cash flow. Powerhouse also assists extensively with capital raising (see below).

- **Market focus.** Powerhouse's staff advise clients to spend equal time on market and product development. The staff work with clients to ensure an in-depth understanding of customer needs; identify beachhead opportunities (for early profitability); and determine product requirements, ensuring the right product-to-market match.

- **Building the team.** Powerhouse's links with the local technology community have enabled it to attract high-quality technical and management staff to client companies.

- **Mentoring of founders.** Because the role and focus of the founding entrepreneur changes dramatically during the early years of a business, Powerhouse provides coaching to company founders to identify their roles in a venture and plan for change.

- **External advice.** Powerhouse calls on an extensive network of local, national, and international experts to guide client companies. This is an essential part of the incubation program.

In addition to this range of business assistance services, Powerhouse provides intensive assistance with the capital-raising process. Powerhouse has raised over NZ$8 million in capital for more than forty ventures.

Powerhouse assists at all stages in the investment process. First, staff help clients determine their financing needs, including when and how much capital will be required, as well as what type of capital should be raised (e.g., grants, equity, debt). Next, incubator staff help clients find the right capital by matching the right investor and type of investment with each company.

Once funding is secured, Powerhouse facilitates the integration of the investors into the entrepreneurial team, assisting with due diligence, term sheets, shareholder agreements, share splits, and share transfers. Powerhouse, along with professional advisors (e.g., lawyers and accountants), assists companies through the process.

Powerhouse helps companies manage relationships with investors and provides assistance with reporting (e.g., quarterly reports).

Powerhouse is a public-private partnership. The company has a contract to manage the three incubators, and the same individuals manage Powerhouse's VC fund, as well.

The VC operation is unique in that it develops new funds annually and in that it attracts capital from high-net-worth individuals (angel investors) who invest anywhere from NZ$10,000 to NZ$250,000 each into Powerhouse's funds and then trust Powerhouse's Investment Committee (whose members also are investors in the funds) to invest that money wisely. The angels also have the option to invest alongside the fund's investments. Angels can diversify their investment among several start-up companies, but they may also choose to invest more cash in a firm that particularly appeals to them.

Since funds are developed each year, Powerhouse can stay focused on early-stage companies. "We want to invest every year in things moving out of the universities," Hampson says. "Multiyear funds eventually don't have sufficient time left to invest early, develop, and get out. Consequently they only do early-stage in the first few years of a fund's life."

But investing in new things each year doesn't stop Powerhouse from making follow-on investments. "We reserve money for follow-on investing," Hampson says. "If we put $200K into a company, we'll reserve $100K for follow-on investing. But we go back out and leverage it."

Typically the angels who contribute to the fund for one year will contribute the following year (some will drop out, some will come in).

The first Powerhouse Fund was launched in 2008 and was to make its first round of three to four investments in the fall of 2009. Powerhouse has a goal of making two investments in companies coming out of the University of Canterbury each year, another two in companies from Lincoln University each year, and up to four investments each year in companies from the private sector. Powerhouse incubator clients can pursue funding, but being an incubator client is not a requirement to receive investments.

Investments range from NZ$100,000 to NZ$1 million, of which approximately 25 percent comes from the fund and the remainder from coinvestors. "Powerhouse's investment leads the deal for angels and corporate investors," Hampson says.

The investors pay Powerhouse a fee for managing their money, and the companies that receive an investment pay Powerhouse a fee based on a percentage of the investment. Hampson says it's too early to analyze investment returns to date, but he expects that eventually returns on investment combined with investment fees will provide sufficient revenue to fund all Powerhouse operations.

Additionally, Powerhouse anticipates that it will develop follow-on expansion capital funds that also will provide revenue.

■ innovacorp

Halifax, Nova Scotia
Dan MacDonald, former president and CEO
David McNamara, vice president, incubation

Originally established as the Nova Scotia Research Foundation in 1948, Innovacorp became a Crown corporation of the province of Nova Scotia in 1995. As a Crown corporation, Innovacorp is owned by the province, which funds 65 percent of the program's annual operating budget. Other sources of operating revenue include incubation fees and investment returns.

Innovacorp's mission is to help early-stage companies commercialize their technology for export, and its daily activities are driven by two broad strategic goals: to accelerate commercialization of client technologies to fuel economic growth and increase competitiveness in export markets; and to collaborate with private and public partners to build a dynamic, high-growth culture of entrepreneurship in Nova Scotia. Key sector targets include information and communications technology, life sciences, and clean technology.

With an annual budget in excess of C$7.1 million, a staff of thirty-five, and over 135,000 square feet of incubation space, Innovacorp has two types of customers. Primary customers are early-stage Nova Scotia entrepreneurs. Secondary customers include a broad, diverse set of stakeholders such as regional and international investors, postsecondary education institutions, and economic development partners.

At the core of Innovacorp is its High Performance Incubation business model. HPI incorporates three critical and symbiotic resources in its program and service delivery portfolio:

- Specialized incubation infrastructure (includes specialized start-up infrastructure, state-of-the-art information technology, and advanced business services)

- Business mentoring (advanced business consulting, marketing and communications, go-to-market strategies, and guidance on access to capital)

- Seed and venture capital investment through Innovacorp-managed funds and partnerships with early-stage investors (regional, national, and international)

Innovacorp positions its HPI services of incubation, mentoring, and investment in the first three stages of the venture growth continuum (idea, start-up, and developmental) to make the company ready for venture capital investment.

"Innovacorp's suite of services is continuously tailored and delivered to help entrepreneurs remove obstacles and bottlenecks that stand in their way," says Dan MacDonald, Innovacorp president and CEO until early 2010.

Armed with a dedicated team of ten highly experienced individuals from diverse private-sector business backgrounds, Innovacorp differentiates its incubation services through a value-added approach to augmenting its clients' business-building savvy. Some examples of how they do this include providing:

- Full-account plans and strategies for the go-to-market activities of each client's ventures

- Target market, target customer, and competitive analysis

- Value proposition, pricing, and packaging development

- A comprehensive, state-of-the-art telecommunications network to handle all client needs (voice, data, server hosting, etc.)

- Postgraduation support, including assisting in lease negotiations

"First we pull up alongside our client companies to ask them the tough questions they need to ask themselves," says David McNamara, vice president for incubation. "Then we provide the maximum support to help the company succeed."

HPI includes a focus on key business needs addressed through a comprehensive suite of services—business development, business planning, R&D, and adequate capitalization of the firm. These services include research and development networks, marketing, sales and distribution strategies, networks and alliances for intellectual property identification and protection, and product development.

Innovacorp takes a unique approach to managing its deal flow and prospects. "In order to run a great incubation process, you have to grow and build a dynamic pipeline of high-quality prospects for your services," MacDonald says. "We constantly review our pipeline to see what prospects are advancing, in need of making a major decision, or need particular assistance from us."

One way Innovacorp maintains deal flow is through its provincewide I-3 Technology Start-Up Competition, which began in 2006. The 2009 competition generated 133 submissions and yielded eleven new clients. (For more on the competition, see chapter 6, "Client Entrance and Exit.")

Whether the result of the competition or walk-in applications, Innovacorp implements strong selection criteria when engaging high-potential start-up ventures. Innovacorp assists its prospects and clients in determining whether they are a good "strategic fit" for the incubation and mentoring services. Prospects can review their eligibility on Innovacorp's Web site or call to schedule a meeting with a senior advisor to review their business concept and its fit with Innovacorp.

Potential applicants are vetted via five specific entry criteria:

- **Stage.** The start-up venture must be a Nova Scotia–based early-stage technology company.

- **People.** The start-up's business plan must be credible, and the team must have management experience, domain expertise, and, preferably, an entrepreneurial track record.

- **Barrier.** There must be a competitive barrier to entry in the form of a unique and/or proprietary technology (product, system, or service), ideally one with defendable intellectual property.

- **Market.** There must be a large national or international addressable market.

- **Fundability.** There must be a high probability or reasonable likelihood of obtaining a fully funded business plan. Consideration is given to how much money it will take to successfully go to market, to commercialize the product or service, and to achieve positive cash flow.

On the basis of this evaluation, Innovacorp prioritizes its resources into actionable categories that define the support menu of services: lab and office space, facilities, and services; information and communications technology infrastructure, services, and support; scientific resources; shared administrative support services; business advice and referral services; networking opportunities; and off-site affiliate client services. These categories include:

01. **Strong prospects of commercial success.** Innovacorp will engage additional resources in these high-potential start-ups to help position the company to obtain venture funding.

02. **Moderate prospects of commercial success.** If appropriate, Innovacorp will work with the start-up to strengthen its attributes and the probability of securing venture funding.

03. **Weak prospects of commercial success.** Innovacorp will disengage from the start-up, providing in-depth feedback detailing the rationale for doing so.

This selection process has allowed Innovacorp to have a highly robust pipeline of deal flow. In a typical quarter, Innovacorp will field ten to twenty-five initial contacts; of those, ten to fifteen will undergo a detailed and critical analysis. Three to eight of those will become clients, and two to four eventually will graduate.

It's not surprising that Innovacorp manages several investment funds to help provincial companies grow and succeed. These include the Nova Scotia First Fund, established by the province in 1989; the HPI Microfund, a seed fund launched in 2004; and the Early Stage Commercialization Fund, established in 2005 to move Nova Scotia's university and community college research to market. (For more on these funds, see the section on access to capital in chapter 8, "Client Services.")

Innovacorp reviews its own operations as critically as those of its prospects and clients. One example is its annual business planning process, which typically takes seven business days over three months. The process begins with a thorough analysis of the strengths, weaknesses, opportunities, and threats for all aspects of Innovacorp operations. The result is a "long, sometimes ugly list" of potential priorities, MacDonald says. Managers of Innovacorp's various divisions rank the competing priorities until a consensus of the most urgent ones emerges. Then, MacDonald solicits feedback from staff and members of his board of directors to ensure buy-in and support. The final business plan, including metrics for achievement of goals, is submitted to the provincial government about a month before the beginning of the fiscal year on April 1. (For more on Innovacorp's business planning process, see chapter 3, "Finances.")

Innovacorp further gauges its effectiveness through an annual third-party survey of clients to solicit feedback on the program's performance. Every year since 2006, Innovacorp has contracted with an independent third party to conduct a telephone satisfaction survey with its clients. Each survey costs Innovacorp about C$5,000; however, there are several free online survey tools, and NBIA members have access to others at low or no cost through the NBIA Partner Program. (For more on the survey, see chapter 5, "Program Evaluation.")

"We have to stay close and be relevant to our clients," MacDonald says. "This extensive survey informs us of what we are doing well and what we can improve on in our services. It also tells us from year to year what our client's value most and how we are delivering on our value-added services."

■ business incubator center

Grand Junction, Colorado
Christina Reddin, executive director
www.gjincubator.org

Founded in 1987, the Business Incubator Center of Grand Junction, Colorado, has solved two significant problems that might have stymied a lesser program: it has developed a comprehensive, yet largely independent, support program for entrepreneurs, including training, business counseling, loan funds, and tax credits, and it has done so in the relative isolation of Colorado's Western Slope. Secondly, it has overcome the disadvantages of a physical structure that is neither beautiful nor easy to get to.

Proving that big ideas can come from smaller, isolated communities, the Business Incubator Center has become the leader in entrepreneurial activities throughout the region, says Executive Director Christina Reddin. "If there are entrepreneurial activities on the Western Slope, we want to be touching them," she says.

Located in Mesa County, Grand Junction is the largest city between the Wasatch and Rocky Mountain ranges, with a metropolitan population of 139,000 people. The community is an economic driver for the region; natural gas, coal, and uranium extraction companies are based there, although mining and gas wells are located throughout this mineral-rich country. Yet Grand Junction is nearly a four-hour drive through snow-capped mountains to the nearest large cities—Denver on the Eastern Slope across the Rockies, and Salt Lake City to the west of the Wasatch Mountains.

The Business Incubator Center—though it started small—is now an independent 501(c)(3) public foundation that offers the following services:

- Financial assistance through its $4.7 million loan fund

- Business development services through its 60,000-square-foot incubator, which offers manufacturing and office space and a commercial kitchen

- Counseling and workshops provided through its Small Business Development Center

- Tax incentives through its Mesa County Enterprise Zone Program

The incubator is 75 percent self-financed. Income is generated through incubator rent and program fees, low-cost SBDC workshops, business loan fund interest income, enterprise zone administrative fees, and property management services for the U.S. Department of Energy, which owns the incubator building and is housed on site. Additional sources of external funding include state grants for the SBDC and the business loan fund, city and county support contracts, and donations

from local private funders. Periodic capital campaigns have raised $2 million in eight years to support renovations to the incubator's campus.

And what about that site and the difficulty of getting there? "You have to drive right out of town, go up a hill, turn around a cemetery, and go down the hill. Then you approach this creepy government building," explains Reddin, who provides pictures of these landmarks during presentations on the incubator. Yet with the many resources and training programs the BIC provides, and a training room that brings monthly Toastmasters' meetings to the incubator, the BIC has made a situation work that could have flummoxed others.

"We are not a threat to local realtors because they'd say, 'Who'd ever want to be down there?'" Reddin says.

The incubator has a staff of eleven, including nine full-time and two part-time employees. This mix includes five full-time business counselors; BIC leverages its staff through tapping the expertise of twenty volunteer business counselors.

"When a potential client comes in the door we throw as many tools at them as possible," says Reddin, who also is an SBDC counselor. "The focus is on service to the client. When a client comes in they're not faced with a bureaucracy. The service level has to match the expectations of people coming through the door."

BIC works with five hundred SBDC clients each year, including the fifty-four incubator clients that reside on site. BIC and SBDC primarily serve manufacturing, agriculture, construction, and retail clients. Results since 1987 include:

- Launching more than two hundred companies

- Generating more than $137 million in revenues from these firms

- Creating 8,982 jobs

- Facilitating investment of $50.6 million in capital

Reddin says she's a big believer in "management by walking around. We do a lot of checking in on clients," she says. Interaction also is encouraged by requiring all clients to come to the front desk to get their mail and packages, and the building hosts at least two SBDC workshops a week in addition to Toastmasters. "There's a lot going on," says Reddin, who doesn't charge nonprofits for use of the BIC training rooms, which brings a constant stream of visitors to the out-of-the-way location.

The diverse staff provides advice on licensing, legal issues, finance, marketing, intellectual property, accounting, and launching a new product or services. The BIC manages the Loan Fund of Mesa County, which makes commercial loans to Mesa County businesses that are not able to get their financing needs met by traditional lenders. An Incubator Bootstrap Fund of $25,000 has been set aside to assist incubator clients, who primarily use it to finance contracts they have obtained—that is, to pay for goods or services required to fulfill contractual obligations that will result in client company income.

"I get to apply my business experience and continue to learn."

– Christina Reddin, executive director, the Business Incubation Center

BIC training programs advertised on its Web site in January 2010 included "Leading Edge Business Planning," a twelve-week program that provides guidance on basic business issues and business plan preparation, as well as "Bookkeeping Boot Camp: Understanding Bookkeeping and Financial Statements," "Tax Plan Workout: Dealing with the Business Tax Maze," "Guerilla Marketing for New Business," "Payroll: the Process in a Nutshell," "Starting a Business in Western Colorado," and "Fast Trac Business Basics." (The Fast Trac program is not affiliated with the Ewing Marion Kauffman Foundation's FastTrac program and is a series of brown bag luncheons focusing on specific business issues.)

In addition to providing training and counseling to incubator and SBDC clients (all incubator clients are also SBDC clients), the incubator offers monthly luncheons for clients to discuss mutual issues and hear informative speakers. It uses Mesa State College interns to assist clients with a variety of projects, and it helps clients develop networks and public awareness by participating in trade shows, open houses, and social occasions at the incubator. Through an agreement with the Colorado Business Incubation Association, BIC also offers its clients free use of CBIA member facilities throughout the state for meetings, networking, and access to technical assistance experts.

The incubator requires clients to have a one-year lease, except for a few short-term month-to-month rentals for up to six months, depending on space availability. The lease also requires that clients consult regularly with incubator/SBDC staff. Space is made available at a percentage of the county fair market rate, beginning at 75 percent and increasing annually. Utilities are included in monthly rents, except for manufacturing spaces. Each client also pays $30 per month in "program fee" charges for access to reception areas, common rooms, the loading dock, and training and break rooms (including a kitchen), and equipment, including copiers, faxes, telephones, computers, word processing software, and an air compressor.

Overhead projectors, laptops and a television are available for short-term use, and the fee also covers janitorial services in common areas and up to two hours per month of light secretarial services, mail services, notary public services, and telephone answering.

Founded by community leaders in 1987 after a regional economic downturn, the incubator was developed to diversify the economy and create jobs. It was originally funded through a Colorado Department of Local Affairs grant that used federal Community Development Block Grants to address slum and blight. The original site, a 40,000-square-foot warehouse, was provided by a local businessman for $1 per year. In 1999, the incubator moved to its Department of Energy campus.

The nine-member board of directors includes representatives of Mesa State College, local entrepreneurs, a banker, a CPA, and an attorney. Ex officio members of the board are Grand Junction and Mesa County economic development officials and a county commissioner. While these ex officio members do not have voting rights, their attendance ensures that they are knowledgeable about BIC activities and value and that incubator staff are up-to-date on local government initiatives.

With a BA in economics from Georgetown University and an MBA from Cornell University (where she cofounded a student-run incubator), Reddin began a business career after graduate school and, as an entrepreneur, became involved with the incubator nearly seven years before becoming its director in January 2007. She and a partner owned Mountain Sprouts, a 2006 BIC graduate.

Reddin is passionate about serving entrepreneurial clients and contributing to local wealth creation and economic development. "I get to apply my business experience and continue to learn. Also you get to work with entrepreneurs every day. The work is meaningful," she says.

Recently Reddin has also become passionate about "economic gardening," embracing efforts to grow second–stage

mpanies, often three to five years old. Pioneered by Chris
bins of Littleton, Colorado, and promoted by the Edward
we Foundation, economic gardening focuses on providing
cond-stage entrepreneurs with information they need to
ive, attending to quality of life and cultural issues, providing
cess to quality employees, and developing networks that can
rove entrepreneurs' ability to grow to the next level.

he core of this philosophy is coaching these clients for
ir next stage of growth, next product line, mapping supply
ains, and innovating—strategically positioning them for the
ure," Reddin says. "All incubator managers know that the
rt-up phase holds many challenges. With incubator clients
erating in our program for five years, we normally see them
ough both the first and second stages of growth. Economic
rdening provides tools that are ideally suited to support our
ents in the second stage, the last few years of the program
d the next few after graduation. In order to really generate
ong, sustainable, job-creating companies, we need to ensure
at clients can not only develop great products and services,
t also became the leaders of great companies."

ddin says that economic gardening best practices are
imately associated with three critical themes:

01. **Infrastructure:** building and supporting the
development of community assets essential to
commerce and overall quality of life (e.g. roads,
education, and cultural amenities)

02. **Connectivity:** improving the interaction and exchange
among business owners and critical resource providers
(e.g. industry trade groups, public sector supporters,
and academic institutions)

03. **Market information:** access to competitive intelligence
on markets, customers, and competitors comparable
to the resources historically available only to large firms

onnectivity is already a strength of the BIC," she says.
herefore our new economic gardening program will focus on
dding market information to our service offering."

■■ environmental business cluster

San Jose, California
Melinda Richter, executive director
www.environmentalcluster.org

The Environmental Business Cluster was established in 1994
in San Jose, California, to assist early-stage companies
developing clean and renewable energy products that have a
positive impact on the environment. Long before environmental
technology, clean technology, and alternative energy were
on the radar screen of investors and technology incubators,
the EBC was established by a handful of stakeholders—
including Pacific Gas & Electric, Joint Venture Silicon Valley,
Union Bank, and Peninsula Conservation Foundation, along
with the San Jose Redevelopment Agency and the San Jose
State University Research Foundation—to further technology
development while improving the environment. The founder,
Jim Robbins, served as executive director until 2009.

Today, EBC serves approximately thirty companies and has
assisted over 160 client companies since its inception. Since
its founding, EBC has increased the number of stakeholders by
adding those with a vested interest in supporting the formation
and growth of clean technology ventures, that were willing to
provide deal flow, and that offer potential clients access to EBC
services by fully or partially subsidizing the expense. Partners
such as the California Energy Commission, Citi Foundation,
and the Cleantech Open business plan competition have
provided companies with access to EBC services.

One example of this innovative approach is the Clean Tech
Commercialization grants provided by the California Energy
Commission since 2005. Under this program, the CEC has
provided one year of EBC incubation and commercialization
services to companies they have invested in.

Core services offered by EBC include, but are not limited to, regular mentoring and strategic coaching sessions in the following areas:

- Market strategy
- Legal and intellectual property strategy
- Operational structure
- Business plan strategy
- Marketing, branding and PR strategy
- Finance strategy and assistance in mapping potential investors using Cleantech Investor DataBase
- Licensing and partnering strategy
- Pitch technique and practice for investor/partner/customer presentations

EBC has also developed innovative programs to further its mission. Examples include:

- **Clean Energy Alliance (CEA) Business Incubation Program.** In 2001 EBC helped the U.S. National Renewable Entergy Lab (NREL) in Golden, Colorado, develop a national network of incubation programs that assist clean and renewable energy start-ups. The network has sixteen participating incubators from all parts of the United States, including California, Georgia, Kansas, New York, and Texas. As a result of this program, EBC clients can receive assistance throughout the United States from CEA member incubators and NREL as they expand and start doing business outside their local market areas.

- **"Meet With" series.** A special program connects emerging companies with access to traditional and alternative funding sources such as Khosla Ventures, Mohr Davidow Ventures, the U.S. Department of Energy, the U.S. Department of Defense, and Bosch.

- **Pro bono office hours and 1-800 hotlines.** Qualified service teams with expertise in legal, insurance, recruitment, benefits, and other issues provide free on-site office hours and a toll-free help line.

- **On-demand "Practice Pitch" sessions.** EBC client companies may practice their funding, sales, or elevator pitches to a panel of experts from the VC and entrepreneurial communities.

- **Monthly workshops and seminars.** Clients have the opportunity to meet with experts and peers on topics relevant to starting a business and critical topics for research and development processes, that provide educational and networking opportunities.

To validate its value proposition, EBC has continually monitored its performance against its mission and the expectations of its key stakeholders. As part of this effort, EBC has documented the following program results:

- Since its inception, EBC has prepared regular return-on-investment analyses for the city of San Jose. These reports showed that the city receives almost $3 in sales tax revenue from EBC client companies for every $1 invested by the city. This analysis—the methodology of which has been presented at NBIA conferences to help other incubators understand the approach—has resulted in twelve years of city of San Jose funding for EBC.

- After using the EBC commercialization program for two and a half years, the California Energy Commission hired ICF, a national consulting firm, to evaluate EBC's results. The study showed that CEC technologies referred to EBC reached the marketplace at a rate ten times greater than that of companies not supported by EBC. When the researchers asked EBC clients whether they would prefer that the funding provided to the EBC to provide services to each company be paid directly to each company, all but one responded that they preferred EBC assistance to direct cash payments. The evaluation concluded that EBC provides good value to client companies and recommended that the program continue to be funded and expanded.

- New Energy Finance in the United Kingdom published a study on Key Success Factors for the Incubation of Clean Technology Companies in 2007. Out of 114 incubators and clean tech centers around the world identified as having a significant focus on clean technology commercialization, EBC was identified as the most successful at market commercialization of client companies.

- EBC reports annual statistics to the Clean Energy Alliance. Although the report is restricted to clean energy companies, EBC in 2007 reported statistical data on forty-eight past and present clean energy companies. Out of twenty-five current clean energy clients, eleven companies had reached the market. These clients had also raised $18.4 million in financing and employed 180 people.

- As part of its tenth anniversary, EBC surveyed every client assisted since its inception and found that 82 percent were still in business and profitable.

In recognition of EBC's excellence, NBIA gave it the 2008 Randall M. Whaley Incubator of the Year Award, which honors the highest achievements among NBIA member incubators.

recognition of the Environmental Business Cluster's
excellence, NBIA named it the 2008 Randall M. Whaley
Incubator of the Year—the industry's highest honor.

afterword

"Best practice" is not just a phrase for NBIA or its member programs. Every day, every year, these and thousands of other incubation programs around the world strive to live up to the standards set by NBIA's board of directors in 1996.

In the introduction, we mentioned the importance of best practices to stakeholders in measuring the effectiveness of business incubation programs. This book is one way to learn how to implement best practices in your program. But NBIA also offers a way for you to measure your compliance with best practices and see instant results.

In 2008, the Appalachian Regional Commission and the Tennessee Valley Authority asked NBIA to develop a system through which the incubators they funded could benchmark their implementation of best practices. As part of that project, NBIA created an online benchmarking tool. Now available to incubator managers everywhere, the tool presents a series of statements that reflect best practices in a number of areas. Participants rank their compliance with the statement on a five-place scale. Users can see how their results measure up to industry standards, as well as to the practices of other programs whose managers have completed the survey.

If you are truly interested in becoming a best practice program—and NBIA hopes you are! —visit www.nbia.org/benchmark to try your hand at this amazing self-measurement tool. With the investment of just a few minutes' time, you can see how close your program is to being a paragon of best practice. If you're not quite there, you can access an online library of resources from NBIA and other content providers that detail how you can improve your practices.

Implementing best practices is important not just for your program but also for the industry as a whole. Incubation is in the political spotlight in a way it has not been since the late 1980s and early 1990s. As the world recovers from financial catastrophe, communities and governments are looking for ways to strengthen their economies. Increasingly, they are looking to incubation. This is our industry's time to shine.

For too long, we have been the best-kept secret of economic development and job and wealth creation. If we are to step into that spotlight and take our place on the world's stage of economic innovation, we have to demonstrate that while incubation is practiced in many ways in many places, it has at its core a set of standards that guide all incubation programs. And that these standards—these principles and best practices—are not just words, but the words we live by. — *Corinne Colbert*

glossary

■■■ THE FOLLOWING ARE DEFINITIONS OF VARIOUS TERMS AS THEY PERTAIN TO BUSINESS INCUBATION.

Admissions Process: See **Client Screening.**

Advisory Board: A dedicated group of business leaders, professionals, stakeholders, and/or specialists that provides competent advice and guidance for the incubation program management team on a regular basis. This group may also advise clients. See **Board of Directors.**

Affiliate Client: A client who is not an occupant of an incubation facility but receives some incubation services for a fee. See also **Virtual Client,** as these terms are sometimes used interchangeably.

Affiliate Program: An orchestrated set of business assistance services that a business incubation program makes available to start-up companies that don't reside in the incubator's physical facility. Affiliate programs also may provide shared administrative and office resources as well as access to conference rooms and specialized equipment. Such programs allow an incubator to better serve its community by serving more clients than it can accommodate in its physical space. Affiliate programs also represent a source of revenue generation for the incubator.

Anchor Tenant: A business or organization that leases space from an incubator but does not receive incubation services. An anchor tenant is usually long term and leases space at market rates, thus providing a steady source of income for the incubator. An anchor tenant also may play a role in the incubation process; for example, an anchor tenant may be a professional service provider that makes discounted services available to client firms.

Angel Investors: High-net-worth individuals who invest money in high-potential start-up businesses in return for an equity ownership position in the company. They provide smaller investments and earlier-stage funding than do professional venture capitalists. Angel investors obtain a return on their investments when the companies in which they've invested experience a liquidity event: are acquired, merged, or have a successful IPO (initial public offering of stock) or are bought out by later-stage investors.

Angel Networks: Connected groups of high-net-worth individuals who are accredited angel investors. Sometimes these individuals join together to collectively invest in high-potential start-up businesses. Angel investments are generally smaller and earlier-stage than professional venture capital investments.

Benchmarking: A method of measuring incubator activities and outcomes against those of recognized leaders to establish priorities and targets leading to improvement.

Board of Directors: A group of individuals bearing governance and fiduciary responsibilities for the activities of an incubation program. These responsibilities include approving the budget and hiring the incubator manager. In many cases, the board of directors handles both governance and client advisory functions. Both types of boards may include the incubator manager and usually include members of the entrepreneurial community, individuals with expertise related to the incubator's mission, and representatives from the finance community, legal professions, host institution, and economic development community.

Business Assistance Services: Intangible services (separate from shared administrative and office resources) an incubation program offers its on-site and affiliate clients. Services include one-on-one business mentoring, business planning assistance, help with accounting/financial management, help accessing capital, and linkages to higher education resources. Often incubation programs utilize outside service providers to provide some of these services.

Business Incubation: The process of accelerating the successful development of entrepreneurial companies through an array of business support resources and services targeted to their needs that are developed or orchestrated by incubator management, either with or without a physical facility. See also **Business Incubator.**

Business Incubator: A program designed to accelerate the successful development of entrepreneurial companies through an array of business support resources and services, developed or orchestrated by incubator management, and offered both in the incubator and through its network of contacts. A business incubator's main goal is to produce successful firms that will leave the program financially viable and freestanding. Critical to the definition of an incubator is the provision of management guidance, technical assistance, and consulting tailored to young growing companies. Incubators usually also provide clients access to appropriate rental space and flexible leases, shared basic business services and equipment, technology support services, and assistance in obtaining the financing necessary for company growth. Incubators vary in the way they deliver their services, in organizational structure and in the types of clients they serve. See also **Mixed-Use Incubator, Special Focus Incubator, Technology Incubator, Service Incubator, Incubator Without Walls, For-Profit Incubator,** and **Nonprofit Incubator.**

Business Incubator Facility: The space or building devoted to housing the business incubation program of services, incubator management, and resident client and anchor tenant companies.

ent: Participant in an incubation program. Clients receive
vices from program staff and the incubator's network of
vice providers, usually for a fee or sometimes in exchange
equity. See also **Affiliate Client.**

ent Screening: An incubator's process for selecting clients.
incubator uses entrance criteria to assess whether an
plicant likely can, with the program's assistance, become
ancially viable and freestanding and meet other program
quirements. As part of this process, an incubator manager
ght conduct an initial interview with a prospective applicant,
iew a completed application and business plan, carry
t credit and reference checks, and perform an in-depth
erview before inviting an applicant into an incubation
gram. An incubator's board of directors or a selection
mmittee might have the final say on accepting applicants.

bt Capital: Funding that must be repaid, e.g., a
mmercial bank loan or U.S. Small Business
ministration guaranteed loan.

veloper/Development Team: An individual or entity that
rks to establish a business incubator in a community. Often
informal leader(s) champions the cause, and a developer or
velopment team takes on the project. A development team
uld have broad community representation that increases
the development process progresses. Developers gauge
level of community interest and support, identify potential
rtners, oversee the feasibility study process, and implement
incubator project.

rly-Stage Company: A new business that is at the beta
ge: It has developed a prototype of its product or service
d is testing that product or service with a few customers
fore making adjustments and launching full-scale. Early-
ge companies may generate minor revenue from these beta
ts, but they often provide their product or service to the
stomer on very favorable terms. These companies usually
funded by angel investors, but some may secure venture
ital funding. Note: The term "early-stage" is often used
describe any prerevenue business. See also **Seed-Stage**
mpany and **Start-Up Company.**

trance Criteria: An incubator's set of standards and/or
delines that help staff determine whether to admit a firm
the incubator during the client-screening process. Criteria
y include potential for job creation, business focus, and
ether the firm has a business plan.

trepreneur: One who organizes, manages, and assumes
risks of a business or enterprise.

Equity Capital: Funding given in exchange for a share of
ownership in a company.

Equity Stake: An incubator's or investor's share of ownership
in a client company, either outright or via stock warrants giving
the option for future ownership. Some incubators take an
equity stake as a deferred payment for services they provide.

Exit Criteria: See **Graduation Policies/Exit Policies**.

Feasibility Study: An objective, systematic analysis to
determine whether an incubation program should be
established in a particular community. At minimum, such a
study examines the market, including the composition of the
available entrepreneurial pool and the needs of prospective
clients; stakeholder buy-in, which focuses on garnering
program champions and community support; short-term and
long-term financial feasibility of the project; and availability of
suitable real estate.

For-Profit Incubator: An incubation program that has among
its primary goals seeking financial returns on investments
for its investors. Three major types of for-profit incubators
have long been recognized—those that anticipate returns on
investment from real estate and service revenues; those that
seek returns on equity stakes in client companies; and those
operated by corporations spinning out technologies (seeking
to recoup investments) or acquiring new technologies with
strategic fit for the corporation.

Graduate: A client that exits an incubation program after
completing a set of benchmarks or goals. These exit criteria
are often part of the lease or service agreement for clients,
although they may also apply to affiliate clients. See also
Graduation Policies/Exit Policies.

Graduation Policy/Exit Policy: Criteria determined by an
incubator's manager or board of directors that specify when
an incubator client is prepared to leave the program. Criteria
usually include benchmarks and goals that are set with clients
individually. These may include having a management team
and board of directors in place, acquiring sufficient financing,
or having sales and profitability that are sufficient for client
success outside of the incubator.

Incubator Network: A set of incubators that work together
to achieve similar missions within a community or region. In
many cases, the incubators fall under the umbrella of a single
organization that operates the network.

Incubator Opening: The date that an incubator opens its
doors for clients to move in and/or receive assistance.

glossary

Incubator without Walls: A program that offers entrepreneurs all of the business-assistance services that a traditional bricks-and-mortar program does without providing a physical facility to house client firms. Like their with-walls counterparts, incubators without walls vary in the way they deliver their services and in organizational structure. See **Virtual Incubator.**

Industry Cluster: A geographic concentration of interconnected companies, suppliers, service providers, and associated institutions in a particular field. A cluster can attract customers, expertise, resources, and capital to a region, thereby creating sustainable local wealth and jobs.

Intern: A student who works with an organization in exchange for pay, course credit, or experience.

Manager: The executive who directs an incubation program's operations. Most managers report to the chief executive officer of the incubator's sponsoring organization; a political leader; a university president; or a board of directors that governs the program. The manager develops and coordinates business assistance services and usually provides one-on-one counseling and referral services to incubator clients. Other tasks include marketing the incubation program, fundraising, client screening, collecting rents and fees for services, and managing other incubator staff. Some incubation program managers have alternative titles, such as "president and CEO" or "executive director."

Manufacturing/Industrial Incubator: An incubation program designed to assist new enterprises primarily engaged in the manufacturing sector. Because clients require manufacturing space in addition to office space, manufacturing incubators tend to occupy more square footage than other types of incubators.

Mentor: An industry expert or business service provider who offers ongoing counseling to an incubator client. A mentor provides a voice of experience on a long-term basis, perhaps through one or more stages of a company's development. Groups of mentors having different areas of expertise may be assigned to individual companies.

Microenterprise: A business that has five or fewer employees; requires $35,000 or less in start-up capital; and does not have access to traditional (bank) financing. Incubation programs for microenterprise clients are often tailored to meet the needs of specific groups, such as welfare recipients, minorities, women, the working poor, and other individuals or business sectors that lack access to credit.

Mission: The guiding statement under which a business incubator operates. A mission statement asserts an incubator's fundamental purpose clearly and succinctly, defining the scope of the incubator's activities, its overall direction, and the clientele it serves. The mission statement should be consistent with client needs, evident in all incubat activities, and appropriate given the incubator's environment

Mixed-Use Incubator: A program that fosters the growth of kinds of companies; the businesses in a mixed-use incubato are not required to fit into any specialized niche. Companies in mixed-use incubators may include service, manufacturing technology, and other types of firms.

Net Leasable Space: The total amount of space in the incubator facility that is dedicated for rental by both anchor tenants and resident clients (excluding administrative offices and shared common space, for example). This term is used interchangeably with "leasable space."

Nonprofit Incubator: A business incubator that is a tax-exempt organization (as defined by the Internal Revenue Service) or operates as a program of another tax-exempt organization. Nonprofit incubators work to achieve various economic development and/or social goals, including creati jobs and wealth for communities, revitalizing neighborhoods diversifying economies, serving women and minorities, or commercializing technologies.

Occupancy Rate: The percentage of leasable or net leasable space available for client lease that is actually being rented b incubator clients.

Postincubation: Services offered to companies that have graduated from the incubation program (i.e., access to specialized facilities as needed, consulting services, CEO roundtables, and networking functions).

Preincubation: Services offered to companies or individuals who have not been formally admitted to the incubation program (i.e., FastTrac or NxLeveL training and business plan reviews).

Research Park: A property-based venture consisting of research and development facilities for technology- and science-based companies. Research parks promote technology transfer and development within a community, usually in partnership with industry and universities, assisting in the growth of new ventures and promoting economic development. A park will often have a contractual formal ownership or operational relationship with one or more universities or other institutions of higher education/ science research. Sometimes called "science park" or "technology park."

ed-Stage Company: A new business that has a firm
ncept and is developing a working prototype of its product
service. Seed-stage companies are funded by family,
nds, and sometimes angel investors.

f-Sufficiency: The ability of an incubation program to cover
erating expenses without external subsidy. Although a
rthy goal, self-sufficiency is unrealistic for some incubation
grams, particularly during program start-up. NBIA supports
 idea of incubator self-sustainability, a more realistic goal.
e also Self-Sustainability.

f-Sustainability: The ability of an incubator to remain on
und financial footing, with predictable, reliable sources
unding. NBIA has set financial self-sustainability as an
ustry best practice. Self-sustainability does not preclude
ancial support from outside sources, making it a more easily
ained goal than self-sufficiency. See also Self-Sufficiency.

rvice Incubator: An incubation program that fosters the
velopment of entrepreneurial firms in the service industry.
ms may range from landscapers, graphic designers,
d accountants to Internet-based companies and Web
velopment firms. An incubation program may target a
ected segment of the service industry.

rvice Provider Network: A stable of business assistance
nsultants who augment the skills of incubator staff. These
ividuals with expertise in specific subject areas, including
rketing, finance, business planning, procurement, and
ent law, usually provide their services for free or low cost
an as-needed basis. Along with incubator staff, these
ividuals provide the value-added service that is the core of
ective business incubation.

ared Administrative and Office Resources: Tangible
vices (separate from business assistance services) an
ubation program offers its on-site and affiliate clients.
vices may include reception and postage; use of office
uipment, including photocopy and fax machines; use of
nference rooms or common areas; and use of video- and
econferencing equipment. Although these services are
nerally integral to the array of services an incubation
gram offers, they are secondary to the business assistance
vices provided by incubator staff and service providers.

all- and Medium-Sized Enterprise (SME): A term used to
er to small- and medium-sized companies in many countries.
ereas the U.S. Small Business Administration generally
ines a small business as having fewer than 500 employees
d uses the term "small business" instead of SME), the
vernments of other countries use different definitions.

Small Business Development Centers: A program of the U.S.
Small Business Administration that provides free business
counseling and assistance to current and prospective small
business owners. By law, SBDCs must assist any business that
asks for help. Many incubators are co-located with SBDCs.

Small Business Innovation Research Program (SBIR):
Federal law requires eleven federal agencies with the largest
extramural research budgets (Defense, National Institutes
of Health, National Aeronautics and Space Administration,
Energy, etc.) to set aside a percentage of those budgets for
research conducted by small businesses. This SBIR program
ensures that small firms may compete for research contracts
in areas of interest to the agencies. While each agency
identifies its own topics of interest, solicits proposals, and
awards contracts, the SBIR program is centrally administered
by the U.S. Small Business Administration. SBIR awards
are an important funding source for technology companies
seeking to determine the feasibility of new technologies.

Small Business Technology Transfer Program (STTR):
Federal law requires five federal agencies with large
extramural research budgets to set aside a percentage
of those budgets to fund research conducted by small
businesses in conjunction with academic and other research
institutions. The STTR program assists firms to work with
research institutions to determine the feasibility of potentially
commercializable technologies. Each participating agency
identifies its own topics of interest, solicits proposals and
awards contracts; however, the STTR program is centrally
administered by the U.S. Small Business Administration.

Special Focus Incubator: An incubation program targeting
a specific industry or economic segment, such as
biotechnology, specialty foods, arts, software, construction,
microenterprises, low-income communities, etc. Special focus
programs offer services tailored to these segments.

Sponsor: Entity that provides regular financial and other
support for a business incubation program. A sponsor may or
may not have developed the incubation program initially, but a
current sponsor maintains ongoing responsibility for managing
or governing the incubator and may provide subsidies to
fund program operations. In some cases, a sponsor may
initiate the program, but if it ceases its financial, governance,
or management role, the incubator likely would then operate
independently with no sponsor. If two or more sponsors
provide financial or management support and there is no
single controlling or primary controlling entity, the incubation
program likely operates with hybrid sponsorship.

Stakeholder: Any nonstaff person who have a vested interest in the success of an incubation program. This definition might include sponsors, service providers, board members, successful entrepreneurs, community leaders, and even community members who would benefit from a strengthened economy. Stakeholders can foster an incubator's success by marketing the program, encouraging promising entrepreneurs to apply for admission, and providing client firms with resources and expertise.

Start-Up Company: A new business that is developing its concept and does not yet have a prototype of its product or service. Start-up companies are usually funded by sweat equity, family, and friends.

Tax-Exempt Organization: An organization that meets the standards and requirements of the guidelines set forth in sections 501(c)(3), 501(c)(4), and 501(c)(6) of the U.S. Internal Revenue Code. Such organizations are exempt from federal taxes on income from activities related to their public or charitable purposes.

Technology Commercialization: The process of turning a technological innovation into a commercial product that is marketed and sold. As part of an economic development strategy, technology commercialization can create new markets, jobs, and wealth. On university campuses, technology transfer offices and business incubators help faculty, staff, researchers, and area entrepreneurs turn research and ideas into companies that help strengthen and diversify local economies. See also **Technology Transfer**.

Technology Incubator: A program that fosters the growth of companies involved in emerging technologies such as software, medical, biotechnology, robotics, and instrumentation. Technology incubator clients may conduct research and development leading to new technologies that can be commercialized or adapt existing technologies for new commercial uses.

Technology Transfer: The transfer, via sale or license, of full or partial rights to a technology from one entity (such as a company, university, or federal laboratory) to another. Some entities use the term "technology transfer" to refer to activities that go beyond technology transfer, into technology commercialization, which implies that products or services derived from the technology have been developed, marketed, and sold.

U.S. Economic Development Administration: A division of the U.S. Department of Commerce established in the Public Works and Economic Development Act of 1965 to create and retain jobs and stimulate economic development in economically challenged areas. U.S. EDA is a leading federal funder of business incubator facility projects.

Valuation: The process of determining a company's worth using various quantitative approaches. Considerations may include earnings, cash flow, and market value of assets. Also the value placed on a company.

Value Proposition: The sum of the benefits offered to customers by a business. For example, a business incubator value proposition to clients might be in its ability to assist a client in finding financing necessary for growth or reducing capital costs by providing access to appropriate space and equipment necessary to its success.

Venture Capital: Money provided by professionals who invest alongside management in young, rapidly growing companies that have the potential to develop into significant economic contributors.

Venture Capitalists: Persons or groups that give cash sums to high-potential start-up businesses in exchange for shares in the company. Venture capitalists always seek an exit strategy in which the company is merged or acquired, or its stock is sold on the public stock markets, permitting the investors to recoup many times their initial investments. Professional venture capitalists generally manage and invest large sums of other peoples' money through a professionally managed entity such as a limited liability partnership.

Virtual Clients: This term may be used interchangeably with "affiliate clients"; however, it also may be used to denote clients that are primarily served via computer and Web-based programs that bring together networks of people and other resources for the purposes of serving client companies that are not housed in any central location.

Virtual Incubator: In the most specific sense, an incubation program that provides services electronically, with little or no face-to-face interaction. However, this term increasingly is used to refer to any program that delivers incubation services to off-site clients. See also **Affiliate Client** and **Virtual Client**.

Volunteers: Persons who accomplish work for the incubation program but are not paid staff. Anyone donating time or services without receiving monetary compensation is a volunteer.

BIBLIOGRAPHY

■ ■ THE FOLLOWING RESOURCES MAY BE HELPFUL IN
NDING AND IMPLEMENTING BEST PRACTICES.

01 governance

ard Source. *The Nonprofit Board Answer Book: A Practical Guide
r Board Members and Chief Executives*. San Francisco: Jossey-
ass, 2007.

lewine, Meredith, and Ellen Gerl, eds. *A Comprehensive Guide to
usiness Incubation: Completely Revised 2nd Edition*. Athens, Ohio:
BIA Publications, 2005.

nopp, Linda. 2006 *State of the Business Incubation Industry*. Athens,
hio: NBIA Publications, 2007.

02 staffing

oyd, Justin. *Incorporating Your Business Incubation Program: How
ax Status and Business Entity Affect Operations*. Athens, Ohio: NBIA
ublications, 2002.

ayhow, Sally, ed. *Human Resources: Finding the Right Staff for Your
cubator, 2nd Edition*. Athens, Ohio: NBIA Publications, 1999.

nopp, Linda. *2005 Compensation Survey of Business Incubator
xecutives*. Athens, Ohio: NBIA Publications, 2006.

———. *2006 State of the Business Incubation Industry*. Athens, Ohio:
BIA Publications, 2007.

03 finances

ammarata, Kathleen. *Developing a Business Incubation Program:
sights and Advice for Communities*. Athens, Ohio: NBIA Publications,
006.

rlewine, Meredith, and Ellen Gerl, eds. *A Comprehensive Guide to
usiness Incubation: Completely Revised 2nd Edition*. Athens, Ohio:
BIA Publications, 2005.

Jarwick, Mal. *How to Write Successful Fundraising Letters*. San
rancisco: Jossey-Bass, 2001.

04 facilities management

ammarata, Kathleen. *Developing a Business Incubation Program:
sights and Advice for Communities*. Athens, Ohio: NBIA
ublications, 2006.

rlewine, Meredith, and Ellen Gerl, eds. *A Comprehensive Guide to
usiness Incubation: Completely Revised 2nd Edition*. Athens, Ohio:
BIA Publications, 2005.

erl, Ellen. *Bricks and Mortar: Renovating or Building a Business
cubation Facility*. Athens, Ohio: NBIA Publications, 2000.

.05 program evaluation

Cammarata, Kathleen. *Self-Evaluation Workbook for Business
Incubators*. Athens, Ohio: NBIA Publications, 2003.

Erlewine, Meredith. *Measuring Your Business Incubator's Economic
Impact: A Toolkit*. Athens, Ohio: NBIA Publications, 2007.

NBIA. *Benchmark Your Business Incubator's Practices*, www.nbia.org/
benchmark. Athens, Ohio: NBIA Publications, 2008.

.06 client entrance and exit

Colbert, Corinne. *A Practical Guide to Business Incubator Marketing*.
Athens, Ohio: NBIA Publications, 2007.

Erlewine, Meredith, and Ellen Gerl, eds. *A Comprehensive Guide to
Business Incubation: Completely Revised 2nd Edition*. Athens, Ohio:
NBIA Publications, 2005.

Hartlen, Stephen P. "A Methodology for Determining the Mentoring
Requirements of Early-Stage Technology Companies." White paper
presented at the annual conference of the Canadian Association of
Business Incubation, Halifax, NS, Canada, September 26, 2006.

James, Carol. *Put It in Writing: Crafting Policies, Agreements, and
Contracts for Your Incubator*. Athens, Ohio: NBIA Publications, 2002.

.07 leveraging innovation

Erlewine, Meredith, and Ellen Gerl, eds. *A Comprehensive Guide to
Business Incubation: Completely Revised 2nd Edition*. Athens, Ohio:
NBIA Publications, 2005.

Friedman, Yali, ed. *Best Practices in Biotechnology Business
Development*. Washington D.C.: Logos Press, 2008.

Kalis, Nanette. *Technology Commercialization through New Business
Formation*. Athens, Ohio: NBIA Publications, 2001.

Kennedy, Wendy. *So What? Who Cares? Why You? The Inventor's
Commercialization Toolkit*. Ottawa, Ontario: Wendykennedy.com, 2006.

.08 client services

Abrams, Rhonda. *The Successful Business Plan*. 4th Ed. Palo Alto, CA:
The Planning Shop, 2003.

Erlewine, Meredith. "Beyond Loans: Where Nontechnology Start-
Ups Find Cash." In *A Comprehensive Guide to Business Incubation:
Completely Revised 2nd Edition*, edited by Meredith Erlewine and Ellen
Gerl (259–64). Athens, Ohio: NBIA Publications, 2004,

Hill, Brian E., and Dee Power. *Attracting Capital From Angels: How
Their Money—and Their Experience—Can Help You Build a Successful
Company*. New York: John Wiley and Sons, 2002.

Osnabrugge, Mark van, and Robert J. Robinson. *Angel Investing:
Matching Start-up Funds with Start-up Companies*. San Francisco:
Jossey-Bass, 2000.

Programs Mentioned

ADVANCED TECHNOLOGY DEVELOPMENT CENTER
Atlanta, GA | Charles Ross, general manager
www.atdc.org

BEN FRANKLIN TECHVENTURES
Bethlehem, PA | Wayne Barz,
manager of entrepreneurial services
www.bftechventures.org

BOSTON UNIVERSITY BUSINESS INCUBATION PROGRAM
Boston, MA | Clifford Robinson, former director
www.bu.edu/otd/about/incubation

BUSINESS INCUBATOR CENTER
Grand Junction, CO | Christina Reddin, executive director
www.gjincubator.org

CENTRAL VALLEY BUSINESS INCUBATOR
Fresno, CA | Kirk Nagamine, CEO
www.cvbi.org

EMERGING TECHNOLOGY CENTERS
Baltimore, MD | Ann Lansinger, president
www.etcbaltimore.com

ENTERPRISE CENTER OF JOHNSON COUNTY
Lenexa, KS | Joel Wiggins, CEO and president
www.ecjc.com

ENVIRONMENTAL BUSINESS CLUSTER
San Jose, California | Melinda Richter, executive director
www.environmentalcluster.org

INNOVACORP
Halifax, Nova Scotia, Canada | Dan MacDonald,
former president and CEO
www.innovacorp.ca

INNOVATION DEPOT
Birmingham, AL | Susan Matlock, president and CEO
www.innovationdepot.net

JUMPSTART, INC.
Cleveland, OH | Chris Mather, president,
JumpStart TechLift Advisors

David Nestic, entrepreneur-in-residence
www.jumpstartinc.org

LA COCINA BUSINESS INCUBATOR
San Francisco, CA | Caleb Zigas, acting executive director
www.lacocinasf.org

LAWRENCE REGIONAL TECHNOLOGY CENTER
Lawrence, KS | Matt McClorey, president and CEO
www.ltrc.biz

LENNOX TECH ENTERPRISE CENTER
West Henrietta, NY | Terry Gronwall, manager
http://htr.org/incubator.asp

LOUISIANA BUSINESS & TECHNOLOGY CENTER
Baton Rouge, LA | Charles D'Agostino, executive director
www.bus.lsu.edu/lbtc

MEYTAV INCUBATOR
Kiryat Shmona, Israel | Orit Shaked, CTO
www.meytavti.co.il

MI KITCHEN ES SU KITCHEN
New York, NY | Kathrine Gregory, director
www.mikitchenessukitchen.com

MISSISSIPPI E-BUSINESS INNOVATION CENTER
Jackson, MS | DeAnna Adams, former director
www.innovationcenter.ms

MISSISSIPPI ENTERPRISE FOR TECHNOLOGY
Stennis Space Center, MS | Charles Beasley, president
www.mset.org

MISSISSIPPI TECHNOLOGY ALLIANCE
Ridgeland, MS | Randy Goldsmith,
former president and CEO
www.technologyalliance.ms

NORTHEAST INDIANA INNOVATION CENTER
Fort Wayne, IN | Karl LaPan, president and CEO
www.niic.net

NORTHEAST OHIO INCUBATOR COLLABORATIVE
northeastern OH | Wayne Zeman, former chairman
http://neoinc.org

NUSSBAUM CENTER FOR ENTREPRENEURSHIP
Greensboro, NC | Sam Funchess, president and CEO
www.nussbaumcfe.com

OREGON TECHNOLOGY BUSINESS CENTER
Beaverton, OR | Steve Morris, executive director
www.otbc.org

POWERHOUSE VENTURES
Christchurch New Zealand | Stephen Hampson, CEO
www.cii.co.nz

PURDUE TECHNOLOGY CENTER—WEST LAFAYETTE
West Lafayette, IN | Tim Peoples, director
www.purdueresearchpark.org

RUTGERS FOOD INNOVATION CENTER
Bridgeton, NJ | Lou Cooperhouse, director
www.foodinnovation.rutgers.edu

SAN DIEGO CONNECT
San Diego, CA | Camille Sobrian, COO
www.connect.org

SAN JUAN COLLEGE ENTERPRISE CENTER
Farmington, NM | Jasper Welch, director
www.sanjuancollege.edu/gcb

SANTA FE BUSINESS INCUBATOR
Santa Fe, NM | Marie Longserre, president and CEO
www.sfbi.net

SOUTHWEST MICHIGAN INNOVATION CENTER
Kalamazoo, MI | Robert DeWitt, president and CEO
www.kazoosmic.com

SPRINGFIELD BUSINESS INCUBATOR
Springfield, MA | Deborah King, former executive director
www.stcc.edu/sbi

TECH FORT WORTH
Fort Worth, TX | Darlene Ryan, executive director
www.TECHFortWorth.org

TECHNOLOGY 2020
Oak Ridge, TN | Shawn Carson, director, operations
www.tech2020.org

TOWSONGLOBAL—INTERNATIONAL INCUBATOR
Towson, MD | Clay E. Hickson, Director
www.towsonglobal.com

UNIVERSITY CITY SCIENCE CENTER
Philadelphia, PA | Kristin Hart,
manager, incubator operations
www.sciencecenter.org

UNIVERSITY OF CENTRAL FLORIDA
BUSINESS INCUBATOR NETWORK
Orlando, FL | Tom O'Neal, director
www.incubator.ucf.edu

UNIVERSITY OF FLORIDA SID MARTIN
BIOTECHNOLOGY DEVELOPMENT INCUBATOR
Alachua, FL | Patti Breedlove, associate director
www.biotech.ufl.org

USC COLUMBIA TECHNOLOGY INCUBATOR
Columbia, SC | Joel Stevenson, executive director
http://incubator.research.sc.edu

VIRGINIA BIOSCIENCES DEVELOPMENT CENTER
Richmond, VA | David Lohr, executive director
www.vabiotech.com/bioincubator

WEST TEXAS A&M UNIVERSITY ENTERPRISE NETWORK
Amarillo, TX | David Terry, executive director
www.IncubationWorks.com

WILLIAM M. FACTORY SMALL BUSINESS INCUBATOR
Tacoma, WA | Tim Strege, executive director
www.williamfactory.com

index

index